ATHENS, THRACE, AND THE SHAPING OF ATHENIAN LEADERSHIP

From the mid-sixth to the mid-fourth century BCE a nexus of connections to Thrace defined the careers of several of Athens' most prominent figures, including Pisistratus, Miltiades, Alcibiades, and Iphicrates. This book explores the importance of Thrace to these individuals and its resulting significance in the political, cultural, and social history of Athens. Thrace was vitally important for Athens thanks to its natural resources and access to strategic waterways, which were essential to a maritime empire, and connections to the area conferred wealth and military influence on certain Athenians and offered them a refuge if they faced political persecution at home. However, Thrace's importance to prominent individuals transcended politics: its culture was also an important draw. Thrace was a world free of Athenian political, social, and cultural constraints – one that bore a striking resemblance to the world of Homeric epic.

Matthew A. Sears is the Theodore Bedrick Visiting Assistant Professor of Classics at Wabash College in Crawfordsville, Indiana. His articles have appeared in *Classical World*, *Hesperia*, and *Mouseion*.

For Jenny

ഉ⊘ ഉ⊘ ഉ⊘ ഉ⊘

ATHENS, THRACE, AND THE SHAPING OF ATHENIAN LEADERSHIP

Matthew A. Sears
Wabash College

CAMBRIDGE
UNIVERSITY PRESS

CAMBRIDGE UNIVERSITY PRESS
Cambridge, New York, Melbourne, Madrid, Cape Town,
Singapore, São Paulo, Delhi, Mexico City

Cambridge University Press
32 Avenue of the Americas, New York, NY 10013-2473, USA

www.cambridge.org
Information on this title: www.cambridge.org/9781107030534

First published 2013

Printed in the United States of America

A catalog record for this publication is available from the British Library.

Library of Congress Cataloging in Publication data
Sears, Matthew A.
Athens, Thrace, and the shaping of Athenian leadership / Matthew A. Sears.
pages. cm.
Includes bibliographical references and index.
ISBN 978-1-107-03053-4 (hardback)
1. Athens (Greece) – Politics and government. 2. Athens
(Greece) – Relations – Thrace. 3. Thrace – Relations – Greece – Athens. I. Title.
DF285.S39 2013
938'.5–dc23 2012016896

ISBN 978-1-107-03053-4 Hardback

CONTENTS

CONTENTS

CONTENTS

LIST OF FIGURES AND MAPS

FIGURES

MAPS

LIST OF ABBREVIATIONS

ARV²	Beazley, J. D. 1963. *Attic Red-Figure Vase-Painters*. 2nd ed. Oxford.
FGrHist	Jacoby, F., ed. 1923–1958. *Die Fragmente der griechischen Historiker*. Berlin.
IG	1873–. *Inscriptiones Graecae*. Berlin.
K-A	Kassel, R., and C. Austin. 1983. *Poetae comici graeci*. Berlin.
LSJ	Liddell, H. G., R. Scott, H. S. Jones, R. McKenzie, P. G. W. Glare, and A. A. Thompson. 1996. *A Greek-English Lexicon*. 9th ed. with revised supplement. Oxford.

ACKNOWLEDGMENTS

I have accumulated many debts throughout the course of this project. First and foremost, it is a pleasure to thank my Ph.D. advisor at Cornell University, Barry Strauss, whose thoughtful and thorough critiques and suggestions, along with his high academic standards, have had an invaluable impact on this book and my work in general. Happily, I have continued to benefit from his sage advice and friendship after completing my degree. I profited from conversations with several faculty members at Cornell, including Annetta Alexandridis, Kim Bowes, Sturt Manning, Hunter R. Rawlings III, and Eric Rebillard. I particularly thank Jeff Rusten for meeting with me several times to offer guidance as I made the transition from dissertation to book. With its impressive resources and vibrant scholarly community, Cornell was the ideal place for my doctoral studies. I am grateful to the school for its generous financial support.

I was fortunate enough to be awarded a fellowship to participate in the Regular Program of the American School of Classical Studies at Athens in 2007–2008, where several of the ideas in this book began to take shape. At the school I gained many good friends, and I thank especially John Oakley and Kirk Ormand. I continue to enjoy my affiliation with such an important institute for the study of Greece. In spring 2008, I traveled to Bulgaria, the heart of Thrace, where I was given a warm welcome and academic assistance from the staff of the American Research Center in Sofia, especially Kevin Clinton and Nora Dimitrova. The Center's staff has continued to aid my research, and Denver Graninger and Emil Nankov kindly secured permission to reproduce an image of one of the countless stunning objects on display in Bulgarian museums.

My current academic home, Wabash College, is a rich and rewarding environment in which to teach and write. I thank my Classics colleagues Jeremy Hartnett, Isabel Köster, and David Kubiak. I thank also the Wabash undergraduates who continually surprised and delighted me in our seminar discussions of Greeks and barbarians.

The two anonymous reviewers for Cambridge University Press offered detailed and keen suggestions, saving me from a host of errors. The Cambridge editorial staff, including editor Beatrice Rehl, senior editorial assistant Amanda Smith, assistant editor Emily Spangler, and copy editor Scott Barker and production editor Regina Paleski were always prompt, professional, and a joy with whom to work.

Finally, I could not have completed this project without the unflagging support of my family. I am grateful for the love and help of my parents, Alan and Jane Ann Sears; my sister, Rebekah Sears; and my parents-in-law, John and Jane Denault. My father read through the manuscript as a whole, along with countless drafts of chapters, and always provided astute comments. My two daughters, Cara and Kallie, made for a joyous home as I worked on the manuscript. My wife, Jenny, from gladly marching around Greece and Bulgaria to enduring the hardships of graduate school and the first years of my academic job, has never ceased to love and encourage. I dedicate this book to her.

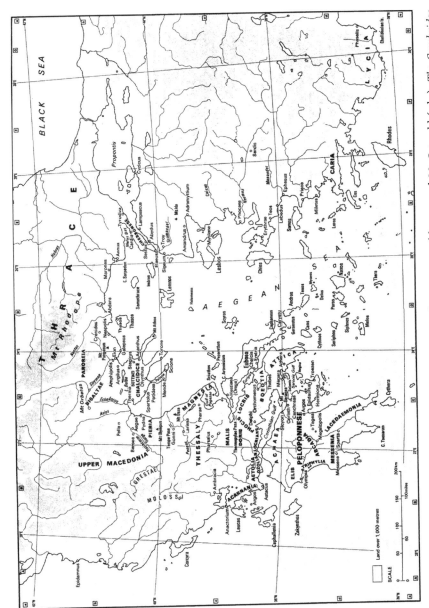

MAP 1. Greece and the Aegean. From D. M. Lewis, J. Boardman, S. Hornblower, and M. Ostwald (eds.), *The Cambridge Ancient History* (2nd ed.), Vol. 6, *The Fourth Century B.C.* © Cambridge University Press, 1994. Reprinted with the permission of Cambridge University Press.

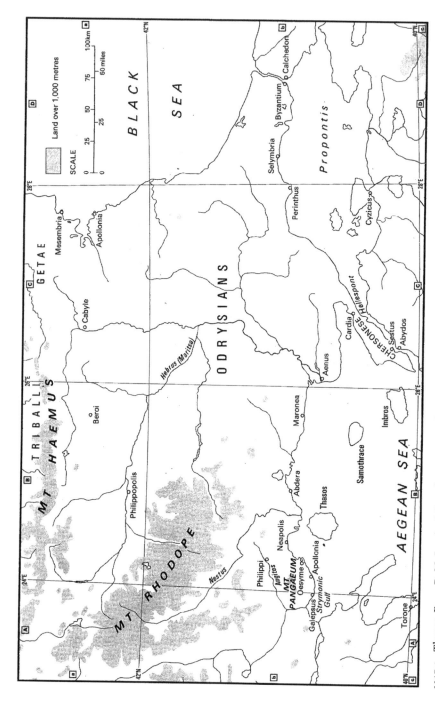

MAP 2. Thrace. From D. M. Lewis, J. Boardman, S. Hornblower, and M. Ostwald (eds.), *The Cambridge Ancient History* (2nd ed.). Vol. 6, *The Fourth Century* B.C. © Cambridge University Press, 1994. Reprinted with the permission of Cambridge University Press.

@⊚ @⊚ @⊚ @⊚

CHAPTER ONE

INTRODUCTION

EGALITARIANISM, AMBITION, AND THE
DISCIPLES OF THRACE

In *Gerytades*, a lost play by Aristophanes dating to the late fifth century, a group of poets gathers to choose envoys to send to their departed comrades in Hades, prompting the following exchange:

(A) And who to the pit of the dead and the gates of gloom has dared descend?

(B) One from each poetic field we chose together, meeting as an assembly: those we knew as Hades-haunters (*haidophoitai*) and regularly fond of yonder parts (*philochōrountes*).

(A) So there are men among you who are Hades-haunters?

(B) By Zeus, there are!

(A) Like Thrace-haunters (*thraikophoitai*)?

(B) You've got it! (F 156 K-A)[1]

Who were these "Thrace-haunters"? What exactly does Aristophanes mean by *thraikophoitai*, a term he seems to have coined?

---

[1] {A.} Καὶ τίς νεκρῶν κευθμῶνα καὶ σκότου πύλας
ἔτλη κατελθεῖν; {B.} ἕν' ἀφ' ἑκάστης τῆς τέχνης
εἱλόμεθα κοινῇ γενομένης ἐκκλησίας,
οὓς ᾖσμεν ὄντας ᾁδοφοίτας καὶ θαμὰ
ἐκεῖσε φιλοχωροῦντας. {A.} εἰσὶ γάρ τινες
ἄνδρες παρ' ὑμῖν ᾁδοφοῖται; {B.} νὴ Δία
μάλιστά γ'. {A.} ὥσπερ Θρᾳκοφοῖται; {B.} πάντ' ἔχεις.
Translated by Rusten (Rusten et al. 2011). Unless otherwise indicated, all other translations are my own. All dates are BCE, unless otherwise specified.

There is an obvious answer to the second question: *thrai-kophoitai* must denote a class of people who not only spent a great deal of time in Thrace but who were also deeply fond of the region. This notion is given further weight by the participial use of the verb *philochōreō*, which generally means "to be fond of or to frequent a place." In Herodotus the residents of Andros use this verb in their complaint that the gods Poverty and Helplessness are always present on their benighted island (8.111). Unfortunately for the Andrians, these malevolent deities are simply fond of Andros. Likewise, *thraikophoitai* found something in Thrace that they liked and consequently spent a lot of time there. According to LSJ, the noun *phoitētēs*, of which *phoitai* is a variant, means one who regularly goes or comes. Often, it specifically refers to one regularly visiting a teacher, in other words, a pupil or disciple. Plato, for instance, often uses the word in this sense (see *Rep.* 563a; *Euthd.* 295d; *I Alc.* 109d; *Laws* 779d). Aristophanes himself employs the related verb *phoitaō* to mean "to go to school" (*Clouds* 938; *Knights* 1235). Even in Modern Greek *phoitētēs* means "student." Perhaps, then, we should translate *thraikophoitai* as "students" or even "disciples" of Thrace. Indeed, they were disciples of Thrace in the full sense of the term, analogous to disciples of a particular teacher. There was a distinct line of Athenians – well known enough in Athens to be the butt of an Aristophanic joke – who went to Thrace time and again, and moreover *learned* from the Thracians as from a respected teacher.

Aristophanes' poets were searching for the ideal representatives to send to Hades, namely, those who were not merely fond of the underworld but were experienced in dealing with its denizens. In Athens, there was a group of people diplomatically valuable because of their ties to Thrace. For over two centuries, from the time of Pisistratus to the Battle of Chaeronea, Athens was keenly interested in securing and maintaining a foothold in the north Aegean, particularly in the regions adjacent to the Hellespont and the mineral-rich areas opposite the island of Thasos and along the Strymon River. Thrace was materially and strategically important for Athens, particularly as Athens became a maritime power. Thracian minerals were a source of wealth (timber from the Strymon was important for ship construction), and the Hellespont waterway provided access to Black Sea trade and formed the bridge between Asia and Europe. Thrace also at times provided military allies and promised a ready supply of fierce and talented warriors to serve as mercenaries. The light-armed peltast, named for his small shield, the *peltē*, was much sought after by several Greek states as a complement to the heavy-armed hoplite. In the interests of furthering its foothold in such an important region, Athens turned to those of its citizens with ties to Thrace and the Thracians, the *thraikophoitai*.

Thrace, though, was not simply a resource exploited for the material and political advantage of the Athenian polis and certain prominent individuals. For the Athenians there was far more to this strange land on the periphery of the Greek world than natural resources and strategic geography. Throughout the Late Archaic and Classical periods, Thrace by turns fascinated and terrified the Athenians. The Thracians were strange and barbaric, decadent and savage. They were also intriguing and mysterious, a source of powerful new gods and the inspiration for aspiring young cavalrymen. The intricate interplay between Athens and Thrace over the course of 200 years can perhaps be best described as a romance. Athens, the center of Greek learning, culture, and political innovation, was enamored of a barbarous people representing the very paradigm of primitive savagery. This is perceptible at every level of Athenian society, and the experiences of the *thraikophoitai*, the disciples of Thrace, afford us the clearest picture of the significance Thrace had for Athenian politics, society, and culture. Despite the historical importance of Thrace for Athens and the Greek world in general, no one has explored how a nexus of Thracian connections defined the careers of several of Athens' most prominent figures.[2] These leaders found in

---

[2] For a good general treatment of the role of Thrace in Greek history, see Isaac 1986.

Thrace both the resources to achieve power and prestige and a type of society that suited their predispositions more than did the Athenian polis. Thrace taught its disciples new ways of gaining wealth and power, new ways of waging war, and new – or perhaps more accurately, old – ways of living.

THE PROBLEM WITH EQUALITY

For the disciples of Thrace, the allure of Thracian cultural practices was combined with the promise of material and political advantages far beyond those available in Athens. Several Athenians grew very wealthy and powerful through their Thracian connections. But they also made full use of Thracian cultural practices in order to live a pseudoheroic lifestyle reminiscent of that enjoyed by Homer's chieftains, the *basileis*. Why was Athens no longer able to satisfy the ambitions of many of its elite? The problem lies with the Greek egalitarian ethos. Every Greek citizen of a polis, especially a polis governed by democracy, was technically the political equal of every other citizen. Though it might seem an obvious inference, ambition and a desire for greater power still stirred in the hearts of certain individuals. Sometimes greater power was achievable, even within the Athenian democracy. Other times it was not.

In his stimulating book on the characteristics of leadership, Waller Newell addresses the appropriate limits to honor seeking or the desire for public recognition, a tension that has plagued every democracy throughout history. Newell focuses on an early speech of Abraham Lincoln's, long before he was president, in which he explains the impediments placed by egalitarian societies to achieving true greatness. Alexis de Tocqueville, for instance, had worried that American egalitarianism would discourage the emergence of great leaders under normal circumstances. For Lincoln, only the crisis of the Civil War eventually enabled him to exercise his leadership qualities to the utmost. As Newell observes, thinkers in the nineteenth century were ever haunted by the specter of Napoleon, a leader with incomparable talents and ambition who disastrously went too far. How is a democracy to restrain the excesses of a Napoleon without preventing the emergence of a Lincoln? Even the Founding Fathers of the United States, having the worst extremes of Classical Athenian democracy in mind, struggled with how to deal properly with ambition.[3] Newell states what he considers the most vexing question of all: "What if the psychological traits of aggressiveness and victory seeking that might lead to tyranny are among the *same* traits displayed by true statesmen?"[4] Athens was never able to achieve the ideal balance between limiting ambition and giving free rein to potential tyrants like Alcibiades. Thucydides himself states that the exile of Alcibiades did as much as anything else to bring about the Athenian defeat in the Peloponnesian War, because Athens had lost a frightening yet uniquely capable leader (6.15).

Despite the case of Alcibiades, there were many ways in which Athenian society tried to cope with the dichotomy of mass and elite, with varying degrees of success. For several ambitious Athenians, Thrace provided both an alternative to the stifling environment of egalitarian Athens and a means to win over the demos and overcome rival claimants to influence. Material resources played a key part in this. In Thrace, an ambitious figure could carve out an autonomous niche, complete with control of lucrative gold mines and the command of what amounted to private armies. Often these resources allowed one to achieve supremacy at Athens. Failing that, an Athenian adventurer could live quite comfortably abroad on his own Thracian estates and at the courts of Thracian rulers, as Alcibiades discovered at the end of his career.

We should not, however, dismiss the cultural draws of Thrace. Athens was egalitarian not only in a political sense but, ostensibly, in a sociocultural sense too. Displays of aristocratic pretension were frowned upon, and the old virtues of athletic and martial prowess and ostentatious wealth did not

---

[3] Newell 2009: esp. 136–62.
[4] Newell 2009: 34.

always guarantee the political power and recognition they once had. Among the Thracians, a determined Athenian could seek status and power as blatantly as he wished – and was in fact encouraged to do so. A good illustration of Thrace's openness to ostentation relative to Athens is that in the fifth and fourth centuries scarcely any gold vessels were buried in Athenian graves, though they had once been common. But we know the Athenians still made quality gold vessels in this period, primarily because many Attic gold cups have been found *in Thrace*, where demand for such ostentation remained high.[5] Many Greeks saw in the Thracians an image of their own past, akin to the heroic world immortalized by the epic poets. Thrace taught a significant number of Athenians how they could live like Homeric *basileis* once again, far removed from the egalitarian ethos of the democratic assembly and hoplite phalanx. This naturally had a profound social and political effect on Athens. It was also important in the military sphere, because several leading Athenians embraced the warlike qualities of the Thracians, coupled with unique and effective tactics that in Greece were stifled by the dominance of the hoplite.

DEFINING THRACE

Thrace, or the territory inhabited in the main by "Thracians," represents a very broad category.[6] The geographical boundaries of what the Greeks and Romans called Thrace varied over time. The Danube might be considered its northern extent, but from antiquity on, many have conceived of territory far to the north of this line as Thracian.[7] To the southwest, prior to the Persian Wars the area west of the Axius River surrounding

---

[5] As discussed by Morris 2000: 26–27.

[6] For the most comprehensive modern treatments of Thrace and the Thracians available in Western European languages, see Danov 1976; Fol and Marazov 1977; Hoddinott 1981; Archibald 1998; Theodossiev 2000b; 2011. See also the collection of papers in Poulter 1983. For more specific treatments of Aegean Thrace, see Isaac 1986; Parissaki 2007; and the collection of papers in Fol 2002.

[7] See, for example, the map provided by Hoddinott (1981: 11–13).

the Thermaic Gulf was inhabited by Thracians, though this region came increasingly under the Macedonian sphere of interest after Xerxes' invasion in 480–479.[8] Even well into the fifth century, though, the Athenians still considered the Chalcidice and Thermaic Gulf region to be part of the Thraceward district for the purposes of collecting tribute.[9] Virtually all the northern Aegean coastline was inhabited by Thracians at some point, including islands such as Thasos, but over time Greek settlements were found increasingly throughout the area.[10] The edge of the Black Sea formed the eastern border, but there were Thracian elements in the Spartocid dynasty as far east as the Crimea in the fourth century.[11] To the southeast, Thracians inhabited the Chersonese – the modern Gallipoli Peninsula – and the northern shore of the Propontis, today's Sea of Marmara. The Greeks considered the lands immediately south of the Hellespont – the strait now called the Dardanelles – and Propontis, including the Troad, to be part of Thrace. Herodotus tells us that the Thracians who had migrated to Asia, that is, to the southern shore of the Black Sea, continued to live exactly as their European brethren, becoming known as Bithynians (7.75). Other writers, including Xenophon, call the Thracians in Asia simply Bithynian Thracians (*Hell.* 1.3.2).[12]

What will be considered Thrace, or at least a "Thracian context" for the purposes of this study, includes the following: all

---

[8] Hammond et al. 1972–1988: vol. 1, 435–40; Baba 1990: 16–17. Buck (1978: 78–81) examines the ancient sources indicating that Thracians at one point lived as far south as Boeotia.

[9] Meritt et al. 1939–1953: vol. 3, 317.

[10] Isaac (1986) provides an account of the Greek settlements in this region, and also eastward to the Hellespont and Propontis. He looks in depth at the level of blending that occurred between the Greek and Thracian populations. For the issue of the ethnic makeup of the population, see also Parissaki (2007), who studies the prosopography of the area. For Thasos, see Owen 2000.

[11] Moreno 2007: 168.

[12] See further Stronk (1995: 59–60, 283), who correctly argues that the entire Propontis region should be conceived of as one "coherent historico-geographical complex" and stresses the historical presence of Thracian tribes in the Troad.

of modern Bulgaria, especially the Haemus (modern Balkan) and Rhodope mountain ranges and the plain lying in between, known as the "Thracian Plain"; northeastern Greece east of the Axius River, including the Chalcidice and all of the northern Aegean coastline; all of European Turkey; a sizable section of northwestern Anatolia, including the northern Troad, the territory abutting the Propontis, and the southwestern shore of the Black Sea; and the northern Aegean islands lying between the Athos peninsula and the Chersonese. It should be noted that many cities in Asia, such as Lampsacus, Cyzicus, and Sigeum, which today are not normally considered to be part of Thrace, were considered so by the ancients and will be treated as such in the following analysis.

In discussing groups of Thracians, the word "tribe" is used for the sake of consistency. Those scholars, such as Archibald and Theodossiev, who write about Thrace all use "tribe" to refer to the different groups living in Thrace. Greek writers, such as Herodotus and Thucydides, variously refer to different divisions of Thracians by *ethnos* and *genos*, and even the Thracians as a whole are labeled an *ethnos*. It seems that *genos* usually denotes a subgroup within an *ethnos*, but the ancient writers show little consistency in the use of these terms in relation to the Thracians.[13] "Tribe" is used to refer to various nonpolitical groups, as opposed to, say, the Odrysian kingdom that incorporated many tribes into a larger federation led by a king.[14] It is uncertain what exactly differentiated Thracian tribes, whether territory, language, origins, or the like. It surely varied from case to case.[15]

---

[13] See J. Hall (1997: 34–36) for the Greek use of these terms, especially in Herodotus.

[14] Archibald (1998: 5) calls the Odrysian kingdom a "supra-tribal polity."

[15] J. Hall (1997) provides the most useful discussion of the concept of ethnicity among the ancient Greeks. For Hall, the Greeks constructed their identity through written or spoken discourse. Genetic traits, language, religion, and even common cultural forms are merely symbols of this socially constructed ethnic identity (2). For the Thracians, of course, we have no recourse to such written texts that might shed

No one can say how many distinct tribes composed Thrace. Strabo, for one, counts twenty-two in the comprehensive treatment of Thrace in his seventh book (7a.48), whereas Pliny the Elder describes Thrace as divided into fifty *strategiae*, a Roman administrative unit that might reflect some sort of ethnic or tribal division (*Nat. Hist.* 4.11.40). The problem is compounded by our inability to ascertain to which chronological period each tribe mentioned in the sources belongs, because Strabo and Pliny wrote centuries after the activities of Athenian Thracophiles. Some tribes were larger and more powerful than others and are consequently better known to us, such as the Triballoi and Getai in northwestern and northeastern Bulgaria, respectively, and the Odrysians, who for a period in the fifth and fourth centuries controlled a grouping of tribes spread over most of southeastern Bulgaria and European Turkey.[16] There were numerous smaller tribes that were at different points incorporated into larger units, such as the Odrysian kingdom, but others seem to have remained independent. For his part, Herodotus judged who should be considered Thracian by a set of criteria that included physical appearance, dress, customs, and traditions of common origin. He was probably influenced by the definition of Thracian then current at Athens.[17] We do not have to accept Greek or Roman notions of tribal and ethnic groups, but as with so much of Classical antiquity we are at the mercy of their terminology. Thracian tribes are thus referred to by the names given to them by Greek literary sources.

The Athenians – as most Greek powers – dealt primarily with the Thracians inhabiting the Aegean littoral. However, some of the tribes with whom the Athenians interacted were from

light on how they viewed their own identity. Archaeology, though, as Hall (111–42) argues, can help identify ethnic groups by illuminating different dietary preferences, the different types of ceramics used, and so forth. For Greek ethnic terminology, see also Fraser 2009.

16 Archibald (1998) offers a useful study of the Odrysian kingdom and provides a map showing the location of the Bulgarian Thracian tribes (108).

17 Asheri 1990: 167.

regions farther inland, such as the inhabitants of the Rhodope Mountains. Also, Sitalces, the Odrysian king allied to Athens in the early years of the Peloponnesian War, ruled tribes quite distant from the Aegean, as did some of his successors. The Odrysian kingdom, however, even at its greatest extent was confined to the southeast corner of Thrace. It should be borne in mind that an Athenian Thracophile usually had a relationship with only one of the many Thracian tribes, centered on a specific region. From Pisistratus to the rise of Philip, Athens was most interested in two particular areas of Thrace: the Chersonese along with the general vicinity of the Hellespont and Propontis in the east, and the mainland opposite Thasos in the west, including the mining region of Pangaeum and the settlements along the lower Strymon River. Other scholars, especially Isaac and Archibald, have produced excellent historical outlines of Greek interest in Aegean Thrace.[18] For the sake of clarity, I provide here a very brief outline of the specific tribes with which Athenians had extensive contact and the relevant historical and geographical circumstances.[19] They are listed in alphabetic order:

- *Apsinthioi*: Known primarily from Herodotus (6.34; 9.119), they lived in the vicinity of the Chersonese and often harried their neighbors, the Dolonkoi. The elder Miltiades was invited by the Dolonkoi to the Chersonese in the mid-sixth century in order to protect them from the Apsinthioi, which he succeeded in doing.
- *Bessoi*: A relatively well-known tribe, they dwelt mostly in the Rhodope range but also perhaps further north, in the Haemus Mountains. They were possibly related to another tribe, the Dioi, who were fierce mercenaries hired by the

[18] Isaac (1986) offers the best general survey of the Greek settlements in Aegean Thrace, including the histories of various sites and an account of the tribes involved. Archibald (1998) focuses mainly on the Odrysian polity, from its origins to collapse, but she also describes Greek interaction with the Odrysians, including Greek colonization efforts in the north.

[19] More complete listings of the ancient sources for these tribes have been usefully gathered in the work of Dechev 1957.

Athenians during the Peloponnesian War (Thuc. 7.28–30). The Bessoi maintained a famous oracle of Dionysus in the Rhodopes (Hdt. 7.111).

- *Bisaltai*: They were inhabitants of the lower Strymon River. According to Herodotus, the king of the Bisaltai cut out the eyes of his sons for participating in Xerxes' invasion (8.116). In the mid-fifth century, Pericles sent out 1,000 settlers to settle among the Bisaltai, possibly at a site known as Brea (Plut. *Per.* 2.5). Members of the tribe were recruited by Brasidas during his campaign against Athens at Amphipolis (Thuc. 4.109.3).

- *Bithynoi*: Herodotus tells us that the Bithynians had once lived along the Strymon but were eventually driven into Asia, where they inhabited the southwestern shore of the Black Sea, or Bithynia. In describing the Bithynian contingent of Xerxes' invasion force, Herodotus says they were dressed and equipped just like the European Thracians (7.75). In 399, the Bithynians carried out some devastating attacks on the remnants of the Ten Thousand as they made their way to the Black Sea (Xen. *Anab.* 6.3; 6.4.2).

- *Dioi*: Dwellers of the Rhodope Mountains, these fierce warriors were dubbed "sword bearers" (*machairophoroi*) by Thucydides because of their fearsome weapons (2.96.2). In 413, 1,300 Dioi were serving as mercenaries for Athens when they massacred the entire population of Mycalessus, a defenseless Boeotian town (Thuc. 7.28–30).

- *Dolonkoi*: They were the inhabitants of the Chersonese that invited the elder Miltiades to the area in the mid-sixth century to protect them against their rivals, the Apsinthioi (Hdt. 6.34–35). Apparently with the full consent of the Dolonkoi, Miltiades and his family ruled the area for half a century.

- *Edonoi*: They dwelt in the lower Strymon region, near Pangaeum, and so might have dealt with Pisistratus in the mid-sixth century. In the 490s, Histiaeus and Aristagoras of Miletus tried to settle amid the Edonians, but Aristagoras was eventually killed by them (Hdt. 5.124; 126; Thuc. 4.102; Diod. 12.68.1–2). In 465, the Athenians sent 10,000 settlers to the region under Sophanes and Leagros to a site known as Ennea Hodoi, or Nine Ways. The members of this expedition were massacred by a coalition of Thracians composed mostly of Edonians (Hdt. 9.75; Thuc. 4.102; Diod. 12.68; Paus. 1.29–45). In 437, the Athenian Hagnon successfully founded a city at the same site, which he named Amphipolis (Thuc. 4.102). Presumably he came to some sort of arrangement with the Edonians.

- *Mygdones*: They were Thracians who inhabited the area around the Axius River and Thermaic Gulf before Macedon came to control the region (Hdt. 7.123–24). They probably dealt with Pisistratus in the mid-sixth century. There were also supposedly Mygdonians near the Troad in Asia, mentioned in the *Iliad* as allies of the Trojans (3.185–87).
- *Thynoi*: They lived on both sides of the Hellespont and Propontis, being, along with the Bithynians, a Thracian tribe dwelling at least partly in Asia. Xenophon says that they were the most warlike of all Thracians and had been a considerable threat to many powerful Thracian rulers, such as Teres, the father of Sitalces (*Anab.* 7.2.22). The Thynians were among the tribes subdued by Seuthes with the help of Xenophon in 399 (*Anab.* 7.4.2).
- *Odomantoi*: Inhabitants of the region of Pangaeum, they worked the mines along with other tribes, such as the Satrai (Hdt. 7.112). Aristophanes' *Acharnians*, produced in 425, describes a contingent of Odomantians brought to Athens as allies. The Athenian ambassador proudly declares them the most warlike of the Thracians (153–56). Thucydides says they lived beyond the Strymon in the plains and were independent, never having come under the sway of the Odrysians (2.101.3).
- *Odrysai*: This tribe came to control a large federation of tribes and ruled much of southeastern Thrace for most of the later fifth century and the first half of the fourth. The Odrysian kingdom was probably the largest and longest-lasting federation of Thracians in antiquity. Thucydides provides a good description of the Odrysian kingdom at the beginning of the Peloponnesian War (2.29, 97). The Odrysians, especially the kings Sitalces, Seuthes, and Cotys, had extensive dealings with the Athenians throughout the period covered by this study.

- *Satrai*: Likely very similar to the Dioi and Bessoi, they lived in the Rhodope Mountains and also worked the mines at Pangaeum. Herodotus says they were the only Thracians never subjected to any foreign power because of their mountainous homeland and warlike character. Herodotus also says that the Bessoi were a branch of the Satrai (7.110–12).

SOURCES AND METHODOLOGY

This study of the more than two centuries of connection between Athens and Thrace incorporates a wide array of sources. For better or worse, the nature of the surviving evidence necessitates an Athenocentric approach because the Thracians left us no writing of their own by which we might discern their motives and views concerning the Athenians. An acute problem for modern scholars is in separating the reality of Thrace from the often ideological perception of Thrace found in literary sources. Several recent archaeologically based studies, though, have made important strides towards illuminating Thracian society on its own terms.[20] For their part, the Greeks had much to say about the Thracians that, though biased and skewed by the incomplete perspective of the foreign observer, can at the very least reveal how the Greeks thought about the Thracians. Because this study is concerned most of all with how the Athenians perceived the Thracians and how they went about exploiting the resources of Thrace for their own advantage, I must plead guilty to the charge of relying in large part on Attic sources. What follows is a survey of the sources most frequently used and the methods employed in approaching them.

Herodotus, Thucydides, and Xenophon are naturally relied upon extensively. Though all three were concerned with the literary qualities of their work, they nonetheless remain

---

[20] See, for example, Archibald's comments on her methodology (1998: 5–6). She advocates moving beyond the traditional categories of investigation derived from the literary sources, such as theories of Thracian kingship and the personalities of individual rulers.

invaluable for reconstructing historical events and context. As with all literary sources, we must approach them with appropriate criticism. In the case of Herodotus, Scott argues in his useful commentary on the sixth book that Herodotus is essentially honest. Scott insists that "for the later books, including book 6, there is no reason to see [Herodotus] as other than a conscientious enquirer, within the limits of his world, and then writing up the results."[21] Despite the intense controversies that have raged regarding Herodotus' accuracy, and especially his use of sources, I am sympathetic with Scott's assessment.[22] But because Herodotus wrote about events that occurred over a huge expanse of the ancient world, usually a generation or more prior to his own researches, we should approach his material cautiously, evaluating how he could have learned about a particular event and whether the event as he describes it is plausible and fits in with what other evidence we have. For Thracian affairs, particularly those pertaining to the Aegean coastline and the Chersonese, Herodotus seems to rely on Athenian sources. While in Athens, he could have consulted members of the large population of ethnic Thracians living in the city. He also visited a number of sites in the north Aegean, including Thasos and the Hellespont, where he encountered both Greeks and Thracians privy to happenings in Thrace and knowledgeable about Thracian customs, *nomoi*.[23]

We will have opportunity to discuss Thucydides throughout this work, not only as a source but also as an Athenian with extensive Thracian ties in his own right. Chosen as the Athenian general in Thrace in the early years of the Peloponnesian War, he controlled mines on the mainland opposite Thasos, and his father had the Thracian name Olorus. A Thracian king named Olorus, probably related to Thucydides' father, had given his daughter in marriage to the younger Miltiades. As for Thucydides' reliability, Gomme sensibly argues that when

[21] Scott 2005: 6n17, 26.

[22] For the extremes of scholarly opinion, see skeptics Fehling (1989) and Armayor (1978); and conversely the response by Pritchett 1993.

[23] As pointed out by Asheri (1990: 132–33).

Thucydides is contradicted in a later source, such as Ephorus or Diodorus, we are to prefer Thucydides unless some new evidence appears in support of the latter.[24] I might add that regarding actual events, as opposed to attestations of motive and the like, Thucydides appears quite reliable.[25] In Thucydides we are fortunate to have a well-informed source regarding many things, but especially in the case of Thrace. And as a figure connected to Thrace himself, he offers special insight into the characters of other such men, though perhaps with a level of bias of which we should be wary. His feelings for the post-Periclean democracy at Athens, for instance, are fairly negative and might bear on his presentation of the democracy's treatment of the elite.[26]

Like Thucydides, Xenophon was a historian and an actor in some of the most significant events he records. Also, like Thucydides, he had extensive experience in Thrace. The last two books of his *Anabasis* give a firsthand account of Xenophon's experiences in Thrace at the head of his troops, the remnants of the Ten Thousand mercenaries who had campaigned on behalf of the Persian pretender Cyrus.[27] Xenophon took up service with the Odrysian dynast Seuthes II and carried out operations through much of southeastern Thrace. Xenophon recounts his personal dealings with this dynast, including a banquet attended by all the Thracian nobles in the region. Here we undoubtedly have a well-informed source, but Xenophon had clear biases from which his history seems

[24] See Gomme's (Gomme et al. 1945–1981: vol. 1, 84–87) principles of historical criticism.

[25] For possible problems concerning the attestation of motives, see Sears (2011) concerning the issues surrounding Thucydides' description of the campaign at Pylos in 425.

[26] See, for example, his comments regarding Alcibiades at 6.15. Though Alcibiades was an arrogant and flamboyant aristocrat, Thucydides argues that because the Athenians turned against him out of their populist paranoia, they brought ruin upon themselves. See Gomme et al. 1945–1981: vol. 4, 242–45.

[27] For a useful commentary on the Thracian portions of the *Anabasis*, see Stronk 1995.

to suffer at certain points.[28] Because he was exiled from Athens
and took up service and residence with the Spartans, he has
been accused of harboring an elitist prejudice against Athenian
democracy.[29] Likewise, his portrayal of the Thracians, especially Seuthes, appears in many places to be a hostile one,
probably because Seuthes failed to deliver the promised
rewards to Xenophon and his troops. What Xenophon tells
about Seuthes' court, however, is in line with other sources
concerning the Thracian nobility, including material remains.
For the period covered by Xenophon we have recourse to
other contemporary accounts, in various states of preservation, that can offer useful corroboration or corrective, as the
case may be. Biases and flaws aside, Xenophon tells us many
useful things about Thrace and Thracophiles, often from a
firsthand perspective.[30]

A great portion of fifth-century Attic literature is represented by drama – tragedy and comedy. Many of the plays
of the great tragedians Aeschylus, Sophocles, and Euripides,
though ostensibly dealing with mythological themes, comment

---

[28] In a seminal introduction to the *Hellenica*, Cawkwell renders a damn-
ing verdict of Xenophon as a historian, highlighting many inexpli-
cable omissions and apparent distortions in his history (Cawkwell and
Warner 1978: 7–46).

[29] The date and cause of Xenophon's exile is a very contentious topic.
Even the ancient sources do not agree, citing reasons ranging from
his mercenary service for Cyrus to pro-Spartan political sympathies.
Rahn (1981) offers convincing arguments that Xenophon was exiled
in 394 once anti-Spartan feeling was again on the rise at Athens,
while Badian (2004) has recently suggested that Xenophon, even
as an exile, remained loyal to Athens. It seems inescapable that
Xenophon had a degree of negative feeling for the democracy that
openly resented his social and economic status as a cavalryman.
The Athenian democracy also executed Xenophon's revered teacher,
Socrates. The same events of history and character traits that led
Xenophon to serve for a period at the court of a Thracian king
would also have prejudiced him against the Athenian system. For
more on this issue, see Chapter Three in this volume.

[30] Two volumes of Xenophon studies have appeared recently that offer
updated scholarly views on a range of issues. See Tuplin and Azoulay
2004; Lane Fox 2004.

on current events.[31] For instance, Euripides' *Hecuba*, staged in 425, is set in the aftermath of the Trojan War, but the villainy of the Thracian character Polymestor was possibly meant as a warning to the Athenians against allying with the Thracians.[32] Likewise, Sophocles' *Tereus*, surviving only in fragments, told in gruesome detail of the rape and mutilation committed by the Thracian king Tereus against Philomela, a daughter of a king of Athens. This, too, might have been meant as a comment on the Thracian allies of Athens.[33] Tragedy offers little by way of factual detail, but yet the attitude of the playwrights towards the relationship between Athens and Thrace was probably shared by at least some other Athenians. We should be cautious in using tragedy as evidence because the writers were pursuing a dramatic rather than historiographical agenda. Tragedy, though, is invaluable in determining how the Greeks conceived of barbarians, including Thracians.[34]

Comedy has often been used as a mine for scholars of Athenian political history. The plays of Old Comedy, in particular, dealt overtly with contemporary events and personalities, especially leading politicians, such as Cleon. As Rusten argues, Old Comic plays survived throughout antiquity, despite their arcane references that would hardly have resonated with later audiences, because the ancients used the plays as sources for Athenian history.[35] The Thracians and Athens' ties to Thrace are mentioned in many places, especially Aristophanes' *Acharnians*. But, as with tragedy, we must be careful in using comedy as

[31] A major exception is Aeschylus' *Persae*, which dramatizes the Battle of Salamis and its aftermath.

[32] For a study of Polymestor's character and the allusion to the Thracians, particularly Sitalces, see Delebecque 1951: 147–64.

[33] For a study of the play's fragments, see Fitzpatrick 2001.

[34] E. Hall (1989) explores how the Athenians sought to understand themselves in comparison to a barbarian other as represented in Attic tragedy. J. Hall (2005: 259–63), however, has recently challenged the notion that the Greeks saw themselves as diametrically opposed to barbarians. Rather, the Greeks might have conceived of themselves and barbarians as occupying opposite ends of a cultural continuum, with an infinite number of blended identities lying in between.

[35] Rusten 2006: 556.

evidence. Facts were routinely twisted and exaggerated to fit comic plots. Also, the relationship between the respective attitudes of comic playwright and audience is not always clear.[36] Like tragedy, comedy can inform us of various Athenian stereotypes of foreigners, such as the Thracians, though perhaps distorted to an even greater extent.[37] In the end, playwrights were concerned with taking the first prize in dramatic competitions and thus they would have written plays that pleased the audience, or at least the judges. If a joke was made concerning the Thracians or an Athenian Thrace-haunter, it probably resonated with the audience.[38]

For the end of the fifth and much of the fourth century, the Attic orators – principally Lysias, Aeschines, and Demosthenes – are often the richest sources we have for Athenian history. This is in many ways unfortunate, not least because, as Harris points out, "nothing aside from the knowledge of the men sitting in judgment and the limits of plausibility restrained the litigant from inventing falsehoods and distorting the truth."[39] A further wrinkle is added by the possible revision of speeches after their oral delivery.[40] The use

---

[36] Sommerstein (1996: 334–37) argues that the playwrights were a "conservative" lot, as were the majority of those who attended the plays. Carey (1994), on the other hand, insists that the lampooning of leading politicians was a means for the mass of citizens to assert authority over their leaders through ridicule. In this way, the comic playwright voiced concerns and attitudes held by the population at large. Henderson (1990: 272) calls the Old Comic poets the "constituent intellectuals of the demos," whose role in influencing and shaping the city's ideology was "an organic feature of the sovereignty of the demos."

[37] For comic representations of barbarians, see Long 1986.

[38] For the role of tragedy and comedy in instructing the audience in moral and ethical matters, see Taplin 1983. Taplin argues that the ancient dramatists did conceive of themselves as playing a didactic role in the polis, though perhaps not to the extent claimed by nineteenth-century scholars.

[39] Harris 1995: 8. Golden (2000), however, cautions against an appeal to plausibility as an indicator of truthfulness. See also Todd (1990) for a survey of the ways in which oratory has been used by historians.

[40] On this issue, see Worthington (1991), who argues for frequent and substantial revisions. MacDowell (2000: 24–26) and Yunis (2001:

made by orators of historical material, involving both the distant and recent past, is a complex issue.[41] At the very least, a speaker would be discriminating and even misleading in the selection, exclusion, and interpretation of historical events. Concerning recent events, orators usually proceeded with the assumption that their audience knew the details, but it is difficult to determine to what extent this was actually true. It is reasonable to assume that recent history could not be treated too cavalierly.[42] As a relevant note on the treatment of historical events in Thrace, Aeschines chides Demosthenes for wearying the Athenians with excessive detail about obscure Thracian matters and places, but he does not impugn the accuracy of these statements.[43] In using oratory as evidence, the context and the intention of the speaker should always be borne in mind; statements about private matters without corroborating evidence should not be trusted; and the speaker's interpretation of even securely attested matters should never be taken at face value, even though the speaker's arguments can shed light on what the audience might have been expected to believe.

The works of two other important fourth-century historians, Theopompus of Chios and Ephorus of Cumae, unfortunately do not survive except in fragments and in the works of

26–27) see revisions as a possibility, only to a lesser extent than Worthington.

[41] See the treatments of Pearson 1941. See also Nouhaud (1982), who is concerned primarily with the orators' use of material preceding a given speech by at least twenty years. He concludes (357–64) that Lysias and Demosthenes were willing to distort and even falsify historical material to suit their purposes, and Aeschines was often mistaken or misinformed in his use of historical examples. Yet Nouhaud concedes that references to contemporary events, especially by Lysias, might be more trustworthy and useful to the modern historian.

[42] See Pearson 1941: 228: "Many such events [after the Peloponnesian War] would have taken place within the lifetime of the audience or might be known to them through older members of their families. In making such allusions the orator would have to be careful not to conflict with private information that some of his listeners might have acquired from their elders."

[43] See Aeschines' comments at 3.82, where he appears to pun on the Thracian place names. For Demosthenes' reply, see 18.27.

later authors, such as Diodorus. Theopompus, quoted chiefly by Athenaeus, should be given serious consideration because he provides an important contemporary perspective on the times in which Iphicrates, Chabrias, Charidemus, and others operated, and in several passages he comments directly on such figures.[44] For his part, Ephorus seems to have provided a fuller picture of the Greek world of the fourth century than did Xenophon, and were it not for Diodorus, who relied extensively on Ephorus, we would be in the dark about many important issues.[45] Ephorus was particularly well informed concerning the campaigns of Greek mercenaries abroad, perhaps hearing from the mercenaries themselves in Athens. His account of Iphicrates' activities in Egypt in 374/3, for example, is given from the perspective of Iphicrates himself, who may have been Ephorus' source, either directly or indirectly.[46]

The Aristotelian *Constitution of the Athenians*, referred to by its Greek title *Athenaiōn Politeia*, rediscovered on papyri in the late nineteenth century, was written probably in the late 330s and revised in the 320s while Aristotle was in Athens. The *Athenaiōn Politeia* consists of two sections, the first a history of the development of the Athenian constitution from its beginnings to the supposedly final reforms of 403. The second gives a detailed account of the workings of the fourth-century Athenian democracy. This study primarily relies on the first half because the author frequently relies on traditions different from those used by Herodotus and Xenophon. It is not always clear which tradition the modern historian should prefer, and

[44] Flower (1994) provides the best modern treatment of Theopompus. See especially pages 66–71 on Theopompus' aversion to luxurious living; and 184–210 for the effect of his moral judgments and concern with motivations on his historical accuracy.

[45] See the treatment of Diodorus' methods in Stylianou (1998: 132–39). But see also Sacks (1990), who attempts a rehabilitation of Diodorus by demonstrating that there is more original thought in his writings than has been acknowledged. In the case of the Ephoran books in particular (11–15), Diodorus seems to have added his own proems, or at least embellished those of Ephorus.

[46] Stylianou 1998: 104–9.

many principles of fourth-century political theory are applied anachronistically to earlier periods, but each case will be judged on its merits.[47]

Cornelius Nepos, a Latin writer of the first century BCE, penned a collection of brief biographies of famous men, *De viris illustribus*, which included a section on Greek generals. Though much maligned by modern scholars for his apparent lack of original research and his hackneyed prose, he does have his defenders.[48] It seems as though Nepos consulted primary sources more than previously thought, and the nature of his work led him to preserve many details left out of historiography.[49] As a repository of anecdotal material, such as certain traits of character and the attitudes held by the contemporaries of important figures, Nepos is often the only source we have. When we can compare his work with other sources, it is clear that he often represents various traditions faithfully.

The first- and second-century CE biographer Plutarch has also suffered at the hands of scholars. Recently, however, he has been rehabilitated as not only a critical user of primary material but also an important literary figure in his own right.[50] Frost presents a convincing image of a Plutarch who is able to consult seminal works while being steeped in an intangible yet vital intellectual and cultural milieu that we today can scarcely hope to appreciate. Though Plutarch's prodigious memory might slip from time to time, he demonstrates vast learning and familiarity with the Greek past.[51] As a biographer, Plutarch was a dedicated moralist. He records the deeds of his

---

[47] Rhodes' 1981 commentary remains the indispensible scholarly aid for the *Athenaiōn Politeia*.

[48] For a disparaging portrait of Nepos, see especially Horsfall's scathing comments in the *Cambridge History of Classical Literature* (1982).

[49] For a reassessment of Nepos, see Titchener 2003.

[50] Duff (1999: 5–9) gives a brief and useful survey of Plutarch's fortunes at the hands of scholars. For Plutarch as an important literary figure, and a discussion of his historiographical methods, see the collection of essays in Pelling 2002.

[51] Frost 1998: 36–53.

subjects, both major public actions and intimate private utterances, in order to present a comprehensive portrait of their respective characters.[52] In so doing, Plutarch hoped to edify his readers. This particular ethic of biographical writing ensures that Plutarch, like Nepos, records many things overlooked or downplayed by historiographical sources. For the careers – and personal traits – of Cimon, Alcibiades, and others, he is invaluable. If the motives he assigns to his subjects are incorrect or inferred from dubious evidence, we can at least gain insight into the reputation and reception of these characters as preserved in the traditions used by Plutarch.

The Greek so-called epigraphic habit, whereby all manner of decrees, laws, dedications, and economic transactions were recorded for posterity on stone, has provided ancient historians with a massive corpus of evidence. The Athenians were especially fond of inscriptions. In addition to filling in the gaps left in literature concerning political history, inscriptions are invaluable for legal and social history. They provide often the only source for local history outside of the main foci of ancient literary sources.[53] In many cases, inscriptions are the soundest pieces of contemporary evidence we have. First of all, they were often inscribed very shortly after the event or decision they record. Also, they have not been subjected to the manuscript tradition, which at certain points might have led to distortions in literary texts. Most probably, the inscription as we have it today is exactly as it was when it was first inscribed, and any subsequent modifications, such as erasures or additions, can usually be detected by examining the stone. Finally, inscriptions have often corroborated and elaborated upon the version of events preserved in literature. For instance, Plutarch tells us that Alcibiades managed to capture the rebellious city of Selymbria largely through treachery and bring it back into alliance with Athens (*Alc.* 30). The inscription preserved as *IG* i^3 118 details the exact arrangements made

---

[52] For his moralizing program, see Duff 1999: 13–98.
[53] Cooper 2008: 10.

between Selymbria and the Athenian generals, and Alcibiades himself is listed as the proposer for honors to be granted to Apollodorus, a Selymbrian citizen and probable associate of Alcibiades. We thus have a much fuller picture of events than Plutarch alone provides, including a glimpse into the personal arrangements that were behind Alcibiades' successful campaigns in the north.

Inscriptions, though, are often poorly preserved, missing large sections of the text and having other sections damaged by erosion and other factors. Although the formulaic language and *stoichidon* lettering of many inscriptions allow epigraphers to make educated restorations to missing lines, Badian has urged caution in reconstructing ancient history from "square brackets."[54] Inscriptions can also be very difficult to date and situate in their proper context. Often a clear date presents itself, such as the preservation of an archon's name. In other cases, epigraphers apply various criteria, from letter forms to grammatical idiom and spelling conventions, but these criteria are necessarily subjective and open to various interpretations. Letter forms, especially, have proven unreliable for dating purposes.[55] A base for a statue of a certain Dieitrephes, one the Thracophiles covered in this study, has been preserved on the Acropolis. The lettering had originally been used to date the inscription to the 440s, too early for our Dieitrephes, but more recently a date closer to the end of the century has been plausibly suggested.[56] Certainty in this case is elusive. We should always remember that the inscriptions we do have form far from a complete record and only survive by chance. More than that, there is no guarantee that what is preserved on inscriptions is accurate. Even in the fourth century, Theopompus accused the Athenians of exaggerating their role at Plataea in the inscription supposedly preserving the oath made before the battle.[57]

[54] Badian 1989.
[55] For dating criteria, see Meiggs 1966; Mattingly 1971; 1999; Henry 1998; 2001.
[56] Keesling 2004.
[57] Theopompus' epigraphical criticism is explored by Pownall 2008.

And finally, the physical placement of the inscription, often on a large and elaborately decorated stele, carried meaning far beyond the written text itself.[58] This meaning is often lost to us, in no small part because the original situation of the inscription cannot be ascertained.

In lieu of Thracian literary evidence, we are fortunate enough to have recourse to a substantial body of archaeological and material evidence from Thracian lands. The first major comprehensive work to deal with Thracian material culture was Danov's 1976 *Altthrakien*, based largely on an earlier work published in Bulgarian in 1968. Danov follows a survey of scholarship on Thrace and his account of the relevant literary sources with a look at what he calls "primary sources," that is, inscriptions, numismatics, and other material and archaeological evidence.[59] More recently, Archibald takes into account the massive amount of archaeological material from Bulgaria in the decades following Danov's work and offers a rich and full survey of a specific area of Thrace from the Early Iron Age to the early Hellenistic period.[60] Archibald urges scholars to move beyond the skewed accounts of Thrace offered in Greek literature and instead to investigate the Odrysians on their own terms. Utilizing material remains, she traces changes in such areas as the symbols used to express wealth and social stratification. From a material perspective, she also explores the interaction between the Odrysians and their neighbors, especially Greeks and Persians.

Although a scholar must treat with caution material finds that have no native literary context with which they might be interpreted, such finds can be used to corroborate what the Greeks wrote about the Thracians. For example, it is difficult to determine what meaning the ornate drinking vessels found among the Rogozen and Panagyurishte treasures had for the Thracians who possessed them.[61] But we can understand how a

---

[58] See Thomas 1992: 78–88.

[59] Danov 1976: 52–89.

[60] Archibald 1998.

[61] See Cook 1989 and Fol 1989 for Rogozen; see Venedikov 1961 for Panagyurishte.

Greek such as Xenophon or Iphicrates would have seen in the use of these objects the type of ritualized ostentation of epic heroes. Likewise, we do not know exactly what significance horse burials, for which we have many surviving examples, had for the inhabitants of Thracian lands, but for the Greeks they might have reaffirmed their view of Thrace as a land of heroic horsemen.[62] By careful use of material evidence, the tension between Greek imagery and Thracian reality can be addressed.

Art objects represent a complex and difficult category of evidence for the historian. Though we have a large body of vase-painting and sculpture, particularly of Attic origin, that depicts Thracians and figures with Thracian attributes, the precise intent and meaning behind such imagery can be elusive. In employing this evidence, the proper context for each object – usually sympotic in the case of vase-painting – must be kept in mind, along with the careful work of art historians. This study is concerned with Athenian attitudes towards Thrace and the Thracians, and therefore artistic material cannot be overlooked. Images of, say, Thracian peltasts might represent their subjects inaccurately, but that peltasts were depicted at all says something about those who consumed such material. There appears to be an acute fascination on the part of the Athenian elite, the primary consumers of art objects, with foreigners in general and Thracians in particular. In many cases, elite Athenians are themselves represented with Thracian attributes, such as distinctive clothing and equipment.[63] In corroboration with literary and other forms of evidence, artistic material can flesh out our understanding of Athens' relationship with Thrace.

PISTIROS: A CASE STUDY IN MATERIAL EVIDENCE

There were extensive contacts between the Thracians and Greeks throughout the Late Archaic and Classical periods,

---

[62] For horse burials, see Archibald 1998: 69; Kouzmanov 2005.

[63] For foreigners in Attic art, see Vos 1963; Lissarrague 1990a. For a general overview of Thracian imagery, see Tsiafakis 2000.

especially in the coastal Greek cities in the north Aegean and in the form of official diplomatic contacts with the upper echelons of the Odrysian court of Sitalces and his successors.[64] A recently excavated Greek settlement in the heart of Thrace provides valuable material evidence for contact and cultural and economic interchange between Greeks and Thracians. This site represents an ideal case study with which to illuminate how material and other forms of evidence can supplement the information found in Greek literary sources.

Over the last two decades, a site identified with the attested Greek trading post, or *emporion*, of Pistiros has been excavated by a joint team of Bulgarian, British, Czech, Polish, and French archaeologists.[65] The *emporion*, flourishing in the fifth and fourth centuries, was officially founded in the mid-fifth century on the site of a preexisting center of tribal trade.[66] It is located near Vetren, on the northern foothills of the Rhodope Mountains and at the extreme eastern part of the Maritsa valley, which was a key route between the Thracian plain and the Aegean. The Rhodope range and surrounding areas were rich in deposits of precious metals, and the Greeks chose the site of Pistiros because of its proximity to the sources of metal extraction and to important transport routes.[67] Pistiros was close to the home of many of the Thracian groups that played key roles in Athenian history, including the Dioi and other independent mountain tribes. The site of Pistiros is invaluable for modern scholarship, both because it is essentially the most completely preserved Greek *emporion* in foreign lands and because it affords us a glimpse of the interaction between Greeks and Thracians well into the interior of Thrace, and relatively far from the view of our main literary sources.[68] The site therefore

---

[64] See Danov 1976: esp. 175–221; Isaac 1986; Archibald 1998: esp. 93–125.
[65] See especially Bouzek et al. 1996; Bouzek et al. 2002.
[66] Domaradzka and Velkov 1994: 8.
[67] See Archibald (1998: 23) for a map of areas of metallurgical extraction in the area.
[68] For the unique importance of Pistiros as an archaeological site, see Domaradzki 2000. The famous *emporion* of Naukratis in Egypt is

offers valuable insight into how Thracians and Greeks – including Athenian Thracophiles – interacted.

Aside from the physical remains at the site, an inscription pertaining to Pistiros – written in Ionic Greek with some Atticisms – was found in the early 1990s at the nearby modern Bulgarian town of Vetren. Likely originating from a Thracian king and successor to Cotys I in the early to mid-fourth century, the inscription outlines some of the benefits afforded by the Odrysian king to the Greek merchants inhabiting Pistiros and other *emporia*, such as exemption from customs dues and guarantees of the preservation of their property.[69] Greek merchants from the coastal cities of Thasos, Maroneia, and Apollonia are also mentioned and granted certain rights. From the inscription, Loukopoulou concludes that the *emporion* of Pistiros was granted to the Greeks by the Odrysians as a mutually beneficial site of lucrative trade, from which the Odrysians could derive considerable tax revenue. The benefits to the Thracian rulers were obvious, so Pistiros and similar settlements were likely part of the general Thrace-centered policy of Athens culminating in an alliance with the Odrysian king Sitalces during the Peloponnesian War.[70] The inscription also deals with territorial disputes between Greeks and locals. After the founding of Pistiros, settlement in the area exploded, with several new sites emerging, especially toward the mountains to better exploit the natural resources.[71] By the time of the inscription, the Greek settlers had gained the upper hand and demanded certain concessions in exchange for continuing to operate in Thrace and benefit the local rulers. For instance, in addition to exemption from certain taxes, the debts of the Thracians to the Greek merchants are mentioned, not the other way around.[72]

probably the best analogue to Pistiros, but the archaeological reports from Naukratis are less than adequate.
[69] Domaradzka and Velkov 1994; Chankowski and Domaradzka 1999; Domaradzka 2002.
[70] Loukopoulou 2005.
[71] Chankowski and Gotzev 2002: 276–78.
[72] Loukopoulou 2005: 17; Domaradzka 2002.

Though the site was clearly Greek, excavations have demonstrated the presence of both Greeks and Thracians in the town. For example, Greek and Thracian names have been found as graffiti on pottery, and distinctively Thracian loom weights and spindle whorls – used by women within the household – were found.[73] Pistiros is a perfect example of the synthesis of Graeco-Thracian material culture in the area. For one thing, the largest amount of fourth-century imported Attic pottery in all of Bulgaria – outside of Apollonia Pontica – has been found there.[74] On the other hand, Pistiros was a metallurgical center where the expertise of Greek craftsmen was blended with local Thracian techniques and styles to produce fine metal goods for consumption by elite Thracians.[75] A bronze appliqué from the fourth century, depicting a comic actor, is a brilliant instance of the combination at the *emporion* of a figure typical of Greek art but rendered by Thracian metalworking technique.[76] Tsetskhladze argues that Greek craftsmen, probably residents of Pistiros, helped to build and decorate the elaborate Thracian tombs found throughout the region. In addition to Greek workmanship, local Thracian tastes are reflected in these tombs also.[77]

There is evidence of religious integration among the inhabitants – Thracian cult objects and altars have been discovered along with the attestation of Greek and Thracian divinities, especially Dionysus.[78] The Vetren inscription itself invokes the typically Thracian god Dionysus as the ideal deity to arbitrate between Thracians and Greeks.[79] Herodotus (7.111) mentions an oracle of Dionysus in the Rhodope range that may give us an idea of the religious and cultural character of the region.[80]

[73] Domaradzka 1996; Bouzek 2002: 347–48.
[74] Domaradzki 2002: 26.
[75] Bouzek 2002: 345.
[76] Lazov 1996.
[77] Tsetskhladze 1998: 73–80.
[78] Lazov 1996; Domaradzka 1996; Domaradzki 2002: 18, 25.
[79] Domaradzka and Velkov 1994: 10.
[80] How and Wells 1912: vol. 2, 168.

A passage from Suetonius confirms that this oracle was famous in antiquity, and he tells us that the oracle predicted Octavian's rise to power, as it had for Alexander the Great (*Aug.* 64). Recent excavations undertaken by a Bulgarian team at a site in the eastern Rhodopes called Perperikon suggest that the place of the oracle may have been found.[81] According to archaeologists, the site was used for cult practices as far back as the Neolithic period, and finds from the Late Bronze Age and Iron Age are abundant. Most interesting are a series of small clay altars and a large open hall with a round altar in its center. The area around Perperikon is littered with troughs and basins, which some archaeologists have equated with wine-making facilities for ritual purposes. According to the excavators, there is also evidence for the practice of Orphic ritual, traditionally connected to Dionysiac worship. All of this evidence points to a cult center, and the location coupled with what appears to be wine-related activity evince Dionysiac activities. Increasingly elaborate structures were built on the site into the Roman period, suggesting continuity of religious activity.

There is some indication of a military relationship at Pistiros, both symbiotic and adversarial. The Greeks would have had some sort of armed protection for an economic center in the heart of foreign territory. The site was fortified in the third quarter of the fifth century with a curtain wall and tower that may have reached over 6 meters high.[82] The fortifications resemble those of Thasos much more than Thracian examples, perhaps reflecting the number of Thasians involved with the *emporion*.[83] These defenses were strengthened in the fourth century. Although profitable contact was made with many of the Thracians in the area, there was still some danger of attack. The Vetren inscription demonstrates that the Odrysian

---

[81] The site's official Web site, sponsored by the Bulgarian Ministry of Culture, is the only comprehensive source on the excavations currently available: http://www.perperikon.bg, accessed on October 11, 2011.

[82] Kolarova 1996.

[83] Bouzek 1996.

rulers protected the Greek merchants at Pistiros, but official protection would have been no guarantee against attack from the independent tribes dwelling in the nearby mountains. In the town itself, some Thracian weapons, including the head from a spear and several arrowheads, have been found on the main road.[84] Chariots, either as transports or weapons of war or both, were present as indicated by their mention in the Vetren inscription and by the presence of distinctive wheel-ruts on the main road and gate.[85] Chariots would have added a distinctively exotic and perhaps even heroic flavor to Pistiros.

Alexander himself found out how much Thracians and Greeks living together in places such as Pistiros could come together militarily. In describing Alexander's campaigns in Thrace, Arrian says that the autonomous Thracians of Mount Haemus – to the north and east of Pistiros – banded together with many armed merchants to oppose Alexander from the heights (*Anab. Alex.* 1.1.6–7). These merchants, or *emporoi*, mentioned by Arrian were most likely Greek inhabitants of *emporia*, such as Pistiros.[86] That the Greeks opted to fight along with the Thracians, and indeed to exploit the mountainous terrain to their advantage in a typically Thracian fashion, demonstrates that Greeks and Thracians dwelling in the heart of the Balkans worked together militarily and learned from one another. It also indicates that many Greeks living in the region were more ready to join forces with Thracians than to capitulate to Alexander.

As a final consideration, Greeks and Thracians had to find some way to communicate with one another in *emporia* such as Pistiros, because they would have had to communicate at the courts of Thracian rulers, on embassies, and as allies on

---

[84] Domaradzki 2002: 16.

[85] Salviat 1999: 266; Bouzek 2002: 344.

[86] This is the reading given by the manuscripts, but most scholars have emended the text to mean "natives" instead of merchants. In light of the discovery of Pistiros, and therefore Greek merchants, so deep in Thracian territory, the manuscript reading must be correct. See Domaradzka and Velkov 1994: 9.

military expeditions. Miller addresses the question of how Greeks and Persians could have communicated and concludes that for the most part interpreters were needed.[87] The same is probably true of Greeks and Thracians, though some Greeks living for extended periods of time in Thrace probably did learn to speak some of the local language. Thracians too, living in and around various northern Aegean Greek settlements, could have learned Greek. There are a few interpreters mentioned in the literary sources, such as the bilingual Carian used by the Persian satrap Tissaphernes in his dealings with the Greeks (Thuc. 8.85). Bilingual Thracians would have been immensely valuable in Pistiros and countless other contexts. Many Thracians lived at Athens in the Classical period, perhaps a majority of whom were household slaves who not only would have learned Greek themselves but could have taught their native tongue to members of the household. We are told by Plutarch that Alcibiades was given a Thracian tutor named Zopyrus by his guardian Pericles (*Alc.* 1.22). This relationship probably paid dividends later in Alcibiades' career when he took refuge on his personal estates in Thrace and had under his command Thracian soldiers. Thracian women were famous in Athens as devoted nurses taking care of their young Greek charges, as shown in literature and on vase-painting. Tsiafakis argues that Athenians knew Thracians better than other types of foreigners.[88] There was no shortage of usefully bilingual Thracians to act as interpreters, and possibly also a good number of Greeks, especially Athenians, who knew some Thracian. Many of the Thracophiles featured in this study were better placed than most to have had extensive contact with Thracian-speakers, even from an early age.

[87] Miller 1997: 130–33.

[88] For Athenian everyday familiarity with Thracians, see Tsiafakis 2000: 365–66. For Thracians as nurses, see the scholiast to Plato *Laches* 187b and Pliny *Nat. Hist.* 35.70; Tsiafakis (373–74) discusses an Athenian red-figure skyphos by the Pistoxenos painter, dating to around 460, that depicts Heracles attended by his aged and loyal Thracian nurse (Schwerin, Kunstsammlungen, Staatliches Museum 708).

INTRODUCTION

THRACE VERSUS OTHER LANDS: THE CASES
OF ALCIBIADES AND CHABRIAS

For the Greeks, other lands – especially Persia – were often perceived as a source of personal enrichment and prestige, and a channel to greater political power. There are significant differences, however, between Thrace and the other lands to which an Athenian might turn, chiefly because of the potential for acquiring autonomous power and territory. Whereas the nations ruled by the Persians were under the thumb of the Great King, and any Greek who was given influence over a territory served at the pleasure of his Persian masters, Thrace was under no such central control. In describing Thrace, Herodotus evokes a land of limitless but unrealized potential. He says that the population of Thrace is second only to that of India, and that if all the Thracian tribes united under a single leader and common goal, no nation on earth could defeat them. Herodotus then qualifies his assessment of Thrace, saying that such a unification could never happen, and thus the Thracians remain weak and divided (5.3). The Odrysian kingdom provides the only exception to a Thrace that was fragmented, and even under the Odrysians, enterprising Greeks could enjoy a great degree of individual power and autonomy. Even though Herodotus himself lived to see the rise of the Odrysian kingdom and knew of the powerful king Sitalces (Hdt. 4.80; 7.137), he persisted in his conception of Thrace as largely ungoverned. It was in this expansive territory in the northern Aegean that ambitious men could establish hereditary dynasties, secure wealth and resources, and acquire private armies of mercenary soldiers. The careers of Alcibiades, who spent time in Persia before turning to Thrace, and Chabrias, who opted for mercenary service in Egypt, can serve to highlight the differences between Thrace and other lands.

Because he was a Thracophile in his own right, Alcibiades will be explored in greater detail throughout this study. To be sure, many Greeks were able to exercise remarkable power and influence within the Persian Empire, and Alcibiades was certainly one of them. For instance, Persia had on many occasions supported Greek tyrants in Ionia, such as Histiaeus of Miletus. But, when Histiaeus and his nephew Aristagoras tried to establish their own niche in Thrace centered around a fortified settlement at Myrcinus on the Strymon, and started to accumulate their own private resources in terms of men and materiel, they began to pose a threat to Darius. Accordingly, on the advice of Megabazus, who warned against such men being given power in advantageous territory, Histiaeus was recalled to Susa (Hdt. 5.23). Aristagoras probably would have been, too, had he not been killed by local Thracians during an attempt at expanding his territory (Hdt. 5.124–26).[89]

Alcibiades had extensive dealings with the Persians. After he fled the Spartans, who had grown to distrust him, he became an advisor to Tissaphernes, the Persian satrap in Sardis. Alcibiades, a haughty, talented, and urbane figure, thoroughly charmed Tissaphernes. The satrap was so enamored with him that he named the most luxurious park in his dominion "The Alcibiades" (Plut. Alc. 24.4–5). Meiggs has argued that it was Tissaphernes' own sophisticated attraction to Hellenism, in stark contrast to the boorishness of the uncultured Spartans, that ensured Alcibiades a privileged position in his court.[90] Perhaps also Alcibiades was himself attracted to the lifestyle and power available among the Persians. Alcibiades advised his Persian host against hastily bringing defeat against either the Athenians or Spartans, insisting that it would be in the Persians' interest to prolong the war between the Greeks until all players were rendered weak. Accordingly, Tissaphernes decided to play both sides, promising, for example, to send money and ships to the Spartans, but delaying at every opportunity. While at the court of Tissaphernes, Alcibiades achieved so great a level of influence that he was able to conduct business personally in the satrap's name (Thuc. 8.45–46). Eventually, the double-dealing that Alcibiades had encouraged Tissaphernes

---

[89] For more on Histiaeus and Aristagoras in Thrace, see Isaac 1986: 15–17.

[90] Meiggs 1972: 354–55.

to adopt backfired. The satrap was forced to arrest Alcibiades after the latter had been denounced by the Spartans to the Great King. Alcibiades eventually escaped this imprisonment (Plut. *Alc.* 27.5).

A few years later, in 409/8, Alcibiades managed to convince Pharnabazus, the energetic satrap of Phrygia, to swear a personal oath to him. The other Greek generals had sworn oaths to the Persians regarding their treatment of the city of Chalcedon. Though Alcibiades was absent at the time, Pharnabazus thought it appropriate that he also be made to give an oath. Alcibiades, however, refused to swear anything unless Pharnabazus in turn swore an oath to him personally. Thus, in addition to making pledges about Chalcedon, both leaders gave private assurances to each other (Xen. *Hell.* 1.3.11–12).[91]

Alcibiades showed himself a master at entering into profitable relationships with the most powerful men in the Persian Empire. The ties he forged with Pharnabazus seemed on the cusp of bearing fruit once Alcibiades was forced to leave his possessions in Thrace following Aegospotami in 405. According to Plutarch, Alcibiades entered the Persian Empire at this time determined to make himself as useful to the Great King as Themistocles had been (*Alc.* 37.4). While in Phrygia, his ally Pharnabazus gave him the town of Grunium, from which he was able to derive 50 talents in revenue annually, a situation analogous to that of Themistocles under Artaxerxes (Nep. *Alc.* 9). Before he was able to gain a position at the court of the king, however, Alcibiades was killed by the agents of Pharnabazus at the request of the Spartan Lysander (Plut. *Alc.* 39).

Powerful as he was, Alcibiades was always subservient to the Persians while in their empire, but in Thrace things were different. Militarily active in the north Aegean, especially around the Hellespont, since at least 411, at some point he established settlements in the area. Xenophon only mentions unspecified

---

[91] For the special relationship between these two, see Hatzfeld 1940: 286.

fortified settlements (*teichē*), but other sources name perhaps three places in the vicinity of Bisanthe and Pactye (Xen. *Hell.* 1.5.17; 2.1.15; Lys. 14.26–27; Plut. *Alc.* 36.3; Nep. *Alc.* 7).[92] It seems that he had secured these fortified places in case he needed a refuge from the Athenians, which in fact he did after the naval defeat under his watch at Notium in 407/6. His settlements were near the territory that had been controlled by other Athenian Thracophiles, the Philaids (which produced the elder and younger Miltiades), in the late sixth and early fifth century. Alcibiades might have consciously emulated the hereditary dominion the Philaids had managed to secure in Thrace.[93] After Notium, he remained in Thrace until the Athenian defeat at Aegospotami left the Spartans as masters of the Aegean. Remaining in coastal settlements, no matter how well fortified, was rendered imprudent in such a climate. Accordingly, Alcibiades fled across the Hellespont to the court of Pharnabazus.[94]

Alcibiades seemed to enjoy a great deal of autonomy while in Thrace, and he was even able to raise sizable armies of Thracians for his own use. In 409, while he was campaigning in the north more or less independently of the official directives of Athens, he seized the city of Selymbria with the forces of the Chersonese and a large number of Thracian troops (Xen. *Hell.* 1.3.10).[95] Plutarch says that the Thracians under his command at this time served Alcibiades zealously because of the goodwill and affection they had for him (*Alc.* 30.4–5). Nepos tells us that when he withdrew to his fortresses after Notium, he raised a force of locals and became the first Greek to penetrate into the interior parts of Thrace. By this action, his fame greatly increased, and he was able to secure alliances with some of the kings of Thrace (*Alc.* 7). Plutarch clarifies that Alcibiades at this time withdrew from the Athenians,

---

[92] For these settlements, see Isaac 1986: 211–12.

[93] Hatzfeld 1940: 319–22.

[94] Hatzfeld 1940: 339.

[95] For the independent status of the Athenian generals in the Hellespont during this period, see Andrewes 1953.

gathered a force of foreign fighters, and on his own initiative attacked some kingless (*abasileutoi*) Thracians and also protected the Greeks living on the frontier from Thracian incursions (*Alc.* 36.3).

These actions appear to have been undertaken by Alcibiades on his own, without the direction of the Athenians or any local Thracian ruler. He did, though, manage to ally himself with Thracian leaders, notably Medocus and Seuthes II. Nepos implies that these alliances were made because of the military success he enjoyed in Thrace. Scholars have surmised that Alcibiades at some point gave aid to these rulers against rebel Thracians. The kingless Thracians mentioned by Plutarch might have been rebelling against the authority of Seuthes. That Alcibiades was able to offer the support of both Medocus and Seuthes to the Athenians at Aegospotami suggests that he had rendered both kings valuable services (Diod. 13.105.3). This is especially interesting given that Medocus and Seuthes were often fierce rivals for power – both claimed legitimate descent from the Odrysian king Seuthes I.[96] Alcibiades was a master at playing both sides, and he appears to have done so in Thrace to his own advantage. He also seems to have had his own force of Thracian peltasts and horsemen at Aegospotami (Plut. *Alc.* 37.2).

There is no indication that he was under the authority of any Thracian ruler. Two of the territories controlled by Alcibiades were later offered to Xenophon by the Thracian dynast Seuthes II. Heraclides of Maronea, a Greek agent of the Thracian ruler, persuaded Seuthes that it was dangerous to give these fortified places to Xenophon, a man with an army (*Anab.* 7.5.8). Heraclides' remark was most likely a thinly veiled reference to Alcibiades' own fortresses, implying that Alcibiades had been a threatening presence in Thrace because he had owned several fortresses and commanded private armies independent of a Thracian authority.[97] Because of their fortified position at

[96] Hatzfeld 1940: 319–20; Archibald 1998: 122–23.
[97] Archibald 1998: 123.

Myrcinus, Histiaeus and Aristagoras had threatened to acquire more power than the Persians could tolerate. Seuthes heeded the advice of Heraclides and ceased mentioning the territories to Xenophon, fearful that with these fortresses the Athenian general would be too powerful and autonomous a force in the area.

Few places could rival Thrace for sheer opportunity. Alcibiades, like the Athenian Philaids before him, was able to sow the seeds of his own fiefdom near the Hellespont, where he commanded great material resources and his own private armies. He at times worked on behalf of the Thracian kings in the area, but he did so to increase his own power and influence, not because of any compulsion from a higher authority. He had enjoyed tremendous, albeit fleeting, influence among the Persians. Yet, he was never able to take charge of his own private forces to do with as he pleased. He could influence and manipulate powerful men like Tissaphernes and Pharnabazus, but he was always under their direct authority and ultimately under the power of the Great King. Estates in the Persian Empire, such as Grunium in Phrygia, were a source of vast revenue for Alcibiades, but they were not his to do with as he wished, as his fortresses in Thrace seem to have been.

Chabrias was a famously competent – and profligate – Athenian general of the fourth century who could not bear to remain among the Athenians, according to Theopompus (*FGrHist* 155 F 105). His extravagance and great wealth are attested in many sources.[98] His military victories were numerous, the most famous being the naval defeat of the Spartans at Naxos in 376. Naxos was widely hailed as the first true Athenian naval victory since the Peloponnesian War, overshadowing even Conon's achievement with a Persian fleet at Cnidus (Diod. 15.35). Chabrias received great personal rewards at Athens for Naxos and other victories, including a bronze statue modeled to reflect his storied tactical ingenuity against

---

[98] These sources are usefully enumerated by Davies (1971: 560–61).

Agesilaus in Boeotia.[99] But, like many other talented generals, Chabrias at times could not bear the Athenians, their fickle support, and their disapproval of his more eccentric traits. So he chose to leave Athens for Egypt, where he acted as a mercenary general for at least two different rulers.

Our sources are explicit in their description of Chabrias' involvement in Egypt as a private enterprise lacking any formal Athenian directive or sanction.[100] Nepos says that Chabrias went to Egypt of his own volition (*sua sponte*) on two separate occasions. In the case of his second journey to Egypt, Nepos explicitly attributes self-interested motives to Chabrias, namely, a desire to reap material rewards equivalent to those given to the Spartan king Agesilaus, who had agreed to serve the Egyptian ruler Tachus as a general (Nep. *Chab.* 2). Likewise, Diodorus says that Chabrias went to aid the Egyptian king Acoris without first securing the approval of the demos, and in the case of Tachus, Chabrias was persuaded to serve privately (*idiai*) instead of being sent publicly (*dēmosiai*) by Athens (15.92.3).

Prior to the King's Peace of 387, which brought an end to the Corinthian War, Chabrias had been sent by the Athenians to aid Evagoras, ruler of Salamis on Cyprus, in a revolt from Persia. Chabrias helped Evagoras consolidate power over all of Cyprus. Xenophon says the Athenians sent Chabrias out with

[99] For the honors after Naxos, see esp. Dem. 20.75, 84–85, 146. Chabrias' statue was designed to mirror the stance he urged his troops to adopt to receive a charge of Agesilaus' hoplites in 378/7. Most of the evidence indicates that he had his soldiers stand at ease, with their shields resting upon their knees, in order to display their contempt of the Spartan forces, who in turn called off their advance. See Anderson 1963; Buckler 1972. The interpretation of Burnett and Edmonson (1961), that the statue depicted a kneeling hoplite, is based on a confused passage of Nepos (*Chab.* 1.3), but the description in Diodorus (15.33.4) should be preferred.

[100] But, see Pritchett (1974–1991: 72–77) who argues that Chabrias, and most of the other infamous generals of the fourth century, actually remained loyal to Athens. Even if Chabrias and others never acted explicitly against Athenian interests, many of their campaigns seem decidedly personal, well outside of any directives from home.

800 peltasts and a large number of hoplites (*Hell.* 5.1.10). This expedition set sail in late 388 or early 387. A year later, Athens was forced to acquiesce to the terms outlined by the King's Peace, which included a cessation of virtually all military activity in the Aegean.[101] The peace would have ended the official Athenian help to Evagoras. Chabrias, though, appears to have remained in Cyprus a while longer before going to Egypt and entering the service of Acoris sometime in 386.[102] It is unclear whether Chabrias maintained a private force that he brought to Egypt, but he did indeed enter the service of the Egyptian king after most likely serving Evagoras privately for a time. Chabrias' position in Egypt was much the same as the Athenian Thracophile Iphicrates – whom we shall examine later – during the same period. Both generals had been abroad leading Athenian forces and both opted not to return to Athens once overseas state ventures were rendered impossible by the terms of the peace.

As Theompompus attests, Egypt was an outlet for Chabrias, much as Thrace was for certain Athenians. How, then, was Egypt different from Thrace in terms of the advantages and opportunities afforded ambitious Athenians? First of all, aside from the sixty-year span between 404 and 343, Egypt was under the control of the Persians for roughly the entire period covered by this study. Essentially, therefore, I regard Egypt as a Persian context. The experiences of Alcibiades reveal the pitfalls of turning to Persia for advancement and as an alternative to Athenian democracy. The levels of autonomy attainable for a Greek in Thrace could not be matched under the Great King and his satraps. Even under Egyptian rulers, haughty Greek commanders could be disappointed by the limitations

---

[101] For the chronology, see Stylianou 1988: 466–69.

[102] The chronology of Chabrias' activities in Egypt has troubled scholars for some time, given that Diodorus (15.29.1–4) relates these events under the year 377/6. Stylianou (1998: 100–101) gives the most plausible solution, suggesting that Diodorus' source, Ephorus, had at this point in his narrative provided a summary of all events in Egypt from 386 until the dispatch of Iphicrates in 380/79.

INTRODUCTION

imposed on them. Agesilaus, for instance, was vexed at being given a military position subordinate to Tachus when he ventured to Egypt as a mercenary (Plut. *Ages.* 37.1–2). At any rate, the volatile nature of Egypt during the period of 404–343, when there were several conflicts with Persia and multiple dynastic quarrels, did offer many opportunities for mercenary service and the acquisition of riches, which Greeks like Chabrias exploited. But, unlike Thrace, Egypt was a venerable and ancient society, civilized centuries before even the emergence of the Greek polis, with entrenched institutions, such as the priesthood and a rigorous code of laws. Wealth and influence aside, perhaps Egypt simply did not offer the same cultural attractions as Thrace. The raw power up for grabs in the lawless regions north of the Aegean were missing in Egypt, not to mention the chariot racing, heroic feasting, and other ancillary benefits so attractive to elite Athenians. Egypt was not a rough-and-tumble frontier for the Athenians in the same way Thrace was. Finally, Egypt did not have the same geographic proximity or quite so long and rich a history of diplomatic and military connections with Athens.[103] Aside from Chabrias, there were very few Athenians whom we could legitimately call Egypt-haunters.[104]

---

[103] Egypt is roughly 600 miles from Athens, with Crete lying in between at about a third of the distance, just under 200 miles. By contrast, the Thracian Chersonese is only 200 miles from Athens, with many friendly islands, such as Imbros, Lemnos, and Scyros, lying in between.

[104] In the late 460s the Athenians launched an expedition to Egypt to aid the Libyan king Inarus in his revolt from Persian control. The expedition, which Thucydides says involved over 200 ships, came to ruin after six years (Thuc. 1.104, 109–10; Diod. 11.71.3–6, 74.1–4, 75, 77.1–5). Thucydides' brief account portrays this venture as one of the Athenian polis, in line with campaigns in Cyprus and elsewhere. We are largely in the dark about internal Athenian politics in this period, and we do not know who advocated the mission to Egypt – whether Cimon, who may have already been ostracized, Pericles, or someone else. See Gomme et al. 1945–1981: vol. 1, 306–7. As such, we cannot evaluate whether this mission was in any way driven by a person somehow tied to Egypt, like those spearheaded by Cimon to the Chersonese and Thasos.

40

OUTLINE OF THE BOOK

This study aims to illuminate the intimate ties between Athens and Thrace that existed for two centuries. These ties were forged and maintained by a set of individuals and families that Aristophanes aptly described as "Thrace-haunters," or perhaps even "disciples of Thrace." Many of these disciples were the most distinguished figures in the polis and were often those who shaped and effected Athenian policy at home and abroad. At the same time, they were frequently denied the power they sought at Athens and were forced to look elsewhere. From Pisistratus' seizure of power with the help of Thracian mercenaries and Pangaeum gold, to Athens' preoccupation with Amphipolis, the colony founded by Hagnon; and from the light-armed troops arrayed against the Spartans at Pylos, to the extreme measures aimed at safeguarding the Chersonese in the face of Philip's expanding empire, Thrace and its disciples had a profound influence on the course of Athenian history.

The following two chapters present in chronological sequence the ways in which Thrace was used to advance the material, political, and military status of certain Athenians within Athens itself. These chapters also explore how Thrace served as an outlet for those individuals who were either unable to achieve sufficient levels of influence at Athens or had fallen out of favor with the demos and thus faced prosecution – or worse. After an introduction outlining the political constraints faced by Athenian elites at home, Chapter 2 turns first to the experiences of the Pisistratids. In the mid-sixth century, Pisistratus was the first, so far as we know, to capitalize on the resources of Thrace, both in terms of soldiers and money, to achieve power at Athens, in this case as tyrant. During the reign of Pisistratus, the elder Miltiades, leader of the Philaid family that included the famous younger Miltiades and Cimon, led a colonizing effort to the Thracian Chersonese – the modern Gallipoli Peninsula. Though in de facto exile, Miltiades was able to rule as a tyrant in his own right, and his family controlled the Chersonese for half a century. In the first half of the fifth century, Cimon was able to recoup his family's lost fortunes and become the preeminent man in the polis, largely because of the successes he enjoyed at the head of several northern expeditions. In the latter half of the fifth century, several figures, notably Hagnon, Dieitrephes, and Thucydides, were appointed to special commands in Thrace, in many cases because of pre-existing ties to the region. They served as "Thrace-experts" on behalf of Athens.

Chapter 3 picks up with the careers of Alcibiades and Thrasybulus. Though having nearly diametrically opposed reputations from antiquity to today, these two figures were linked closely both militarily and politically. Both were tied to Thrace and campaigned extensively in the north Aegean during the final years of the Peloponnesian War. Once Alcibiades was exiled from Athens for the final time, he turned to his own private estates and private mercenary forces in Thrace. Thrasybulus returned to Thrace in the early fourth century at the head of an Athenian expedition, being sure to forge his own personal relationships with local Thracian rulers and provide for himself a place of refuge in case of trouble at home. Though revered as a democratic hero for defeating the Thirty Tyrants in 404–403, Thrasybulus did not always enjoy a cozy relationship with the demos. While the Ten Thousand were marching back from the Battle of Cunaxa at the turn of the fourth century, Xenophon was offered estates, women, and other lavish rewards in return for military service on behalf of the Thracian dynast Seuthes II. Though Seuthes ultimately failed to deliver the promised rewards, Xenophon seemed genuinely attracted to the prospect of life in Thrace on his own richly appointed estates. The last figure covered in depth is Iphicrates, the preeminent mercenary leader of the early fourth century, who spent two lengthy periods in Thrace at the court of the Odrysian king Cotys. Iphicrates went so far as to marry Cotys' daughter and to fight a naval action against the Athenians. Drawing together the cases treated in both Chapters 2 and 3, I conclude that Thrace was a vital political alternative to Athens. It afforded many elites a decisive advantage at

Athens itself, while also sparing Athens considerable political turmoil by channeling the more egregious ambitions of some of the most divisive figures in the polis.

In Chapter 4, I discuss Athenian ambivalence towards Thrace and the Thracians. The Thracians were by turns attractive and terrifying to the Athenians. The two differing views of Thrace provided respectively by Herodotus and Thucydides are the starting point of the discussion. Herodotus presents the Thracians at the beginning of his fifth book as foreign and strange; Thucydides lays out in the introductory passages of his history how barbarians simply live as the Greeks themselves once had. The Athenian populace as a whole seemed to be divided between these two perceptions of the Thracian other. Next, I explore the experience of Thracians living at Athens. The Athenians' eager acceptance of the Thracian cult of Bendis is juxtaposed with the fact that Thracians made up the largest share of Athenian slaves. The last section of the chapter outlines the various responses the Athenians had to the Thracophiles themselves. It seems that the disciples of Thrace were particularly controversial figures, frequently censured because of their ties to a foreign land and people.

In Chapter 5, as a complement to the discussion of elite political discontent in Chapter 2, I begin with an exploration of why Athens failed to satisfy some of its citizens culturally and socially. Next I turn to the different uses of Thracian imagery on the part of the Athenian elite. Following scholars such as François Lissarrague, I argue that Thracian attributes were used by some elites to distinguish themselves as superior in terms of social class. The discussion continues with a description of various Thracian practices – including the use of gold funerary masks, chariot racing, heroic individual combat, and hero-cult – that would have appealed to self-conscious elites. Thracian court life, too, enticed those eager to emulate the aristocrats of old in the conspicuous display of wealth and reception of obeisance from subject populations. In the end, for the disciples of Thrace the search for political and material advantages need not have been divorced from cultural and social considerations. In Thrace they were able to live as aristocrats should.

Chapter 6 investigates the ways in which the connection between Thrace and Athens affected Greek military practice. I begin with the elder Miltiades, who built a wall across the entire Gallipoli Peninsula in order to keep out the Thracians who regularly invaded his territory. It seems that this fortification was inspired by the type of enemy Miltiades faced, namely, loosely organized raiding parties instead of regular armies. The evidence indicates that this fortification inspired several similar types of wall throughout antiquity. Miltiades' nephew, the younger Miltiades, took over control of the family territory on the Gallipoli Peninsula and ruled it for many years before returning to Athens in 493. At the Battle of Marathon in 490, in which the younger Miltiades acted as Athenian commander, several tactical decisions were made – including charging the Persians to eliminate the effectiveness of archers and emancipating slaves (perhaps to serve as light troops on the flanks) – which might have been inspired by his experiences in Thrace. The next section deals with Athens' use of Thracian mercenaries before and during the Peloponnesian War. Thracian tactics were used to great, if sometimes horrifying, effect during the war, including the capture of Spartan hoplites near Pylos and the attack against Mycalessus (Thuc. 4.28.4; 7.28–30). By leading groups of Thracians, several Athenian commanders of this period learned important lessons in the use of diverse infantry tactics. In 404–403, Thrasybulus led the democratic resistance against the Thirty Tyrants. Thrasybulus made extensive use of Thracian troops, both mercenaries and aliens resident at Athens, in the defeat of the Thirty. Because of his previous campaigns in Thrace, Thrasybulus knew best how to use Thracian fighters, from setting ambushes to leading them over mountainous terrain. In the final section, I turn to Iphicrates, who was credited in antiquity with the introduction and regularization of the peltast in Greek armies. Though he certainly did not introduce the peltast to the Greeks, Iphicrates learned from his campaigns with Thracians and developed a versatile infantry soldier who was a cross between a Greek hoplite and Thracian peltast. I conclude that for some Athenians, Thrace – not the hoplite phalanx composed of citizen equals – served as their military academy.

The Epilogue outlines the activities of the Athenian generals Chares and Charidemus, who earned considerable notoriety from their private military campaigns, particularly in the Thraceward region. To round out the study of the Atheno-Thracian connection, I emphasize the lot of Chares and Charidemus after the rise of Macedon as the dominant power in the Greek world. Following Philip's conquest of virtually all of Thrace, including the areas within Athens' traditional sphere of influence, Thrace could no longer serve as an outlet for ambitious and unscrupulous Athenians. These two were just the sort of military adventurers who could have found a home among the Thracians, but in a Macedonian world they had to resort to other options. After serving the Persians as a mercenary against Alexander – suffering an ignominious defeat in the process – we last hear of Chares commanding a group of mercenaries on Cape Taenarum in the southernmost point of the Peloponnese. Charidemus entered Persian service, where he was killed by Darius III after a piece of advice too freely given. Thrace attracted hard military men, and Chares and Charidemus were able to make quite a career for themselves in the northern Aegean before Philip fundamentally changed the geopolitical environment.

@/@ @/@ @/@ @/@

CHAPTER TWO

THRACE AS RESOURCE AND REFUGE I

THE PISISTRATIDS TO THUCYDIDES

INTRODUCTION TO CHAPTERS 2 AND 3

In the fourth century, many Athenian generals abandoned Athens in favor of their own private operations abroad, which Demosthenes attempts to· explain in the *Second Olynthiac*, delivered in 349:

If I am to say something factual about the generals, then why do you think, men of Athens, all the generals you send out flee this war only to pursue their own private wars? Because this war is fought for prizes that are yours collectively (for if Amphipolis were taken, you would be immediately advantaged), but the commanders bear the danger themselves and yet receive no pay. In private wars, the danger is small and the rewards go to the commanders and the soldiers – Lampsacus, Sigeum, and the things plundered from ships, for example. Therefore each one turns to that which pays best. (2.28)[1]

---

[1] τίνος γὰρ εἵνεκ', ὦ ἄνδρες Ἀθηναῖοι, νομίζετε τοῦτον μὲν φεύγειν τὸν πόλεμον πάντας ὅσους ἂν ἐκπέμψητε στρατηγούς, ἰδίους δ' εὑρίσκειν πολέμους, εἰ δεῖ τι τῶν ὄντων καὶ περὶ τῶν στρατηγῶν εἰπεῖν; ὅτι ἐνταῦθα μέν ἐστι τἀθλ' ὑπὲρ ὧν ἐστιν ὁ πόλεμος ὑμέτερα (Ἀμφίπολίς γ' ἂν ληφθῇ, παραχρῆμ' ὑμεῖς κομιεῖσθε), οἱ δὲ κίνδυνοι τῶν ἐφεστηκότων ἴδιοι, μισθὸς δ' οὐκ ἔστιν· ἐκεῖ δὲ κίνδυνοι μὲν ἐλάττους, τὰ δὲ λήμματα τῶν ἐφεστηκότων καὶ τῶν στρατιωτῶν, Λάμψακος, Σίγειον, τὰ πλοῖ' ἃ συλῶσιν. ἐπ' οὖν τὸ λυσιτελοῦν αὐτοῖς ἕκαστοι χωροῦσιν.

In urging the Athenians to commit the requisite resources to check Philip's growing power, Demosthenes gives a straightforward, sensible reason why commanders have taken to pursuing their own "private wars." Fighting on behalf of Athens carried great risk for a commander in the case of defeat and very little reward in the case of victory.[2] Demosthenes was addressing the situation in his own day, but the Athenian generalship had always been a hazardous occupation. Capable of bringing great glory to a victor, such as for Miltiades after the Battle of Marathon, it virtually guaranteed harsh and immediate consequences after defeat, as it did for the very same Miltiades following his failure at Paros. Such were the consequences of popular control over the leaders of the polis.

In his 352/1 speech *Against Aristocrates*, Demosthenes characterizes those generals who were attracted to Thrace as desirous of *exousia* (license and authority) (23.57).[3] Throughout the speech, Demosthenes deals with Charidemus of Oreus, one of the more notorious military leaders of the mid-fourth century. Charidemus was originally from Euboea, but as a mercenary light infantryman in the 360s he served under Iphicrates and accompanied him on a mission to Amphipolis. When Iphicrates failed to take the city and decided to remain

---

[2] Although many scholars have followed the scholiast to this speech in suggesting that Demosthenes means to single out Chares in particular as the general who pursued his own interests instead of bringing aid to Olynthus, I agree with Ellis (1967: 109), who argues that Demosthenes is alluding to all Athenian generals.

[3] ἀπαλλαγῇ μὲν ἐκ Θρᾴκης, ἐλθὼν δ' εἰς πόλιν οἰκῇ που, τῆς μὲν ἐξουσίας μηκέτι κύριος ὢν δι' ἧς πολλὰ ποιεῖ τῶν ἀπειρημένων ὑπὸ τῶν νόμων, "Suppose [Charidemus] should leave Thrace, coming to live in some civilized city, no longer enjoying the license through which he now commits innumerable violations of the law." Demosthenes supplements the sections of historical narrative in this speech with many pieces of documentary evidence. As Sealey (1993: 131) notes, Demosthenes acquired the copious knowledge of Thrace demonstrated in the speech from his service as a trierarch in the region in 360–359. Sealey also suggests that, though a Hellenistic scholar listed Euthycles as the actual litigant who delivered the speech, perhaps Demosthenes prosecuted Aristocrates himself.

in Thrace, Charidemus did likewise and spent the rest of his career oscillating between service to the Athenians and to Thracian kings. To Demosthenes' mind, Charidemus was loyal only to his own advancement. Demosthenes carefully contrasts the civilizing and constraining laws of the Athenian polis – particularly the legal safeguards and recourse available to aggrieved citizens against the more powerful – with the *exousia* available in Thrace to the unscrupulous. Like his protégé, Iphicrates seems to have been attracted to the *exousia* of Thrace when denied what he deemed to be suitable power in Athens.

For a long time, scholars maintained that the generals in the fourth century were tied less and less to the demos and behaved largely as condottieri, the mercenary generals of late medieval and Renaissance Italian city-states. Some have likened them to the professional generals of the seventeenth and eighteenth centuries who rose to prominence in the armies of foreign powers.[4] Also, mercenary soldiers came increasingly to replace the traditional citizen hoplite as the mainstay of Greek armies, as was received opinion at least.[5] Iphicrates, with his storied leadership of Thracian mercenaries and perfidious actions in the service of Thracian kings, appeared to be the very paradigm of these trends in Greek warfare. But, the observations of Demosthenes are also apt with respect to many prominent Athenians in the fifth and even the sixth century. In the context of post-Solonian Athens, Thrace had long beckoned leading political and military figures with the promise of ever greater *exousia*.

It is a truism that there will always be elites in any given society, regardless of the particular political, social, and

---

[4] For a discussion of the problems with labels such as condottieri, see Pritchett 1974–1991: vol. 2, 59–116. Pritchett argues that these generals remained loyal in the service of their polis. He seems to overstate his case at certain points, however, because many of the Athenian leaders did at times forsake Athens in favor of their own campaigns.

[5] For a study of this phenomenon, see Burckhardt 1996: 76–153. Pritchett (1974–1991: vol. 2, 104) thinks the sources, especially Demosthenes and Isocrates, exaggerate the dependence on mercenaries.

cultural framework by which the society is defined. In the case of ancient Athens – although by the end of the sixth century a new form of government took hold that in theory afforded ever greater numbers of adult male citizens a full share in the running of the polis and the benefits derived therefrom – there remained individuals who strove for a disproportionately great share of power. Sometimes these figures were able to achieve such power, but they were often left disappointed. Scholars have long wrestled with how democratic Athens reconciled the opposing interests of mass and elite, not to mention the fierce competition among the elites themselves.

Ober argues in his seminal *Mass and Elite in Democratic Athens* that the elite communicated with the masses in the public sphere by means of a complex set of symbols, especially evident in the rhetoric used by professional orators. The meanings and ideology behind these symbols were assigned by the masses themselves, thereby constraining the elite.[6] More recently, he has explored further the ways in which the Athenian democracy met the challenges posed by what was in reality a socially diverse citizen body. He calls democracy "diversity management," and acknowledges that such a system inevitably left some disappointed. Ideally, though, the political and social ledger would be balanced over time.[7]

Moreno has recently argued that, by contrast, the elite were in fact able to maintain power over the masses in Athens, achieved principally through control of the grain trade. For Moreno, foreign connections with the Aegean settlements (*klērouchies*) and allies in the fifth century and with the kingdoms in the grain-producing Crimea in the fourth were crucial to elite control of Athens. These elites were cynical enough to call themselves democrats while fostering despotic rule in the northern Black Sea in order to cement their position within the democracy. According to Moreno's model, the rhetoric employed by orators was not indicative of mass control

---

[6] See Ober 1989: esp. 339.
[7] Ober 2005: 1–26.

over the elite, but rather a tool used by the elite to mask their unsavory and undemocratic foreign connections and the true nature of their control of the grain trade.[8]

In addition to tensions between mass and elite, there was also acute competition among the elites themselves. In an important study, Forsdyke shows that members of the elite throughout pre-democratic Greece had employed exile as a means of removing their competitors. This, however, rendered the political situation in many states inherently violent and unstable. Forsdyke maintains that the Athenian democracy finally softened and took ownership of the weapon of exile through the institution of ostracism. With its ten-year limit, ostracism was an ingeniously mild form of exile, which at once showcased the democracy's restraint while still preventing dangerously ambitious and influential individuals from posing a threat to the balance of power.[9]

To add to these discussions of the power balance between mass and elite, Thrace was a place to which the elite could remove *themselves* should they be unwilling or unable to engage in the prevailing ideological system and should mechanisms such as ostracism fail to bring about the desired result, such as the removal of their more powerful competition. Not every ambitious Athenian was willing to suffer political and social disappointment in the hopes that the situation would even out in the end. In this way, removal of oneself to Thrace served as a type of voluntary ostracism. Furthermore, it seems that Athens was not always as susceptible to elite capture as Moreno contends. Even if it were, not a few notable Athenians would still have been largely excluded from power. Instead of using foreign ties to maintain their influence at Athens, many elites turned abroad when the desired level of influence proved unattainable, either because the democracy would not countenance elite capture or because rival elites held the reins of power. For this reason, Thrace proved a vital alternative to

[8] See Moreno 2007: esp. 204, 322–23.
[9] See Forsdyke 2005: esp. 1–3.

Athens, providing a power base and an outlet for elites unable to achieve their goals at home. The ambitions of the elder Miltiades, for example, were stifled because of Pisistratus' firm grip on power in the second half of the sixth century, so he turned to the Thracian Chersonese. This is not to say that connections to Thrace did not also allow elites to achieve greater influence at Athens itself. For his part, Pisistratus overcame rival aristocrats once and for all and was established as tyrant largely because of the mercenaries and money he was able to amass from the region around Mount Pangaeum in the northern Aegean.

The extent and nature of the role Thrace played in the contest for political power among Athens' elites has gone unnoticed by modern scholarship. In the 1970s, Pritchett, in discussing Iphicrates, commented that "we are in need of a study of nuptial ties of mercenary chieftains with Macedonian and Thracian princesses."[10] Little has been done to remedy this situation. As this study will show, for Athens such ties went far beyond the nuptial and involved several leading figures beyond those traditionally seen as mercenary chieftains. In his invaluable reference work for Aegean Thrace, Isaac identifies some of the personal ties established between Athenians and Thrace. For instance, in discussing the ties of Thucydides and the Philaids to the region opposite Thasos, Isaac stresses the long-standing relationship forged by one of Athens' most elite families with Thrace, based largely on cooperation rather than enmity with local Thracians.[11] But Isaac is interested in such connections only insofar as they pertain to the local history of certain sites. He therefore provides only a cursory account.

Archibald's 1998 *The Odrysian Kingdom of Thrace: Orpheus Unmasked* provides the most comprehensive survey to date of the region of Thrace most directly connected to the Athenians. In discussing Athenian activities in Thrace during

[10] Pritchett 1974–1991: vol. 2, 66n33.
[11] Isaac 1986: 34.

the Pentacontaetia, she says that "the relationship between official civil and military activities and unofficial, private ones is occasionally perceptible in our sources but is otherwise an unexplored dimension of these developments." Archibald does recognize that the personal interests of elite Athenians were central to Athens' foothold in Thrace, but she stresses that Athens' principal aims in the north were economic and strategic.[12] There is no in-depth exploration of how pervasive these personal ties actually were, and no study of the full range of factors that led to elite Athenian interest in Thrace irrespective of the wider aims of the polis. Also, Archibald distinguishes between the personal ties made by Pisistratus and the Philaids, especially Cimon, with what appear to have been official "civic" ventures from the mid-fifth century on.[13] Even in the later fifth century, though, the personal connections of the elite continued to play a pivotal role, and there was not as much of a shift in Athenian diplomatic machinery as scholars such as Archibald contend.

Thrace was both a resource for those seeking greater power at Athens and an alternative setting when sufficient levels of power were unattainable within the Athenian system. In short, the disciples of Thrace could obtain the *exousia* they desired. Thrace was also a source of refuge for those facing prosecution – or worse – at home. This chapter will provide a chronological account of the experiences of Athenian Thracophiles, ranging from Pisistratus in the mid-sixth century to Thucydides in the latter half of the fifth. Chapter 3 will cover the period from Alcibiades in the late fifth century through the career of Iphicrates spanning into the mid-fourth.

THE TYRANT: PISISTRATUS

So far as we know, Pisistratus was the first Athenian who found in Thrace the resources that could tip the balance of

---

[12] Archibald 1998: 115–16.
[13] Archibald 1998: 112.

power in Athens. For Pisistratus, in the mid-sixth century, these resources were large sums of money and mercenary soldiers. He had tried to secure autocratic power in Athens on two occasions prior to turning to Thrace, and both times he was eventually overcome by his aristocratic rivals. After his second expulsion from the city, he turned to the Thermaic Gulf, where he established a settlement and evidently made connections with the local ruling elite. He also went to the region surrounding Mount Pangaeum, recruiting soldiers and growing wealthy from the area's mines. Only then did he move south and amass his Greek allies from various poleis to help overwhelm his rivals at Pallene. Once back in power, Herodotus says, he maintained his position by means of revenue from Thrace and by retaining a force of mercenaries, presumably those he recruited from Thrace. Pisistratus' enemies at Athens were utterly bested, unable to challenge the tyrant's authority again. A new element had been introduced into Athenian politics that would be of central importance for the next 200 years.

Pisistratus first seized power in Athens sometime in the mid-sixth century. Taking advantage of the factional strife that plagued the post-Solonian polis – namely, that between the people of the coast led by the Alcmeonid Megacles and the people of the plain under Lycurgus – Pisistratus championed the cause of a new third faction, the people of the hills.[14] Shrewdly drawing upon the fame he acquired in

---

[14] The fullest accounts of Pisistratus' tyranny are given by Herodotus (1.59–64) and the Aristotelian *Athenaiōn Politeia* (14–19). For the chronological problems involved, see Rhodes 1981: 191–99. How and Wells (1912: vol. 1, 81) see these factions as the natural consequence of Solon's reforms, which eroded the traditional rule of the *eupatridae*. They argue that the real division was between the old landed aristocracy and the rising mercantile class. For recent scholarly treatments of Solon's reforms and the political situation in Athens at the time, see the collection of essays in Blok and Lardinois 2006, especially the offerings of Raaflaub and van Wees. Raaflaub argues that there were basically two, rather than four, classes in Solon's time, the cavalry leaders (*hippeis*) and hoplite followers (*zeugitai*); but van Wees posits that Solon merely reinforced the preexisting agrarian class divisions.

a war against Megara, and addressing the grievances of a large underprivileged segment of the Athenian population, Pisistratus managed to obtain (by vote) a bodyguard with which he occupied the Acropolis and became master of the polis (Hdt. 1.59; *Ath. Pol.* 14.1–4).[15] Soon, however, his aristocratic rivals joined forces and drove him from Athens. How was Pisistratus to overcome the traditional elite weapon of exile?[16]

In order to regain power, Pisistratus devised a scheme in conjunction with his former rival Megacles whereby he was escorted into Athens by an exceptionally tall woman in full panoply on a chariot. The Athenians were told that this was Athena herself bringing Pisistratus home. The ruse worked (Hdt. 1.60.4).[17] The fourth-century Athenian Atthidographer Clidemus says that this woman, named "Phye the daughter of Socrates," became Hipparchus' wife (*FGrHist* 323 F 15). In the Aristotelian *Athenaiōn Politeia*, we are told of a tradition that this woman was a Thracian flowergirl (*stephanopōlis*) or courtesan (*hetaira*), living in the deme Collytus (14.4). In introducing the passage from Clidemus, Athenaeus preserves her designation as a flowergirl, which was unknown to Herodotus and Clidemus. Jacoby thinks that her label as a Thracian was an insertion, perhaps originally a marginal note on the *Athenaiōn Politeia*. As he argues, it would not be surprising for a tradition to take root that made Hipparchus' wife a nameless Thracian, as appears to have happened in the case of the mother of another famous Athenian, Themistocles (Plut. *Them.*

See also Rhodes 1981: 183–87. For the general importance of conflict among elites in this period, see Stahl 1987: 60–105; Forsdyke 2005: 103–7.

[15] The *Athenaiōn Politeia* labels Pisistratus as *dēmotikōtatos*, as opposed to Megacles and Lycurgus. Rhodes (1981: 186) thinks that this account of the rivalries between aristocrats is broadly correct.

[16] See Forsdyke (2005: 101–33) for a study of the role of exile during the Pisistratid period.

[17] How and Wells (1912: vol. 1, 83) believe this story. The sons and grandsons of those who had seen this peculiar procession would still have been alive at Athens.

1.1–2).[18] As we shall see, this was a stock slander in Athenian political history.[19]

The Pisistratids hedged their bets with far-flung alliances. Clidemus says that Pisistratus chose for his son Hippias the daughter of the polemarch Charmus, which would have secured the loyalty of a powerful Athenian. Herodotus tells us that Pisistratus installed his own illegitimate son, Hegesistratus, also called Thessalus, as tyrant in Sigeum after driving out the Mytileneans by force.[20] It was to Sigeum – a city in the Troad – that the Pisistratids fled after their expulsion from Athens (Hdt. 5.94; Thuc. 6.59.4). After the death of Hipparchus, Hippias made an alliance with Hippocles, the tyrant of Lampsacus – a city on the southern shore of the Hellespont – by marrying his daughter to Aeantides, a son of the tyrant (Thuc. 6.59.3). Others too contracted such alliances, even with foreigners. The younger Miltiades married the daughter of a Thracian king, probably to strengthen his position in the Chersonese.

Moreover, if the ethnic designation of Thracian was meant to slander Hippias, why does the author of the *Athenaiōn Politeia* (or the writer of the marginal note) preserve only part of the slanderous tradition without mentioning that this woman was married to Hippias? It seems that there were two traditions about the wife of Hippias: one that she was the daughter of a prominent Athenian, the other that she was a nameless Thracian. Perhaps the slander lay in the allegation that she was an unknown flowergirl rather than the daughter of an important figure in the Thraceward region where Pisistratus would soon demonstrate extensive ties. We cannot safely disregard either version of the story.[21]

---

[18] See Jacoby's discussion in *FGrHist* (3T, b, vol. 1, 70–72; vol. 2, 73–74).

[19] For Themistocles, however, there is strong evidence that his mother actually was a Thracian woman from the Chersonese, or at the very least a Greek living in this Thracian territory. See Bicknell 1982; Lewis 1983.

[20] See How and Wells 1912: vol. 2, 55–56.

[21] Interestingly enough, the Thracians were often characterized as unusually tall. Valerius Flaccus, for example, refers to the *immanes*

Pisistratus' second period of tyranny also did not last long because he again fell afoul of Megacles. Pisistratus was soon forced abroad, where he set about marshaling the support of his friends. Herodotus says that the he spent ten years gathering a force from Thebes, Argos, Naxos, and other places while based in Eretria on Euboea. Finally, he landed at Marathon, defeated his Athenian enemies, and took control of Athens, this time for good. He maintained power by means of many mercenaries and the great deal of money he derived from Athens and the area around the Strymon River in Thrace (Hdt. 1.61–64).

The account preserved in the *Athenaiōn Politeia* explains this reference to the Strymon. During his decade-long exile, Pisistratus had first ventured to the Thermaic Gulf – near modern Thessaloniki – where he established a settlement at a place called Rhaecelus.[22] At this time, the area was very prosperous and still inhabited by Thracians, as the presence of wealthy Thracian burials attests.[23] Cole conjectures that the Greek verb used, *synoikizō*, implies a joint colonization venture, perhaps with supporters from Athens, or more likely with a group from Eretria.[24] Soon Pisistratus went to the region of Mount Pangaeum, adjacent to the Strymon and famous for its mines. Here he grew wealthy and hired soldiers. Cole suggests that Pisistratus might have introduced the large-scale worship of Dionysus in Athens as part of an arrangement with the Edonian Thracians dwelling near Mount Pangaeum, analogous to the later introduction of the Thracian goddess Bendis

Bessi (2.229). The Bessoi were a Thracian tribe inhabiting the western Rhodope range, not far from the northern stretches of the Strymon. See the map in Archibald 1998: 108.

[22] For the location, see Edson 1947: 89–91.

[23] For this material, see Baba (1990), who discusses the material from several sites, including Sindos. Many of the grave goods consist of luxury items, including gold funerary masks reminiscent of those from Grave Circle A in Mycenae. For the masks, see also Theodossiev 1998; and the catalogue of the Sindos finds, Vokotopoulou 1985. The region fell within the Macedonian sphere of influence after the Persian Wars, as implied by Thucydides (2.99–100). See Hammond et al. 1972–1991: vol. 1, 435–40; Cole 1975: 42n1.

[24] Cole 1975.

in Attica. These Thracians did famously worship Dionysus.[25] After a decade in the north, Pisistratus moved to Eretria to gather his Greek allies (*Ath. Pol.* 15.2). Best offers compelling additional evidence that his mercenary force in Athens was based on Thracian solders – at precisely this period, Thracians began to appear in Attic vase-painting.[26]

Forsdyke argues that Pisistratus mollified the traditional aristocratic rivalries that often led to expulsion by involving a larger portion of the population. She also argues that he allowed his rivals to have a suitable level of power in Athens rather than resorting to the weapon of exile. Yet, as I shall demonstrate in the following section, the elder Miltiades went into de facto exile. In order to account for Miltiades' exile, and the attested exile of the Alcmeonids during the Pisistratid period, Forsdyke faults Herodotus' sources and very grasp of the situation. She attributes the account as preserved to Philaid and Alcmeonid propaganda in the oral tradition.[27] Why, though, would Herodotus uncritically accept such propaganda, aimed at dissociating these families from the Athenian tyrants, while at the same time expressly labeling Philaid rule in the Chersonese as tyranny?

Thrace played a crucial role in cementing Pisistratus' third and lasting tyranny, a role that has gone largely unnoticed. Lavelle, followed by Forsdyke, thinks that Pisistratus relied on trade and temporary exploitation of Thracian resources by force in order to acquire resources during his exile, but any sort of permanent control of the mines of Pangaeum would have been unfeasible in light of the strength of the local Thracians.[28] Such arguments, however, ignore Herodotus' comment that Pisistratus continued to rely on money from the Strymon in maintaining power at Athens, as is indicated by the use of the present participle *syniontōn* (1.64.1). Also, Hippias, once expelled, was offered Anthemus on the Thermaic Gulf

---

[25] Cole 1975.
[26] Best 1969: 1–15.
[27] Forsdyke 2005: 121–24.
[28] Lavelle 1992; Forsdyke 2005: 118–19.

by Amyntas of Macedon, which suggests that lasting ties had been established by the Pisistratids in the region (Hdt. 5.94).[29] Although Pisistratus enjoyed a level of popular support in Athens, and many Athenians joined his side in the Battle of Pallene, in which he defeated his rivals (Hdt. 1.61.3–4; *Ath. Pol.* 15.3), the Thracian mercenaries constituted the backbone of his military resources.[30] These soldiers remained loyal to their paymaster regardless of any change in the political mood.

Pisistratus seems to have been the first Athenian to use Thrace as a springboard to power. Unfortunately, we are not told why he chose to go north during his second exile or how he learned of the region's advantages. If during his second period as tyrant he did indeed choose a Thracian wife for his son, a prior connection to Thrace is implied. The moves he made to acquire influence in the northern Troad demonstrate that he was well aware of the strategic importance of that part of Thrace. His ability to found a colony at Rhaecelus and to secure mining rights around Pangaeum attests to his skill in dealing with the indigenous inhabitants of the Thermaic Gulf and Strymon valley. The forging of inroads in the north paid off for Pisistratus by allowing him to seize lasting power in Athens, and his successors benefited from a suitable place of refuge after they were exiled. Scholars such as Cole have appreciated that Pisistratus set off a long-lasting Athenian interest in the Pangaeum region and that he demonstrated an especial diplomatic talent in doing so.[31] No one, though, has fully recognized that Pisistratus initiated a clear and pervasive pattern that was followed by several elite Athenians for the next two centuries. The aristocratic rivalries at Athens had made Pisistratus' position unstable. At one moment he was an ally of

[29] Baba (1990: 16–17) suggests that Pisistratus gave aid to the Thracians in the Sindos region against their northern enemies and thus secured their friendship.

[30] Forsdyke (2005: 119–21) mentions these mercenaries, but only in passing. For her, the support of the Athenians was the linchpin of Pisistratus' success.

[31] See also Isaac 1986: 14–15.

the powerful Megacles; at another he was driven from the city. The money and soldiers of Thrace proved to be an advantage that Pisistratus' rivals could not overcome.

The Exile as Tyrant: The Philaids

While Pisistratus held power in Athens, the Dolonkoi, an otherwise obscure Thracian tribe that inhabited the Chersonese, found themselves continuously under threat from their neighbors, the Thracian Apsinthioi. Rivalries between tribal groups were the norm for the region, which lacked a dominant governing power. Around 545/4, the Dolonkoi set out for Delphi to inquire of the god as to how their situation might be remedied. The oracle replied that they should take as a founder for their land the first person who should offer them the traditional tokens of guest-friendship (*xeinia*). The first person to do so was the elder Miltiades, an Athenian, who noticed the foreigners from the porch of his country house as they walked by (Hdt. 6.34–35).[32] Herodotus' account of the Athenian foray into the Chersonese in the mid-sixth century gives the distinct impression that the elder Miltiades desired more personal power than he was able to exercise in Pisistratid Athens. As such, he jumped at the chance to leave Athens and rule over a foreign land and people.

In deciding to leave Athens, the elder Miltiades seized an opportunity to carve out a niche in greener pastures, literally – the Thracian Chersonese abounded in fertile land for crops and pasturage, a thing decidedly lacking in Attica. Also, the straits provided access to Black Sea trade. It would have been in any state's interest to control important ports along this trade route in order to impose duties and attract the business of traveling mariners. The Black Sea eventually became crucially important as a source of imported grain, though likely not before the late

[32] As Scott (2005: 165) says, there is no a priori reason to reject this story of Thracians consulting the Delphic oracle. Many other non-Greeks did too.

fifth century.[33] Miltiades, however, did not seem to rule the Chersonese on Athens' behalf. For the next five decades, he and his family lived like kings in the north Aegean.

As it turned out, the fringes of the Greek world proved just the place for the horse-loving Philaids. The extent to which sheer necessity lay behind such overseas ventures and colonization efforts is hotly debated by scholars. A consensus is emerging that emphasizes adventurism over pragmatism.[34] Moreno calls the younger Miltiades, nephew of the founder of the Chersonese territory, an "aristocratic buccaneer."[35] Beyond the call of adventure, Thrace served as a social safety valve whereby elite Athenians could achieve their full aristocratic potential without the constraints of Athens' political system, be it democracy or Pisistratid tyranny. Moreno contends that achieving power in Athens was always the ultimate goal of the Philaids and those like them.[36] The elder Miltiades, though, accepted that the door to advancement in Athens was closed. He was not simply an old-fashioned aristocrat opposed to a populist tyrant. There is good evidence that *he* wanted to be a tyrant. Later generations of Philaids distilled an additional advantage from this Thracian power base, namely, the ability to

[33] For the vigorous scholarly debate surrounding the settlement of this region, see Isaac 1986: 159–66. For a comprehensive history of the Chersonese, see Tzvetkova 2008 (in Bulgarian, but with an English summary). For the grain supply, see Moreno 2007.

[34] De Angelis (1994) argues that problems of overpopulation and other traditional explanations for colonization played less of a role in the settlement of Selinous in Sicily than did the thrill of new opportunities. The role of the Hellespont in the Athenian grain trade is disputed. Garnsey (1985; 1988) argued that Athens was more self-sufficient in terms of grain than previously thought, so the colonization of the Hellespont was driven by adventurism. Keen (2000), conversely, attempts to show that Athens did use Black Sea grain before the Peloponnesian War. More recently, Moreno (2007: 140–43) has shown that Athens used Aegean *klērouchies* to provide the city with grain throughout most of the fifth century, and did not turn to the Black Sea until the fourth. In his model, the missions of Phrynon, the Philaids, and others were aimed at securing land for the elite.

[35] Moreno 2007: 142.

[36] Moreno 2007: 140–41.

court the Athenian populace and bolster their position within the new democracy. But, even for talented leaders enjoying privileged access to the resources of Thrace, the politics of the democracy proved too volatile. Pisistratus had largely kept rivals to his power at bay, but the Philaids struggled to maintain lasting influence once back in Athens.

In introducing Miltiades, Herodotus outlines the political situation then current in Athens: Pisistratus held all the power, but Miltiades was still a man of influence.[37] To clarify Miltiades' station, he is said to have had a household wealthy enough to race four-horse chariots, an indicator of vast resources. Furthermore, his illustrious ancestry, tracing back to Aeacus of Aegina and connected to Athens via Philaeus (hence, Philaids) the son of Ajax, is outlined in detail.[38] Miltiades' father, Cypselus, was most likely the grandson of the Corinthian tyrant of the same name and had been eponymous archon in 596/5. Thus, the Philaid family was among the old aristocracy, the *eupatridae*, who had monopolized political power at Athens before Solon's reforms.[39]

Miltiades offered the Dolonkoi shelter and hospitality (*xeinia*) once he had noticed their foreign clothing and the spears they were carrying. Thucydides remarks that by his time only barbarians and some of the less civilized Greeks still regularly carried weapons out of their fear of bandits (1.5.3–6.2). The spear-brandishing Dolonkoi were readily identifiable as foreigners. Because of Pisistratus' use of Thracian mercenaries

---

[37] Pisistratus held all the power: εἶχε μὲν τὸ πᾶν κράτος; Miltiades was still a man of influence: ἀτὰρ ἐδυνάστευε καὶ Μιλτιάδης. Scholars dispute the chronology of much of the Philaid colonization of the Chersonese. The most comprehensive general treatment is given by Kinzl 1968. This passage, coupled with Miltiades' connection to Croesus, suggests that Miltiades set out during Pisistratus' third and lasting period of tyranny, probably in 545/4. Some scholars argue that one of the earlier tyrannies is indicated. For a concise account of this debate, see Scott 2005: 166.

[38] For family claims of descent from gods or heroes, see Scott 2005: 167–68.

[39] Bradeen 1963: 193–96.

at Athens, it is possible that Miltiades was familiar with their specific style of clothing and weapons and recognized them as Thracian.

Miltiades was amenable to the request of the Dolonkoi that he accompany them to the Chersonese. He was unhappy with Pisistratus' reign and wished to remove himself from the way, to be *ekpodōn*. Many scholars think that Pisistratus himself sent Miltiades as part of a comprehensive foreign policy, which included the Hellespont, and that Herodotus is offering a sanitized, pro-Philaid version of events, with Pisistratus' involvement removed. Even if this were true, Miltiades probably did resent the tyrant's grip on power and was eager for a way to advance his own interests. In that case, both men would have something to gain from the venture: Miltiades by finding an outlet from Athens, Pisistratus in removing a powerful rival. On balance, however, one can reasonably trust Herodotus' version of events.[40] Seeing the Dolonkoi in their Thracian clothes, and having in mind the precedent set by Pisistratus, Miltiades eagerly embraced the opportunity to establish personal ties with the foreigners. The hospitality so willingly offered the Dolonkoi might have been a deliberate first step in forging a formal guest-friendship (*xenia*).[41]

Before setting out for the Chersonese, Miltiades assembled all of the Athenians willing to take part in such an expedition, offering them a chance to join him (Hdt. 6.36.1). A large number of Athenians probably went along, perhaps as many

[40] For Herodotus relying on a pro-Philaid source, see Scott 2005: 163, 169–70. But Scott also argues (366–67, 526–27, 531, 643) that for the younger Miltiades, Herodotus made use of an anti-Philaid tradition, namely, that derived from the prosecution's arguments at Miltiades' tyranny trial, which emphasized the link between his family and the Pisistratids. Why the inconsistency on the part of Herodotus? Herodotus seems to have been aware of both traditions, those for and against the Philaids, and for some reason felt the version he chose to be the more likely. The most vigorous argument in favor of the private nature of Miltiades' expedition (and also Pisistratus' activities at Sigeum) is given by Berve 1937: 26–28; 1967: 62, 80.

[41] Herodotus mentions *xeinia* in the context of formal diplomatic relations in 2.115.4.

as 400 to 600, if we are to judge by the several settlements that were founded.[42] This group most likely included other ambitious Athenians dissatisfied with their prospects for advancement under the tyranny, possibly even the father of Themistocles.[43] If Pisistratus had brought some Athenian supporters along with him to settle Rhaecelus during his second exile, Miltiades would have had a ready precedent.

This entire episode bespeaks a Miltiades jealous of Pisistratus' power (archē) and searching for an outlet for his own ambitions. The advent of the Dolonkoi seeking help against their rivals, the chance to be a prestigious city founder, and the legitimacy of power that could only be conferred by the Delphic oracle furnished the ambitious aristocrat with the means of creating his own archē only a few days' sail from Athens.[44] He was evidently satisfied enough with his position in the Chersonese: he died there between 525 and 516, having ruled for at least two decades.[45] Unlike Pisistratus, he never ventured to return to Athens and make a bid for power, in spite of being able to call upon significant numbers of both Thracians and Greeks living in his domain.

As holders of power in the Chersonese, the Philaids exercised what was tantamount to regal authority, treating the region as their personal property. Herodotus calls them tyrants, applying the verb tyranneuō and the nouns tyrannos and tyrannis to their rule, explicitly equating it to the power wielded by Pisistratus in Athens (6.34.1, 36.1). The elder Miltiades was superior to many of the Thracian rulers in the area, because the kings (basileis) of the Dolonkoi willingly surrendered their power to him. Accordingly, he took possession of the land once he arrived in the Chersonese. He ruled the Dolonkoi by virtue

---

[42] As conjectured by Scott (2005: 170).

[43] Bicknell 1982: 168–73.

[44] Herodotus indeed calls the Philaid principality in the Chersonese an archē (6.34.1), a term that had strong resonances in the time he wrote his history. For the complexity of Herodotus' views on the Athenian archē of the mid- to late fifth century, see Fornara 1971b: 37–58.

[45] For the date of his death, see Scott 2005: 174.

of their invitation and because he fought on their behalf and offered them security by building a wall across the Chersonese to keep out their Thracian enemies. After Miltiades' death, possession of the land remained within the Philaid family. Many Athenians evidently disapproved of the exercise of such authority, even in a foreign land. Once the younger Miltiades, heir to the family dynasty, returned to Athens in 493 he was tried by his political enemies on a formal charge of tyranny, but he was acquitted and elected general shortly afterwards (Hdt. 6.104.2).

The elder Miltiades' nephew, Stesagoras son of Cimon, succeeded him as tyrant. When Stesagoras was assassinated by an enemy during a war with Lampsacus, the younger Miltiades, another son of Cimon, was sent out by the Pisistratids to succeed him around 515/4 (Hdt. 6.38.2–39.1).[46] This Miltiades was more heavy-handed than his uncle and his brother had been. He seized total control of the area by tricking the regional chieftains (*dynasteuontes*) and having them all imprisoned. It seems that the various indigenous leaders were unable to unite in order to pose a challenge to Miltiades' power. Miltiades then maintained a force of 500 mercenaries in order to avoid his brother's fate, and he held the Chersonese as his possession (Hdt. 6.39.2). It is unclear whether these mercenaries were Greeks or Thracians. It is likely that Pisistratus had shown the Philaids how useful Thracian mercenaries could be.

According to Nepos, Miltiades carried himself among the inhabitants of the Chersonese with a regal demeanor (*dignitate regia*) and secured for himself lifelong rule (*perpetuum imperium*). It should be noted that Nepos seems to conflate the careers of the elder and younger Miltiades, so the exercise of regal and perpetual authority might therefore apply to the elder.[47] Nepos says that Miltiades obtained such power largely through his

---

[46] For the date, see Scott 2005: 178–79.

[47] Hammond (1956: 122–27), against the opinion of most scholars, argues that Nepos actually fills in some of the gaps concerning the younger Miltiades' career and does not in fact confuse the two men. Scott (2005: 164) argues that already in the fifth century there was a confusion of

justice and magnanimity and that he had the full support of the Athenians, both those who had sent him on the mission and those who had accompanied him (*Milt.* 2.3). This support was the natural result of the great benefits he conferred, such as granting those Athenians who were with him tracts of land and enriching them through frequent raids into adjacent territories (Nep. *Milt.* 2.1). To be sure, the legitimacy of Philaid rule had been founded upon, and was increased by, the continued support of the Dolonkoi. Even though the younger Miltiades seems to have had a more authoritarian style of rule than his predecessors, once he had fled the Chersonese because of a threat of Scythian invasion, the Dolonkoi of their own volition asked him to return and reinstated him in power (Hdt. 6.40).[48]

During the course of the campaigns to secure his position on the Hellespont, the elder Miltiades was captured by his rivals from Lampsacus. According to Herodotus, the safety of Miltiades was then of great concern to Croesus, which suggests the two were political allies. Croesus threatened the Lampsacenes with total destruction should they fail to release their prisoner, and Miltiades was accordingly set free (Hdt. 6.37). The war with Lampsacus, a city on the Asiatic side of the Hellespont, indicates that Miltiades aimed at complete control of the straits. Croesus, under threat from the growing power of Persia, doubtlessly desired to cultivate an alliance with the ruler of a territory as strategic as the Chersonese.[49] Perhaps, also, Croesus sought to increase his standing in the Greek cities of Asia Minor and to acquire influence with the Thracians, a potential target for future conquest, through Miltiades.[50] In any case, there was a personal connection between Miltiades and the Lydian king that benefited both parties.

the elder and younger Miltiades, which was picked up by Ephorus and in turn Nepos.

[48] Scott (2005: 181–82) discusses the chronological and other problems with this Scythian invasion. In any case, Herodotus' text implies the esteem the Dolonkoi had for Miltiades.

[49] Isaac 1986: 171; McQueen 2000: 114; Scott 2005: 173.

[50] Danov 1976: 246.

Once in the Chersonese, the younger Miltiades, though previously wedded to an Athenian woman, married Hegesipyle, daughter of a Thracian king named Olorus (Hdt. 6.39.2). Emphasizing its importance for Miltiades' position of authority, Herodotus lists the marriage along with the other measures Miltiades took to seize power, namely, imprisoning all potential rivals and maintaining a private mercenary force. It was Hegesipyle, rather than Miltiades' Athenian wife, who was the mother of the famous Cimon. The historian Thucydides' father was a man named Olorus, and Thucydides himself controlled mines in Thrace and wielded considerable influence among the local inhabitants (Thuc. 4.105.1). There was certainly a relationship between Thucydides and the Philaids, centered on Thrace. It stands to reason that Miltiades' father-in-law, Olorus, was a king in the region near Mount Pangaeum or on the mainland opposite Thasos where Thucydides later had connections via his father of the same name. In addition to strengthening his position in the Chersonese, perhaps Miltiades also had an eye to securing some of the resources of Olorus' territory.[51]

Marriage alliances among the aristocracy of Greek poleis were common in the Archaic period, and in the northern kingdoms of Macedon and Thrace the custom was the norm throughout much of antiquity. Hammond argues that many Archaic Greek aristocrats and tyrants often resorted to polygamy in order to cement marriage alliances. Thus, they were essentially a "law unto themselves," paralleled most closely by the Macedonian royals.[52] There is some evidence that Miltiades' first wife was a relation, or even the daughter, of Hippias.[53] Sometime after the marriage alliance between Olorus and Miltiades, Hippias seems to have withdrawn his support for the venture in the Chersonese, instead throwing in his lot with Lampsacus. Perhaps this was in response to Miltiades' actions during Darius' Scythian

---

[51] Scott 2005: 180–81. How and Wells (1912: vol. 1, 343) suggest that Miltiades had rendered Olorus some military service, but there is no direct evidence of this.

[52] Hammond 1956: 120n3.

[53] Davies 1971: 302.

campaign of 513, when Miltiades had attempted to betray the Persians by having their bridge across the Danube destroyed, leaving them at the mercy of the Scythians (Hdt. 4.137).[54] After this episode, it has been argued that Hippias attempted to ingratiate himself with Darius and thus abandoned Miltiades and the territory on the European side of the Hellespont.[55] Other scholars have suggested that Hippias might also have been motivated by family pride to break ties with the Philaids after Miltiades took a Thracian wife.[56] Perhaps, then, Miltiades' first wife, a relative of Hippias, was still alive when the marriage to Hegesipyle took place.

Herodotus portrays the Thracians as polygamous (5.5). If Miltiades was still married to his first wife when he took Hegesipyle as a bride, in all probability Olorus would have had no qualms with the arrangement. In this way, members of the Archaic aristocracy might have been more at home among the Thracians than with their fellow Greeks. By marrying the daughter of a powerful local dynast, Miltiades prefigures Greeks such as Iphicrates and Charidemus who married Thracian princesses in the fourth century in order to cement their own political influence in the north. The historian Xenophon too was offered the daughter of the Thracian Seuthes in exchange for military services, but he declined. As tyrant, Miltiades was adept at employing local customs in consolidating his position. It seems that many of these particular customs fitted in well with his aristocratic predispositions.

At the end of his tenure in the Chersonese, Miltiades filled five triremes with his personal possessions in the area

---

[54] The historicity of this story was long ago called into question, principally because Miltiades' supposed betrayal of the Persians would have served the Athenian general well during the Persian Wars. See the note in Asheri et al. (2007: 667), which provides a full account of the scholarly treatment of this passage, concluding that Miltiades was justified in caving in to the Scythians because the Scythians posed an imminent threat to the Thracian Chersonese. Darius, thus, would not have seen Miltiades' actions as a betrayal in the strictest sense.

[55] Wade-Gery 1951: 218–19.

[56] Davies 1971: 302; Scott 2005: 180–81.

and fled the region under threat from the Phoenicians, who were engaged in the Persian annexation of territory after the Ionian revolt (Hdt. 6.41.1). Five triremes' worth of goods and settlers bespeaks the vast amount of wealth the Philaids were able to acquire during the course of their rule.[57] The crews of these ships were probably men of Athenian descent who were brought back into Athenian society upon their return to Athens. Scott estimates that those accompanying Miltiades in his flight from the Chersonese numbered between 500 and 900 men, women, and children, along with Miltiades' personal fortune. That Miltiades owned this many triremes is not out of the question because even at this time triremes were sometimes owned by wealthy families and rulers as an emblem of their power and status.[58] These ships of war added greatly to his ability to control the Hellespont.

The Phoenicians managed to catch up with part of Miltiades' fleet and to capture his son Metiochus, the offspring of his first marriage. The Phoenicians thought they had a great prize to present to Darius because of Miltiades' alleged treachery during the Persians' Scythian campaign. In spite of this, Darius did not harm Metiochus. Rather, he gave him a house and a Persian wife, by whom Metiochus had children. As far as we can tell, Metiochus never returned to Athens. We are told that his children lived as Persians (Hdt. 6.41.2–4). Scott interprets this passage as an example of the trope of Persian magnanimity towards prisoners.[59] But, as McQueen suggests, it is likely that Xerxes would have had uses for Metiochus if the invasion of 480 had been successful.[60] The Persians surely saw the potential benefit of securing the services of a Greek of such high standing, and for his part Metiochus was schooled in dealing with

[57] As Scott (2005: 183) argues, though the typical Greek trireme did not afford much room for baggage, if Miltiades' ships were closer to the Phoenician design, fewer rowers would be needed. This might have allowed more space for material wealth.

[58] Scott 2005: 183.

[59] Scott 2005: 184–85.

[60] McQueen 2004: 120.

foreign monarchs. His great-uncle had enjoyed advantageous ties with Croesus, and his father had married into a Thracian royal house. That Miltiades was part of Darius' Scythian campaign suggests that the Philaids had prior experience at the Persian court itself.

The career of the Philaids to this point demonstrated to any astute Athenian the opportunities Thrace could afford in terms of territory, material wealth, and political power. Archibald contrasts the activities of Pisistratus and the Philaids – that is, the *personal* foreign ties they cultivated irrespective of any coherent Athenian policy – with the "civic enterprises" of the Classical Athenian polis once it had developed the "institutional machinery" of international relations.[61] Yet, personal connections, and usually by extension individual private interests, continued to play an integral part in Athens' relationship with Thrace.[62] Athens might have become more sophisticated in its use of diplomacy, and a definite foreign policy might have been advanced by the polis as a whole, but prominent individuals who more or less conformed to the Philaid paradigm continued to drive that policy. And they did not always subordinate their own aims to those of Athens.

RECOVERING HIS FAMILY'S THRACIAN FORTUNE: CIMON

Though the younger Miltiades successfully defended himself against a charge of tyranny and gained renown from his role at Marathon, he never reacquired his family's territory in Thrace. Instead, he died in disgrace after being fined 50 talents for the

[61] Archibald 1998: 112.
[62] Herman (1987) explores in depth the tension between lingering interpolity personal ties and the emerging importance of civic duties in the Classical period. According to Herman, even though the civic model became dominant, the ties of guest-friendship remained and had an impact on the civic model itself. The persistent loyalty on the part of elites to their foreign guest-friends came to be conceived of by the demos as tantamount to treason (116–61).

failure of an expedition to Paros in 489. It was left to his son Cimon to pay the fine, and as a result the family was reduced to poverty and relative political insignificance for some time (Hdt. 6.132–36; Plut. *Cim.* 4.3). Isaac, following Perdrizet and Ehrenberg, argues that Miltiades' expedition to Paros was merely a prelude to a concerted effort to acquire the gold mines opposite Thasos and thus enrich Athens substantially. Paros, after all, was the mother city of Thasos, and its reduction was a fitting first step in challenging Thasian interests in Thrace. Also, Olorus, Miltiades' father-in-law, was probably a king in the vicinity of the Thasian-controlled gold mines, a connection the Athenian leader surely hoped to exploit. Finally, the Parians set up a grave monument to a certain Tokes on the mainland opposite Thasos between 525 and 490 or so, which shows continued Parian interest in the region shortly before the time of Miltiades' expedition.[63] But, with Miltiades' disgrace and death, and the consequent penury of his surviving family, Philaid influence in Thrace seemed at an end.

Cimon eventually attained prestige and political power at Athens, largely through his wealth and acts of philanthropy. He regularly entertained and feasted the citizens of his deme Laciadae, and he let any who wished pick fruit from his extensive estates. All of this personal generosity was in addition to his liberal execution of liturgies. To combat such wealth and the public favor it fostered, Pericles, Cimon's rival, was forced to offer the citizens of Athens jury pay (*Ath. Pol.* 27.3; Plut. *Cim.* 10.1–3). The financial straits in which Miltiades had left the family had been remedied and more, largely through Cimon's own campaigns in Thrace. As scholars point out, in Thrace Cimon was careful to appear as Athens' champion, all the while enlarging his own personal fortune through conquest.[64] He had learned from his father that vast wealth and territory were up for grabs in the northern Aegean, and though Miltiades failed in his final attempt to expand his

---

[63] Isaac 1986: 5–7, 18–19.
[64] Isaac 1986: 34; Archibald 1998: 114.

own power and that of Athens in the region, Cimon enjoyed tremendous success.

In 476, Cimon led a force of Athenians to Thrace. For this first campaign he concentrated on the region opposite Thasos and along the Strymon, fulfilling his father's thwarted ambitions. After a destructive siege of Eion, a city on the Strymon under the control of the Persian governor Boges, Cimon expelled the Persians from the city and also ravaged the local Thracians who had been bringing the Persians supplies (Hdt. 7.107; Thuc. 1.98.1; Plut. *Cim.* 7–8.2). Though Eion itself had been destroyed by the Persians at the end of the siege, Plutarch tells us that the surrounding countryside was beautiful and fertile and that Cimon turned it over to the Athenians for settlement (*Cim.* 7.3).[65] Plutarch additionally remarks that by this feat Cimon achieved greater fame in Athens than either Themistocles or Miltiades had. At Cimon's insistence, stone herms were dedicated in Athens celebrating his victory, even though Miltiades and Themistocles had received not so much as a laurel crown. Plutarch guesses that the Athenians were so thrilled by Cimon's achievement because, whereas the other great generals of Athens were primarily engaged in defending their city from external enemies, Cimon had brought the offensive to the enemies themselves and had in the process acquired new territories for the Athenians to settle (*Cim.* 7.3–8.2). Isaac suggests that Cimon's success on the Strymon brought such great excitement because of the possibility of the untold riches of Thrace falling into Athens' hands.[66]

In 466, following the Battle of Eurymedon, the Chersonese was brought back under Athenian influence by another expedition of Cimon. The Persians in the area had enlisted the help of Thracians to the north, perhaps tribesmen connected to the

---

[65] See Isaac (1986: 19–20) for the extent of the Athenian settlement on the Strymon organized by Cimon, which may have included an expedition to Ennea Hodoi and the first attempts to found a city at the future location of Amphipolis, as indicated by Nepos (*Cim.* 2). For the date of the campaign, see Archibald 1998: 114n101.

[66] Isaac 1986: 21.

very Thracians whom the elder Miltiades had driven from the Chersonese, in order to fight against Cimon. With but a few ships and vastly inferior numbers, according to Plutarch, Cimon defeated the combined forces of the Persians and Thracians, both on land and sea, and won for Athens the entire Chersonese (*Cim.* 14.1). Philaid influence on the Hellespont was thus restored, though Cimon ostensibly gave the land to all Athenians.

Immediately following this victory, Cimon put down a revolt on Thasos. From our sources, it is clear that Thasos and Athens disputed the control of the *emporia* on the mainland opposite the island, along with the lucrative gold mines in the vicinity (Thuc. 1.100.2; Plut. *Cim.* 14.2).[67] After a victory at sea and a successful siege of Thasos, Cimon acquired for Athens the disputed mainland territory along with its mines.[68] His victory was so complete, in fact, that many Athenians thought he should capitalize on his gains by moving against Alexander of Macedon. That Cimon failed to do so brought upon him the charge of taking bribes from Alexander, for which his enemies prosecuted him at Athens. Cimon's defense consisted of insisting that he was not a foreign advocate (*proxenos*) of wealthy Thessalians or Ionians, as some other Athenians were, but rather of the frugal Spartans. All the riches gained by his campaigns were funneled directly into the city of Athens. By implication, he would never be swayed by a bribe (Plut. *Cim.* 14.2–3). In reality, though, Cimon was greatly enriched by his activities in the northern Aegean, in no small part from the very mines he had wrested from Thasos.

[67] Meiggs (1972: 79–82) discusses the date of the Battle of Eurymedon and Cimon's subsequent expeditions to the Chersonese and Thasos. From the evidence of a surviving casualty list (*IG* i² 928), which contains a record of the fallen from both the Chersonese and Thasos, a coherent and comprehensive campaign in the north Aegean led by Cimon is indicated.

[68] Thucydides (1.100.2) tells us that at about the same time, Athens attempted to establish a colony at Ennea Hodoi, later Amphipolis, with 10,000 settlers, which ended in disaster at Drabeskos. For this colonization attempt, see Isaac 1986: 24–30; Archibald 1998: 115.

Cimon made great gains for Athens in the north Aegean, reestablishing Athenian control on the Chersonese, making the first major inroads up the Strymon valley, and securing lucrative mines and territory on the mainland opposite Thasos. All of these areas figured prominently in Athenian foreign policy for over a century following Cimon's career. It is also clear that Cimon's own personal fortunes were vastly improved by these activities – he became one of the wealthiest men in Athens and a leading political actor. His innate military talent was combined with extensive connections in the region to achieve his aims. In the case of the Chersonese, Plutarch is explicit that the Persians disdained Cimon because of his small number of ships, but still Cimon was successful. Perhaps Plutarch insists on a small number of ships in order to glorify Cimon. Perhaps, though, Cimon really did overcome a deficit in numbers by drawing on his family ties in the area, with Greek settlers and friendly Thracians alike, to drive the Persians and enemy Thracians from the peninsula. He followed in his father's footsteps by bringing the fight to Thasos in order to open up new sources of revenue for Athens. Again, family connections probably played a key role. Cimon, the grandson of the Thracian Olorus, would have had useful friends in the area, friends who might have been a help in his earlier siege of Eion and colonization efforts on the Strymon.

As the ignominious end of Cimon's father, Miltiades, reveals, the Athenians could be a very fickle people. Even the hero of Marathon was not immune from prosecution and humiliation at the hands of a vengeful demos. Athens' impatience with its generals and political leaders is a prominent theme of ancient history. Pericles was of an exceptionally rare breed in that he managed to maintain the favor of the Athenians until his death, though had not the plague killed him in the early years of the Peloponnesian War, there is no telling how long the city would have abided his policies. Many of the fallen stars of Athens turned to Thrace as a place of refuge. The elder Miltiades had set out for the Chersonese because the political situation in Athens was unbearable and there was no room for so prominent a rival to Pisistratus. Once driven from Athens, the Pisistratids themselves found refuge with their friends at Sigeum. Like his father, Cimon too fell out of favor with the democracy at home. Though his Thracian connections had led to power and prestige at Athens, Cimon was overshadowed and driven from the city by his political rivals Ephialtes and Pericles in 461 (Plut. *Cim.* 17.2). His family, by contrast, had managed to hold onto power in the Chersonese for half a century. In the case of Pisistratus, Thrace turned out to be a source of power at Athens itself. But under the increasingly entrenched democratic constitution, the zero-sum game of Athenian politics proved too volatile even for men as capable as Cimon. We are in the dark concerning Cimon's whereabouts during his period of exile. He seems not to have returned to Thrace, where he might have been able to reassume his family's tyranny free of his democratic rivals.[69]

THRACE-EXPERTS: HAGNON, DIEITREPHES, AND THUCYDIDES

In 431, as the war with Sparta loomed on the horizon, Athens resorted to the traditional instrument of proxeny to establish an alliance with Sitalces, king of the Odrysian Thracians who controlled much of southern Thrace in this period. Proxeny is usefully defined by Hornblower as a consular arrangement whereby a citizen of city A looked after the interests of city B in city A. It was largely a public variant of the guest-friendship (*xenia*) relationships that existed between

---

[69] He appears in Boeotia at the Battle of Tanagra in 457 and offers to fight on Athens' side against Sparta (Plut. *Cim.* 17.3–5). Plutarch tells us that Cimon was recalled to Athens in 451, on a proposal by Pericles no less, to negotiate a truce with Sparta (*Cim.* 17.6). Gomme et al. (1945–1981: vol. 1, 325–29), however, argue based on the testimony of Theopompus (*FGrHist* 115 F 88) that Cimon was recalled in 357 after only five years in exile. See also the discussion of Hornblower (1991–2008: vol. 1, 167–68), who argues that Theopompus is guilty of some telescoping. Thucydides tells us little about Cimon in this period, so we are largely in the dark.

notables throughout the Greek world for centuries.[70] In a very detailed account, Thucydides tells us that Nymphodorus of Abdera, who had given his sister in marriage to Sitalces, was made an Athenian *proxenos* and acted as the negotiator between Athens and the Odrysian king (2.29).[71] Through Nymphodorus' agency, Sitalces' son Sadocus was brought to Athens and made an Athenian citizen in order to cement the alliance. Courting Sitalces' favor might also have been partially behind the Athenian public adoption of the cult of the Thracian goddess Bendis at this time. The Odrysians were persuaded to send cavalry and peltasts to aid Athens in the Thraceward region. Nymphodorus also arranged an alliance between Athens and Perdiccas of Macedon, whereby Athens restored Therme to the Macedonians, and the Macedonians in turn aided the admiral Phormio in an expedition to the Chalcidice. Thucydides is unusually explicit in recording the Athenian motives in these dealings, probably because of his own interest and expertise in the region. Hornblower wonders whether Thucydides actually had a hand in encouraging the Athenians to ally with Sitalces.[72] That Thucydides was in favor of an Odrysian alliance explains his unusual polemic aimed at correcting Athenian misconceptions of Sitalces' father, Teres, who had been slandered as a descendant of the savage Tereus (2.29).[73]

[70] Hornblower 1991–2008: vol. 1, 285. For a comprehensive treatment of *xenia* relationships, see Herman 1987. See also Mitchell (1997) for an in-depth study of how the polis as a whole made use of private relationships between elites of different polities, primarily in the selection of envoys.

[71] See also Herodotus (7.137), who says that Nymphodorus had captured Spartan envoys to Asia and sent them to Athens, where they were executed. This is also related by Thucydides (2.67), but with no mention of Nymphodorus' involvement. For Nymphodorus' proxeny and the alliance between Athens and Sitalces, see Gomme et al. 1945–1981: vol. 2, 89–90; Walbank 1978: 167–68; Isaac 1986: 99–104; Hornblower 1991–2008: vol. 1, 284–89; Archibald 1998: 118.

[72] Hornblower 1991–2008: vol. 1, 286.

[73] Gomme et al. (1945–1981: vol. 2, 90) suggest that Thucydides aimed at correcting Hellanicus, and perhaps Sophocles.

Though the institution of proxeny was already ancient and well established by the time of the Peloponnesian War, Athenian Thracophiles were responsible for a majority of Athenian diplomatic gains in the north.[74] The use of Nymphodorus as an agent in Thrace appears to be the exception rather than the rule for Athens during this period. In Thucydides' history, Nymphodorus is the only Athenian *proxenos* in Thrace of any consequence.[75] Instead, much more emphasis is given to the activities of Athenians in the Thraceward region, men such as Alcibiades – and Thucydides himself. For example, though Athens had *proxenoi* in such northern places as Sciathos and Selymbria, these men seem to have been connected personally to Athenians with interests in the area, namely, Dieitrephes and Alcibiades.[76] In spite of the role played by Nymphodorus in initiating the alliance between Athens and Sitalces, soon certain Athenian individuals dealt directly with the Odrysian king. Because of their connections and experience, the disciples of Thrace acted as Thrace-experts on behalf of the Athenian polis. Not that they were motivated primarily by Athens' interests; rather, they used their Thracian ties to obtain for themselves positions of power at Athens, usually in the form of special military commands.

This was not a phenomenon unique to Thracian connections. Mitchell, for instance, usefully gathers the examples of appointments made on the basis of personal foreign connections from the time of the Peloponnesian War through the fourth century, and at Athens it is apparent that leaders were selected based on ties to many foreign powers.[77] But the

[74] For the history and origins of proxeny, see Wallace 1970.

[75] As Hornblower (1991–2008: vol. 1, 285) points out, only five of the ninety-four fifth-century Athenian *proxenoi* collected by Walbank (1978) are mentioned by Thucydides.

[76] Oiniades of Sciathos is honored as a *proxenos* of Athens in a decree proposed by Dieitrephes. See Walbank 1978: 444–48. Apollodorus of Selymbria is similarly honored in a decree proposed by Alcibiades. See Walbank 1978: 432–44; and Chapter 3 herein.

[77] Mitchell 1997. See pages 90–110 for Athenian appointments to various offices, including the generalship, based on foreign ties. Of the

importance of Thrace in terms of strategic location and abundance of resources, coupled with the sheer number of leading Athenians who had connections in the region, meant that Thrace did play a larger role in this aspect of Athenian politics than did other locales.

Following the activities of Pisistratus around the Thermaic Gulf and Mount Pangaeum, and the ties established by the Philaids in the Chersonese and on the mainland opposite Thasos, there is a relative lacuna in our knowledge of Athenian activities in Thrace. The sources pick up again in 437/6, when an important Athenian named Hagnon was sent out as the leader of an expedition to the Strymon River to found a colony where several other attempts had failed. In 497, Aristagoras of Miletus went to Thrace after the Persians had recalled his uncle and father-in-law, Histiaeus, from the region. After conquering the territory of Myrcinus on the Strymon, Aristagoras was killed by Edonian Thracians, probably at the site known as Ennea Hodoi, or Nine Ways (Hdt. 5.124; 126; Thuc. 4.102; Diod. 12.68.1–2). In 465, at the time Cimon was putting down the revolt on Thasos and acquiring territory for Athens on the mainland opposite, an Athenian expedition of 10,000 settlers was sent to the site of Ennea Hodoi. The leaders of this venture were the Athenians Sophanes and Leagros. Our sources tell us that this group, along with its leaders, was massacred by a force of Thracians, mostly Edonians, at the nearby Thracian site of Drabescus (Hdt. 9.75; Thuc. 4.102; Diod. 12.68; Paus. 1.29.4–5).[78] The site of Ennea Hodoi was very advantageous, occupying an elevated position surrounded on three sides by the Strymon.[79] But the major attempts to settle it by the

twenty-three Athenian generals listed (105), six were connected to Thrace. So, for the period covered by her study (435–323), over a quarter of the generals selected directly because of their foreign connections were tied to Thrace.

[78] For this settlement attempt and the battle at Drabescus, see Isaac 1986: 24–30.

[79] For the topography, see Pritchett 1965–1992: vol. 3, 298–346. In point of fact, Ennea Hodoi may have been situated on Hill 133, just slightly to the north of the later Amphipolis.

mid-fifth century had met with bloody failure at the hands of the local Thracians. Hagnon, however, succeeded in founding a lasting Greek city in 437/6, which he named Amphipolis.

After giving a brief synopsis of the history of the site, Thucydides describes Hagnon's foundation. From their base at Eion on the coast, which had been earlier established by Cimon, the Athenians drove the Edonians out of the area. Hagnon named the new city, 3 miles from the port at Eion, Amphipolis because it was surrounded on both sides by the river. He built the city in such a way that it was conspicuous from land and sea, and he planned to fortify it with a long wall stretching from one portion of the river to the other (Thuc. 4.102). Athenian citizens formed the backbone of the new settlement's garrison, but a majority of the population was non-Athenian, mostly from the nearby city of Argilus (Thuc. 4.103.5, 106; Diod. 12.68.3).[80] We do not know why Hagnon was specifically chosen to lead this venture. He was already prominent, having been an Athenian general at Samos in 440/39 (Thuc. 1.116–117.1), and Cratinus labels him as from a family of "old money (archaioploutos)" (F 171 K-A), but it is unknown whether he had prior Thracian connections. Most scholars assume that the colonization of Amphipolis was part of Pericles' overall expansionist policy, but it is uncertain to what extent Hagnon and Pericles were political allies.[81]

In 429/8, Sitalces invaded Macedon at the head of a massive coalition of tribes. Sitalces was accompanied by several Athenian ambassadors who happened to be in the area. Moreover, Hagnon was to act as commander (hēgemōn) of the expedition, showing

---

[80] For Hagnon's settlement and the city's population, including the relative civic status of the Athenians and non-Athenians, see Isaac 1986: 36–40. It seems that all were citizens, but that the Athenians may have formed a separate group among themselves. Certainly, the loyalty of those from Argilus to the Athenians was weak, for they eagerly handed the city over to Brasidas (Thuc. 4.103).

[81] Isaac (1986: 36) calls the colonization of Amphipolis Pericles' "most ambitious project in the north Aegean." For questions surrounding the supposed alliance between Hagnon and Pericles, see Pesely 1989: 198–203.

that he had gained a measure of influence in Thrace. For their part, the Athenians were to send a fleet and as many troops as possible to aid Sitalces in subduing the Chalcideans (Thuc. 2.95). The Athenians never made good on their promise of added support, but so far as we can tell the Athenian ambassadors went along with Sitalces nevertheless, and Hagnon did act as a military leader for the invasion. A group of Thracians known as the Dioi had come down from the Rhodope range to serve as prominent members of this army, composing the most fearsome contingent in the infantry (Thuc. 2.96.2, 98.4). Members of this same tribe played a significant, if gruesome, role later in the war. It seems that Hagnon alerted the Athenians to the potential usefulness of the Thracians – including the particularly fierce tribe of the Dioi – as mercenaries and military allies.

Hagnon remained prominent at Athens well after his foundation of Amphipolis. At least in part because of his past success in Thrace, he was appointed to the board of *probouloi* in 413, a body created after the Sicilian Expedition and meant to be a check on the excesses of democracy. His son Theramenes was a key player in the oligarchic coup of 411 and also the overthrow of democracy in 404 (Lys. 12.65; Xen. *Hell*. 2.3.30).[82] Theramenes, inheriting his father's northern connections, took part in Athenian campaigns in Thrace and the northern Aegean from 411 to 407.

In 413, the Athenians were facing immense difficulties as the Peloponnesian War entered a new phase. According to Thucydides, not only were the Athenians engaged in a war with Sicily, a war on the same scale as that which they had been waging against the Peloponnesians, but they were also facing financial ruin, largely from the damage caused by the Spartan fortification of Decelea. It was in this context that one of the most gruesome episodes of the war took place (Thuc. 7.27.1–2, 28–30).

A contingent of Thracian fighters, from the same tribe of the Dioi that had factored largely in Sitalces' expedition, had

---

[82] For a thorough study of Hagnon's life and career, see Pesely 1989.

arrived in Athens to aid the general Demosthenes in Sicily. Unfortunately, they arrived too late. The Athenians, not willing or able to cover the expense of keeping these soldiers on the payroll, sent them back to Thrace under the command of Dieitrephes. While sailing back to Thrace through the Euripus Strait, the Athenians had instructed Dieitrephes to inflict as much damage as possible on the enemy. After plundering Tanagra, the Thracians moved farther inland and attacked the town of Mycalessus, catching the inhabitants entirely off guard. Mycalessus was supposedly far enough from the sea to prevent a seaborne attack, and the walls of the city had been neglected to the point of disrepair and were crumbling in several sections. The band of 1,300 warriors stormed into the town and systematically butchered all they encountered, sparing not even the livestock. Most shockingly, they entered into the region's largest boys' school and slaughtered all the children found inside. Thucydides insists that this attack represented an utter calamity for the town of Mycalessus, a disaster as complete and pitiable as any that occurred during the long war (7.30.10). Eventually, the Thebans sent their cavalry and hoplites to the aid of Mycalessus, and catching a sizable group of the Thracians still who involved in looting the town, killed many of them. The Thracians who managed to retreat in an orderly fashion performed well against the Thebans, adopting the tactics of their native land by charging at the enemy in small groups and subsequently falling back again. Having lost 250 out of 1,300 men, the Thracians escaped to their boats and sailed north.

Thucydides is an author fond of paradigms. For example, although many outbreaks of civil strife (*staseis*) occurred during the war, he chose to describe only the one at Corcyra (3.69–85). The brutality and horrors of the civil strife among the Corcyreans, so vividly illustrated by the historian, served to inform the reader's picture of subsequent revolutions that took place in various cities throughout the course of the war, without the need for Thucydides to go into such detail again. Other paradigmatic descriptions can be found, such as the famous passage concerning the plague in Athens (2.47–55).

In the same way, the episode at Mycalessus was employed by Thucydides to paint a striking portrait of the levels of brutality and cruelty to which the war had descended. Other terrible atrocities had been committed, but the slaughter at Mycalessus provided a powerful enough image to serve as a paradigm.[83] But terrible as it was, this attack was nothing more than the logical result of decades of Athenian military involvement with the Dioi and other similar Thracians. For his part, the Athenian commander Dieitrephes was tied to the Thracians through his own family. Because of his own ties to Thrace and the prior experiences of Hagnon, Dieitrephes likely knew the character of the Dioi well.

The evidence indicates that Dieitrephes' family was distinguished in Athens. Ostraka dating to around 460 were found in the Agora depicting the name Dieitrephes, son of Euthoinos.[84] The date indicates that this was an older relative, probably two generations removed, of the Dieitrephes of 413. Candidacy for ostracism signifies one's political prominence dangerous enough to threaten the egalitarian democratic order. The son of this elder Dieitrephes, Nicostratus, was a prominent general in the first half of the Peloponnesian War and was placed in command along with Nicias of an expeditionary force to attack the Thraceward cities Mende and Scione in 423 (Thuc. 4.129.2).[85] In this force were 1,000 Thracian mercenaries and an undisclosed number of peltasts from Athens' northern allies.[86] This

---

[83] See, for example, Lateiner (1977), who argues that Thucydides often uses events of little significance (such as the massacre at Mycalessus) to serve as a paradigm for the *pathos* of war. See also Quinn 1995: 573n2.

[84] See Vanderpool (1968), who includes a genealogical table for this family. For an alternate genealogical table, see Fornara 1971a: 56–57, 64–68; Develin 1989: nos. 830, 2177.

[85] Nicostratus, a general for at least five years during the war, is also mentioned in Thucydides (3.75, 4.53, 4.119, and 5.61) and was killed at Mantinea in 418/7.

[86] For the phenomenon of Greek poleis in the Thraceward area adopting peltast tactics for themselves, see Best 1969: 12–13. They were doubtlessly also mustering points for Thracian mercenaries entering Greek service.

Nicostratus is mentioned in Aristophanes' *Wasps* as addicted to sacrifices (*philothutēs*) and fond of foreigners (*philoxenos*, 81–84).[87] His connection to the Thracians explains the second label, and perhaps the first is a slur against the foolish superstition that is often attributed by the Greeks to barbarous peoples.[88] Aristophanes tells us that Nicostratus' deme was Scambonidae. Thus, he was a both a co-general and fellow tribesman of Thucydides, who was appointed to Thrace in 424/3, and in 418/7 he was co-general with his fellow demesman Alcibiades, who had Thracian connections of his own.[89] By extension, the younger Dieitrephes, who was also from Scambonidae, conceivably had an association with Alcibiades.

Nicostratus was heavily involved in trying to prevent violence between the democratic and oligarchic factions at Corcyra in 427 (Thuc. 3.75). He was a mediator between the two sides, but the oligarchs benefited most from his interventions because the democrats were prevented from going on an extrajudicial killing spree. Nicostratus' efforts in preventing a massacre contrast poignantly with the inaction of another Athenian general, Eurymedon, who sat idly by with his sixty ships while the democrats butchered their opponents (7.81). Nicostratus may simply have been a better man than Eurymedon, or he may have had more sympathy for the oligarchic Corcyreans, who were threatened with violence from the democrats.

Although Thucydides gives no patronymic for the Dieitrephes of 413, the rarity of the name strongly implies that

---

[87] Even though *philoxenos* often denotes hospitality or the entertaining of guests, Strabo at least (10.3.18) uses the verb *philoxeneō* to mean "fond of foreign fashions" while discussing the Athenians' taste for all things foreign, particularly Thracian and Phrygian religious practices. For the identification of the comic Nicostratus with the general, see MacDowell 1965; Fornara 1970.

[88] The scholiast to these lines says that those who are *philothutai* are irrationally superstitious (*deisidaimones*). For an alternate interpretation of these lines, see MacDowell (1988: 140–41), who argues that these words are terms of praise rather than reproach, and are brought up primarily to make fun of Philoxenos.

[89] Fornara 1970: 41n3; Canfora 2006: 6–7, and note 12.

he was a relative, if not the son, of this Nicostratus, and in any case the grandson of the elder Dieitrephes.[90] By the time of his command in 413, men from at least two generations of this family had been put in charge of Thracian forces, suggesting a family connection to Thrace and the Thracians.[91]

Other prominent members of this family are known to us. Herodotus names a champion in the *pankration*, Hermolycus the son of Euthynos, as the most conspicuous fighter among the Greeks at the Battle of Mycale (9.105). Euthynos is almost certainly the same man Euthoinos named in the above-mentioned ostraka, signifying that Hermolycus and the elder Dieitrephes were brothers.[92] Pausanias relates that he saw a statue of Hermolycus the pankratiast on the Acropolis (1.23.10).

Near the image of Hermolycus, Pausanias also saw a statue of a Dieitrephes, which he equates with the younger Dieitrephes who led the Thracians in 413 (1.23.3–4). The probable base for this statue was found in 1839 between the Propylaia and the Parthenon with an inscription mentioning a Hermolycus the son of Dieitrephes as the dedicator, along with the name of the sculptor, Cresilas (*IG* i³ 883). Pliny the Elder attributed to Cresilas a famous work of High Classical sculpture, called the *volneratus deficiens*, which depicted a mortally wounded man (*Nat. Hist.* 34.74). This piece, which may be the very sculpture of Dieitrephes seen by Pausanias, is represented by several extant Roman copies depicting a hoplite pierced by arrows. It has been suggested that the statue Pausanias saw actually represented the elder Dieitrephes, Nicostratus' father. In this case, Pausanias simply got the identification wrong because

---

[90] Inscriptional evidence, for example, furnishes only sixteen instances of the name in Attica (twenty-two in the entire inscriptional record). Including the ostraka and inscriptions already mentioned, there are a total of only four examples from the fifth century. By way of comparison, the name Nicostratus appears in Attic inscriptions 293 times.

[91] See Andrews in Gomme et al. 1945–1981: vol. 5: 156–57; Connor 1971: 156n75.

[92] The manuscripts of Herodotus give several variant readings for the name, Euthoinos being among them.

the younger Dieitrephes was the more famous figure.[93] Scholars are also divided as to whether the extant statue base belonged to the statue of Hermolycus the pankratiast or to that of Dieitrephes, especially because the inscription on the base had been dated to around 440. Recent epigraphic scholarship, however, indicates a date toward the end of the fifth century, a date that would indeed correspond to the younger Dieitrephes.[94] In any case, a family link between the Hermolycus of Mycale fame, the elder Dieitrephes, and the younger Dieitrephes is manifest.

A red-figure vase now in the Getty Museum, dated to the first half of the fifth century, includes the inscription *Hermolykos kalos*.[95] On the vase are depicted young men locked in athletic combat. The name, date, and sport portrayed point to this vase representing the same Hermolycus mentioned by Herodotus. It is clear that Hermolycus, a warrior and athlete, was a famous and leading figure in early fifth century Athens, justifiably so according to Herodotus' account. The bulk of the evidence, therefore, indicates that Dieitrephes' family was one of considerable means and prominence both politically and militarily.[96]

Was command over the group of Thracian mercenaries in 413 a prestigious appointment or a lowly task reserved for a leader of little import? The campaign in Sicily was at this time the focus of Athens' military objectives, led by Nicias and newly reinforced by a group under the prominent general Demosthenes. It is unclear whether or not Dieitrephes was officially a general in 413, but that he was not in Sicily need not imply he was somehow out of favor and relegated to minor tasks. Demosthenes himself, the hero of Pylos, did not go to Sicily

---

[93] Stevens 1936; Dinsmoor 1941: 163–64; Vanderpool 1968.

[94] Earlier date: Stevens 1936; Dinsmoor 1941: 163–64; Vanderpool 1968. Later date: Keesling 2004.

[95] J. Paul Getty Museum, 83.Ae.217; see *Greek Vases in the J. Paul Getty Museum* 4 (1989), 66–69, figs. 1A–F.

[96] Connor (1971: 156–57) also argues for the political and military prominence of this family, in spite of the seeming comic slander against them as nouveau riche.

until several months after the beginning of the expedition, when additional forces were called for. Command of Thracians was often given to Athens' most illustrious men. Hagnon, who enjoyed prominence in Athens even up to 413 when he was made *proboulos*, was sent to aid Sitalces in 429/8. Nicostratus had shared command over his Thracian mercenaries with no less than Nicias. The group of Thracians under Dieitrephes was initially intended to serve under Demosthenes in Sicily, a leader who had previously sought out and employed Thracians and other light-armed troops to great effect at Pylos. Finally, if Dieitrephes was not in fact a general in 413, his command would have been a special one granted by the city, implying a certain amount of prestige. Thucydides never calls Dieitrephes a general (*stratēgos*). Jordan argues that there existed a military office subordinate to the *stratēgoi*, called the *archōn*, and that Dieitrephes' official title in 411 was *archōn epi Thraikēs* ("commander in Thrace") rather than *stratēgos* (234).[97] In 413, he may have been in a similarly subordinate, or even unofficial, command.

In 411, two years after the massacre at Mycalessus, Dieitrephes was appointed by the oligarchic regime, which then held power in Athens, to take overall control of the Thracian area. His first action upon arriving in the region was to install oligarchies in various states, most notably Thasos (Thuc. 8.64). This special command tells us several things. First of all, Dieitrephes had at least a moderate degree of antidemocratic feeling to be used as an agent of the oligarchy. Antidemocratic tendencies are evinced also by his task of replacing democracies with oligarchies in the north Aegean. The oligarchy had been formed in Athens in order to affect the recall of Dieitrephes' fellow demesman and Thrace-haunter Alcibiades (Thuc. 8.76.7), which might further suggest an association between the two.

Second, that Dieitrephes was given such a high-level post a mere two years after the brutal massacre over which he presided is interesting to say the least. Certainly his experience

[97] Jordan 1970.

with Thracians would have been useful for the operations he carried out on behalf of the oligarchy, allowing him to rely on local connections and networks to support his political objectives in the Thraceward area. The evidence indicates that Thasos and the other north Aegean poleis contained large numbers of Thracian inhabitants, on whose sympathies Dieitrephes might have relied.[98] Thucydides is silent on Dieitrephes' role at Mycalessus in 413. He is also silent as to the general Athenian reaction to this slaughter of a defenseless population. The events of 411 would indicate that the upper echelons of Athenian society, those backing the oligarchy, did not condemn Dieitrephes for his role two years earlier. Either Dieitrephes was powerless to stop his soldiers from committing the atrocity, in which case his competence to hold an effective command in the Thraceward area would be called into question, or he was complicit in the destruction of the town. If the latter is true, his assignment in 411 indicates that his fellow elites not only approved of his connection to the Thracians, even to a group as murderous as the Dioi, but actively rewarded it. At the very least, they appreciated Dieitrephes' usefulness. The leadership qualities of Dieitrephes and the sort of Thracians he was accustomed to commanding were embraced by a significant portion of the Athenian elite as a way of furthering their cause in the north.

In 409/8, the Athenians passed a decree to honor one Oiniades of Sciathos for his service to the Athenians (*IG* i³ 110). Dieitrephes is listed on the inscription as the proposer of the decree. We know that Sciathos had long been an ally of Athens, in fact a member of the Delian League. As a league member, Sciathos was listed as part of the Thracian district, even

---

[98] Isaac (1986: 289–92) discusses, among other things, the high level of religious and cultural assimilation between Greeks and Thracians in the poleis of the north Aegean and the need for cooperation between the two peoples in order for the Greek settlements to be successful. Owen (2000) presents the possibility that the Greek settlers of Thasos respected and adopted preexisting Thracian cult practices on the island, implying some level of assimilation and co-habitation.

though fairly far south, just off the coast near Mount Pelium (*IG* i³ 269.II.30). Dieitrephes' role in the honors bestowed upon Oiniades shows that he was still involved in the affairs of the Thraceward area in 409/8, after democracy had been restored in Athens. Evidently, he continued to be concerned with maintaining his connections in the north Aegean, and his work on behalf of Oiniades, securing for him *proxenos* status among other privileges in Athens, was conducted with that end in mind.[99] Dieitrephes' ability to thrive in both democratic and oligarchic climates speaks either to his skill as a politician, to his indispensability as a leader, or both.

The statue of Dieitrephes on the Acropolis, as seen by Pausanias, depicted a figure pierced by many arrows. Pausanias is at a loss to explain the arrows, commenting that among the Greeks only the Cretans were known for their use of the bow. It is true that archers were not a particularly prominent part of Greek armies, but they were a mainstay in the armies of other peoples, particularly the Scythians and also the Thracians. Archaeological evidence attests to the bow being, along with the javelin, a key weapon for the Thracians – many arrowheads have been found in Thracian tombs.[100] The northern Thracian tribes, such as the Getai, were armed much like the Scythians, that is, as mounted archers (Thuc. 2.96.1). Thucydides' account of the battle at Pylos in 425 tells us that Cleon led a force of light-armed troops that included peltasts from Thrace via Aenus along with many archers from foreign lands (4.28.4).[101] It is reasonable to assume that some, at least, of these archers were Thracians. Perhaps Dieitrephes continued in his role as soldier and leader of mercenaries even after the attack on Mycalessus, finally to be memorialized by his son as bravely fighting and dying among barbarian archers in northern lands.

Like Hagnon and Dieitrephes, the great historian Thucydides seems also to have been appointed to a prestigious command

---

[99] See Walbank 1978: 444–48.

[100] Archibald 1998: 203.

[101] See Isaac (1986: 153) for Aenus as a mustering point for Athens' mercenary peltast forces.

in the north because of personal ties to the region. Thucydides
is a crucial source for our study here not only because of his
incomparable history of the Peloponnesian War and much of
the fifth century but also importantly because he was tied to
Thrace in his own right. He tells us that he had many connections in Thrace, mostly because of his control of gold mines
on the mainland opposite Thasos (4.105.1). The biographical
tradition of Thucydides, attributed largely to one Marcellinus,
adds that the historian owned estates in the region (Marc. *Vit.
Thuc.* 14).[102] Plutarch says that Thucydides inherited these
mines from Cimon, who was probably a kinsman, and from his
own father, Olorus (*Cim.* 4). It is nearly certain that Thucydides
was related to Cimon and the Philaid family. There is ancient
testimony of a monument or tomb of Thucydides at Athens
located among those of the other members of the Philaid family, though scholars are divided as to the historicity and nature
of the monument.[103] At any rate, Thucydides' father was a man
named Olorus, which was the name of the Thracian king who
married his daughter Hegesipyle to the younger Miltiades.
Some sources attribute the name Hegesipyle also to Thucydides'
mother. It is possible, then, that Thucydides was a grandson of
the elder Miltiades – there almost certainly existed some sort
of familial relationship.[104]

Thucydides was one of the Athenian generals specially
charged with affairs in Thrace (*stratēgos epi Thraikēs*) for 424/3
(Thuc. 4.104.4). Following the loss of Amphipolis to Brasidas –
in part owing to Thucydides' failure to arrive from Thasos in
time to prevent the city from defecting – Thucydides withdrew to his possessions in Thrace, at Skaptesyle across from

---

[102] For Thucydides' biographical tradition, see Maitland 1996.

[103] Marc. *Vit. Thuc.* 17. For a discussion of the problems relating to the
monument, and for Thucydides' biography in general, see Canfora
2006.

[104] It has also been argued that Thucydides the historian was related to
Thucydides son of Melesias, also a kinsman of Cimon. For a proposed
stemma of the family, see Wade-Gery 1932: 210–11. See also Gomme
et al. 1945–1981: vol. 3: 578; Davies 1971: 233–34.

Thasos. According to both Plutarch and Marcellinus, there he completed the writing of his history (Plut. *Cim.* 4; *Mor.* 205c; Marc. *Vit. Thuc.* 46–47). Marcellinus adds that Thucydides married a woman from Skaptesyle and remained very rich and in possession of mines (19). In light of his role in the loss of Amphipolis, which was psychologically devastating for the Athenians, Thucydides might have opted for voluntary exile.[105] His career trajectory resembles that of several figures examined in this study: he gained a prestigious command because of his ties to Thrace, and once out of favor in Athens he relied on those same connections to provide refuge.

[105] Canfora (2006: 16–17) argues that Thucydides' exile was voluntary, and that he may have returned to Athens for a brief period after the exiles were recalled in 413; after 411, he left Athens again, perhaps because of his connections with the oligarchy of that year. Canfora's arguments, however, are not without critics. In Thucydides' own account we are told that he was an exile for a period of twenty years after Amphipolis, but the language is ambiguous as to whether voluntary or forced exile is meant (5.26.5). This passage is a vexing one. Canfora has argued that it was in fact penned by Xenophon, and others have suggested various emendations. Dover, though, accepts the text as it appears (Gomme et al., 1945–1981: vol. 5, 431–32). Hornblower (1991–2008: vol. 3, 50–53), who insists that this passage is authentic and sound, thinks Thucydides returned to Athens after the war, in 404.

@@ @@ @@ @@

CHAPTER THREE

THRACE AS RESOURCE
AND REFUGE II

ALCIBIADES TO IPHICRATES

ALCIBIADES AND THRASYBULUS

Thrasybulus was the iconic figure of Athenian democracy at the end of the fifth century. After the destruction of the Athenian fleet at Aegospotami and the subsequent subjection of the city to Lysander's puppet regime, the murderous Thirty Tyrants, it appeared as though the broadly based democracy of Pericles had been on the wrong side of history. Yet, starting out with only seventy supporters, Thrasybulus managed to capture the Attic stronghold of Phyle and eventually defeat the forces of the Thirty decisively in the Piraeus, thereby bringing about a restoration of the democratic constitution. As a sign of the ultimate magnanimity, he was a major proponent of the famous amnesty law that prevented a violent backlash against the oligarchs once the democrats were back in power.

Alcibiades had a decidedly different reputation in antiquity. Haughty, vain, and ambitious, he was a talented politician and general who worked towards his own advancement rather than that of Athens. Upon falling out with the Athenian demos, Alcibiades had no qualms about aiding the Spartans and even the Persians. The duplicitous and treacherous opportunism of Alcibiades ensured his place as one of the archvillains of Greek history. At the same time, nearly all ancient authorities

90   @@

agree that his talents exceeded those of his contemporaries and that following the death of Pericles he alone was in a position to win the war for Athens. After the failure of the Sicilian Expedition, Alcibiades' naval commands and his alliance of sorts with Tissaphernes kept Athens afloat for several years, and had the Athenians heeded his advice at Aegospotami, they might well have defeated the Spartans. He captivated ancient writers as much as modern – his complicated story provides endless fodder for sophisticated historical analysis and amusing anecdotes alike.

Thrasybulus and Alcibiades were close political and military allies from the time of the Ionian War, the period of predominantly naval conflict that followed the Athenian disaster in Sicily. In fact, Alcibiades owed many of his greatest successes to Thrasybulus, including his recall to Athens and subsequent position as supreme leader of the Athenian war effort. As Nepos says, Thrasybulus accomplished many things without Alcibiades, but Alcibiades did nothing without Thrasybulus. However, because of certain traits of character and the vagaries of fortune, Alcibiades managed to secure the credit for himself (*Thras.* 1). As partners, both men were tied to Thrace. After the naval battle at Abydos in 411, Alcibiades and Thrasybulus remained in the north Aegean, exacting financial contributions from cities in the area, putting down revolts against Athenian authority, and dealing individually with Thracian rulers. They both also secured the services of Thracian soldiers and used them at times almost as private armies. Whereas Alcibiades employed his Thracian forces mainly for his own purposes as an exile in Thrace, Thrasybulus made use of Thracian fighters in Athens itself during the battle to restore democracy in 404–403.

We catch a first glimpse of collaboration between Alcibiades and Thrasybulus in 411. Thrasybulus, one of the leading Athenians at Samos during the tumultuous period of the oligarchic coup at Athens, persistently advocated the recall of Alcibiades (Thuc. 8.81). As such, he seemed to stake his political future on Alcibiades' potential successes in the service of Athens.[1] Once Alcibiades had regained Athens' trust, the two men worked together in the Hellespont from 411 to 407, combating Sparta's navy and its Persian support and bringing cities over to Athens. During this period, the Athenian generals in the Hellespont, led primarily by Alcibiades but with Thrasybulus also playing a central role, worked more or less independently of the newly restored democracy back home.[2] It was at this time that Alcibiades and Thrasybulus began making connections in the Thraceward region that played a decisive role in the remainder of their respective careers.

The campaigns in the Hellespont were necessitated by the dire situation at Athens following the Sicilian Expedition, which had ended in disastrous defeat in September 413. The massive force the Athenians had sent to Sicily had been utterly annihilated, resulting in the loss of perhaps 3,000 citizen hoplites, 9,000 lower-class thetes, and many thousands of metics. Of the Athenian ships, 160 had been destroyed, leaving only 100 or so left in the Piraeus.[3] The loss of so many men, whom the Athenians saw as irreplaceable, and materiel was compounded by the paltry funds remaining in Athens' treasury. The high cost of the war effort, exacerbated by the economic ruin wrought by the Spartan presence in Decelea, left no money to build more ships.[4] Even if there had been ships, there were no men to fill them. In such straits, the Athenians despaired of their own survival (Thuc. 8.1.2).

Athens' principal source of revenue had been its empire, which was in danger of falling apart. Thucydides says that the Athenian defeat in 413 had made all the states in Greece eager

---

[1] Strauss 1984: 42, and notes 21–22.

[2] For their activities in this period, see especially Andrewes 1953.

[3] For these numbers, see Kagan (1987: 1–11), who gives a comprehensive account, along with a survey of scholarship, of the consequences of the Sicilian disaster. See also Strauss (1987: 179–82) for a rendering of all Athenian casualties during the war, especially those of the thetic and metic classes.

[4] For the effect of Decelea, see Kagan 1987: 3. See also Kallet (1999), who discusses the moral and psychological effects of this financial devastation, which culminated in the massacre at Mycalessus.

to turn against Athens, the subjects of the empire in particular, a result the Spartans and Persians were all too eager to precipitate (8.2.2; 8.5.4–6.1). When the Spartans sent a fleet to the Hellespont and Propontis in 411, eventually causing the revolt of Byzantium, Athens' grain supply and very survival came under threat (Thuc. 8.80). In response, the Athenians sent out a fleet under the command of Thrasybulus, which defeated the Spartans at Cynossema, marking Thrasybulus' first significant victory (Thuc. 8.100–106).[5]

From 411 to 407/6, Thrasybulus was continuously active in the north, involved with the other generals in raising money (Xen. *Hell.* 1.1.8), and reelected general several times, even in absentia (Xen. *Hell.* 1.4.10).[6] His activities included bringing several cities back over to Athens, beginning in early 410 after a victory at Cyzicus (Diod. 13.64.3), and retaking both Thasos and Abdera with a fleet of thirty ships (Xen. *Hell.* 1.4.9; Diod. 13.72.1–2). Diodorus says that Thrasybulus won a battle at Thasos and followed up with a successful siege. Xenophon tells us that Thasos had been reduced to a miserable state from continuous war, revolution, and siege-induced famine before submitting to Thrasybulus. Even before Cyzicus, Thrasybulus had been active at Thasos, attempting to bring the city back under Athenian control (Xen. *Hell.* 1.1.12).

Krentz suggests that sometime during this period Thrasybulus had been appointed by Athens as the overall commander in the Thraceward area, just as Dieitrephes had been shortly earlier by the oligarchy in 411.[7] Such an appointment made perfect sense, especially in light of Thrasybulus' focus on Thasos. Dieitrephes was chosen by the oligarchy of 411 to establish an oligarchic government on Thasos, which promptly revolted from Athenian control mere weeks after Dieitrephes had left the island. As Avery persuasively argues,

---

[5] For this campaign in the Hellespont, see Kagan 1987: 211–16, and 218n31 for Thrasybulus' position as commander in chief. See also Buck 1998: 31–32.

[6] For his reelection as general, see Buck 1998: 40n112.

[7] Krentz 1989: 127.

though Thasos revolted from Athens, it maintained an oligarchic government of some form. The anti-Athenian oligarchs were supported by Athens' enemies, specifically the admiral Timolaus of Corinth (*Hell. Oxy.* 7[2].4).[8] Thrasybulus, a man quickly cementing ties in Thrace, was chosen by the reestablished Athenian democracy as a Thrace-expert to combat the rebellious Thasian oligarchs. Athens had the greatest chance of regaining Thasian allegiance by crushing the island's oligarchs and restoring democracy. The juxtaposition of the missions of Dieitrephes and Thrasybulus neatly demonstrates that both oligarchs and democrats saw the value in maintaining an Athenian foothold in the north Aegean and that Thracian ties could be as important to a democrat as they were to an oligarch, depending on the political situation. Thrasybulus' mission also shows that a "good democrat" was not above breaking the will of recalcitrant allies through siege and famine.

Alcibiades was similarly engaged during this period. After Abydos he collected money along with the other generals before he was briefly imprisoned by Tissaphernes (Xen. *Hell.* 1.8–10). Subsequent to a period of relative inactivity following Cyzicus, he turned his attention to attacking the interests of the Persian satrap Pharnabazus along the Asiatic shore of the Hellespont and Propontis.[9] The literary sources agree that Alcibiades did great damage to the territories of the King, and Diodorus tells us that he secured enough goods from the Persians not only to satisfy his men but also to lessen the tax burden (*eisphorai*) levied against Athenian citizens for the prosecution of the war (Diod. 13.64.4). As Strauss points out, revenue from the empire was a main guarantee against excessive taxation for Athenians.[10] Alcibiades' activities met with the approval of the Athenian masses. He soon turned his attention to fortifying Lampsacus and made an excursion against

[8] Avery 1979: 236–38.
[9] For the issue of his inactivity after Cyzicus, see Hatzfeld 1940: 274–80.
[10] Strauss 1987: 51.

nearby Abydos. Spending the winter at Lampsacus, he conducted further raids into Persian territory.

Following these activities, he set out for Chalcedon, which
had revolted from Athens. The people of Chalcedon had gathered all their movable property and handed it over to their
allies, the Bithynian Thracians. Alcibiades, through the help of
his imposing forces, struck his own deal with the Bithynians
and seized the goods of the Chalcedonians. He then set about
walling off Chalcedon and in the process defeated both the
forces of Hippocrates, the Spartan governor of the place, and
Pharnabazus, who had come to the city's aid. Alcibiades continued in this manner, heading to the Hellespont and Chersonese
to raise money, and in the process he recruited many Thracians
and the entire population of the Chersonese to his cause. He
took Selymbria by betrayal, bringing in a small force of Greeks
and Thracians and having his friends on the inside arrange for
the city's surrender. Once the city was in his hands, if Plutarch
is to be believed, Alcibiades feared that his Thracian troops,
who were fiercely loyal to him out of goodwill and affection (*eunoia*, *charis*), would plunder the city. So, he sent the
Thracians out and left the city and its territory intact, leaving only a garrison and collecting a sum of money (Plut. *Alc.*
30.4–5). Finally, he besieged Byzantium and took the city, once
again with the collusion of his friends on the inside.[11]

As is evident from our sources, Alcibiades and his lieutenants struck their own agreements with the peoples in the
north. With the Bithynian Thracians, Alcibiades concluded
a treaty of good faith or friendship (*pisteis*, Xen. *Hell.* 1.3.4;
philian, Plut. *Alc.* 29.3); with Chalcedon, his lieutenants, principally Theramenes, arranged that the same tribute should be
paid to Athens as before (Xen. *Hell.* 1.3.9; Diod. 13.66.3; Plut.
Alc. 31.1); from Selymbria he exacted a sum of money after
establishing a garrison (Diod. 13.66.4; Plut. *Alc.* 30.4–5); and
he arranged to return the city of Byzantium to its own citizens

---

[11] For all of these events, see the accounts in Xenophon (*Hell.* 1.2.15–3);
Diodorus (13.64.4–67); and Plutarch (*Alc.* 29–31).

after making them allies (Diod. 13.67.7). Though Alcibiades and the other generals were at this time acting on their own initiative, the epigraphic record confirms that many of the arrangements made in 410–408 were subsequently ratified at Athens once Alcibiades made his return to the city.[12]

During this period Alcibiades depended heavily on his friends in the north, principally as betrayers of cities, as he relied on local forces, both Thracian and Greek, to accomplish his ends. While Athens reacquired many of its interests in the north and gained some much needed revenue, Alcibiades, raising substantial numbers of local troops who were loyal to him personally, consolidated his own position among the Thracians. At some point between 411 and 407, he established several fortified settlements in the Hellespontine region, which later served as his refuge from the Athenians once he fell out of favor after the Battle of Notium in 407/6. From his base in Thrace, Alcibiades waged campaigns with his own private Thracian armies and forged alliances with several Thracian kings. By these campaigns he enriched himself and increased his fame. He offered his own forces, plus those of the Thracian rulers Medocus and Seuthes, to the Athenian generals at Aegospotami, which those generals refused to their own ruin (Nep. *Alc.* 7–8; Plut. *Alc.* 30.4–5, 36.3, 37.2; Diod. 13.105.3–4).

In 407/6, Alcibiades had left his fleet at Notium under the command of a subordinate, for reasons not entirely known.[13] In his absence, the Athenians were defeated by the Spartans under Lysander, most likely because of the folly of the officer Alcibiades had left in charge (Xen. *Hell.* 1.5.10–15; *Hell. Oxy.* 8[4].1–4). Following the defeat, the anger of Athenians burned against their erstwhile hero Alcibiades, and he was dismissed from command. He then fled to his Thracian strongholds

---

[12] See, for example, *IG* i³ 118 for the ratification of Alcibiades' treaty with Selymbria and *IG* i³ 119 for his treaty with Daphnous.

[13] For this campaign and the scholarly issues surrounding it, see Buck 1998: 43–46. It seems Alcibiades had left in order to lend support against oligarchic exiles at Clazomenae (Diod. 13.71.1) or to confer with Thrasybulus at Phocaea (Xen. *Hell.* 1.5.11).

(Xen. *Hell.* 1.5.17–18). Alcibiades perhaps had an eye to making himself indispensible to Athens. Athens had demonstrated a keen interest in the Hellespont since the seventh century. By setting up his own autonomous fiefdom in the region, Alcibiades might have hoped to offer the Athenians the chance to regain their influence in a key strategic area. As such, he once again could have regained Athens' favor.[14] Even so, he was acting with his own interests, as always, in the forefront. To reemerge once again as Athens' savior, and to have personal control over a piece of territory the city so desired, would have made him more powerful still. After Notium, Thrasybulus also fell out of favor at Athens. It seems he was considered guilty by association with Alcibiades. As evidence of Thrasybulus' political decline, he failed to be elected general the following year.[15] He remained out of the spotlight until he led the overthrow of the Thirty in 404–403, a feat that catapulted him to unprecedented stardom. In this conflict, he employed Thracian soldiers, which will be discussed in Chapter 6.

In 390–389, Thrasybulus again ventured to the Hellespont, and he is mentioned as the overall commander in the region (ἦρ[χεν], *IG* ii² 24). Here he made great gains for Athens, not least of which was effecting an alliance between the quarreling Thracian rulers Medocus and Seuthes, joining them both to Athens in the process (Xen. *Hell.* 4.8.26). Xenophon tells us that by so doing, he figured that not only would he gain powerful Thracian allies for Athens but the Greek cities in the area would be much more inclined towards Athens. His campaigns continued down the Ionian coast, where he exacted money by any means necessary. Eventually, he ended up in Aspendus, where he continued his financial exactions. The people of Aspendus were so angered by the raiding and looting of Thrasybulus' men that some locals stormed into the Athenian camp at night and killed Thrasybulus in his tent (Xen. *Hell.* 4.8.26–30; Diod. 14.94, 99.4–5).

---

[14] For these plans of Alcibiades, see Hatzfeld 1940: 321–23.
[15] Buck 1998: 46.

During the period of the Ionian War and in the early fourth century, legitimate means of raising money were not sufficient to keep any sizable military venture going. Pritchett argues that the so-called condottieri of the fourth century, that is, Greek generals who seemed to operate independently of their home polis, were forced to resort to brigandage in order to pay for their soldiers and supplies. The financial situation in the fourth century was so poor that the poleis themselves, Athens included, sanctioned such activity.[16] The situation was similar for Athens during the last decade of the fifth and first decade of the fourth centuries. It seems that Thrasybulus, who had worked closely with the Thracians, famous as thieves and brigands, and with Alcibiades, a proven master at raising money by any means necessary, had learned well how to exact funds from unwilling peoples. The Athenians demonstrated their implicit approval of Thrasybulus' activities by sending out Iphicrates as his replacement in the Hellespont. Iphicrates had already shown himself to be a resourceful and cunning commander of irregular troops, and a man close to the Thracians. Accordingly, he was sent out with 1,200 peltasts (Xen. *Hell.* 4.8.34).

Many scholars have suggested that Thrasybulus, a staunch democrat, wanted to restore Athens' former empire in the early fourth century, and his activities in the Hellespont were aimed at such an end.[17] Democracy itself was arguably in much need of empire. Moreno, discussing the connection between Athens and the grain-producing polities in the Crimea, remarks that the despotic governments of the northern Black Sea were cynically influenced and supported by Athens, a democratic polis. Athens' very food supply was dependent upon overseas

---

[16] Pritchett 1974–1991: vol. 2, 59–116, esp. 68–70.

[17] Seager 1967; Cawkwell 1976; Buck 1998: 97–98, 115–18. Cawkwell argues that the main point of rivalry between Thrasybulus and Conon was the extent to which the Persians should be included in the restoration of Athens' empire. Thrasybulus wanted to exclude them utterly, but Conon saw them as a potential asset. It seems, though, that both men were guided more by personal rivalry and a pragmatic desire for personal power rather than any sort of democratic or anti-Persian ideals. See Strauss 1984.

to prevent her from revealing his crime. Once Procne learned of her husband's deeds, she conspired with her sister to kill her own son by Tereus, and serve his remains to Tereus as a meal. When the awful truth was revealed, Tereus was transformed into a hoopoe in full armor, Procne into a nightingale, and Philomela into a swallow. The myth existed before Sophocles' play, but it seems that Sophocles innovated by setting the action in Thrace.[7] It is likely, though, that Sophocles made use of a preexisting tradition in which Thrace had rendered military aid to Athens at some point in the epic past.[8]

The myth of Tereus was popular in Athens during the time of the Peloponnesian War. Tereus is a central character in Aristophanes' *Birds*. He is also mentioned by Thucydides in connection to the Athenians' Thracian ally Sitalces (2.29). Sitalces' father was a man named Teres, and clearly some Athenians had connected Teres with the mythological Tereus, a notion Thucydides attempts to disprove. In the early fourth century, the Thracian dynast Seuthes II appears to make use of the same mythological kinship in dealing with Xenophon, as recounted in the *Anabasis* (7.2.31; 7.3.39).[9] Although the Thracians tried to use the myth to their advantage by highlighting a history of military alliance between Athens and Thrace, writers such as Sophocles possibly employed the myth as a cautionary tale. Like Polymestor, Tereus was a cruel and untrustworthy ally. Thus, Athens was cautioned to think twice before working with his descendants.[10]

The Thracians were noted for their propensity for warfare. Euripides describes the fearsome god of war Ares as the lord of Thrace of the golden *peltē*, that is, the crescent shield wielded by peltasts (*Alc.* 498). Herodotus claims that Ares, along with

---

[7] Fitzpatrick (2001) presents an in-depth look at Sophocles' fragments and attempts to determine the plot of the *Tereus*, including the elements Sophocles inherited and those he invented.

[8] Hall 1989: 137.

[9] See Stronk 1995: 52–53.

[10] Stronk (1995: 53) argues that Sophocles' play was meant to flatter Sitalces. Given the nature of the plot, this hardly seems likely.

Dionysus and Artemis, was one of the only gods worshipped by the Thracians (5.7). Herodotus also says that the Thracians considered a life of working the land the least worthy of honor, but they reckoned that warfare and plunder provided the finest mode of living (5.6). Herodotus rounds out his description of Thracian bellicosity by stating that the most valuable prizes in Thracian athletic competitions were awarded to the victors in single combat (5.8). Thucydides' account of the Mycalessus massacre paints a terrifying picture of Thracian brutality (7.29–30). In the fourth century, Isocrates equated seaborne pirates with peltasts (4.115). Even into the Roman period, the Thracians continued to be famous for fighting. Vergil calls Thrace the land of Mars (*Aen.* 3.13), and Horace describes it as a country literally mad with war (*Carm.* 2.16.5). Tacitus blames the outbreak of a Thracian rebellion in 26 CE on the lawless and ferocious character of mountain-dwelling tribes (*Ann.* 4.46.1). As Martin and Woodman argue in their commentary on this passage, Tacitus probably knew little about the actual campaign and instead relied on stock imagery.[11] In order to please his readership, Tacitus' description of the Thracians was made to fit with Roman stereotypes, which appear to have differed little from those held by the Greeks.

Thracians, as other barbarians, were purported to be drunkards. Aristophanes, in his *Acharnians*, ridicules the Athenian envoys to Sitalces by suggesting that they were held up so long in Thrace by continuous drinking parties (141). The Persians are also similarly mocked in the play (73–78), yet the Thracians seem to have had more of a flair for rowdy drunkenness. Plato lists the Thracians along with the Scythians as the quintessential drinkers, taking their wine neat and letting it crudely drip all over their clothes. Even the women partake in such activities. In this way, the Thracians and Scythians reckon that they are following a noble and prestigious custom. The Persians, however, also drink great quantities, but they do so with considerably more decorum (*Laws* 1.637d–e). Xenophon

---

[11] Martin and Woodman 1989: 206–7.

5. Votive relief depicting the Thracian goddess Bendis (right) and her worshippers, found in the Piraeus, early fourth century; British Museum 2155. Reprinted by permission of the British Museum. © The Trustees of the British Museum.

of as Thracian in the fourth century. In fifth-century representations, in addition to attributes such as Thracian boots, cloak, and double javelins, Bendis wears a fox-skin cap with flaps extending down the back and sides of her head, much like the caps described by Herodotus and worn by Thracians on contemporaneous vases.[86] In the fourth century, however, Bendis is consistently portrayed on vases and in sculpture with a cap in the exact shape of the tiara-like helmet (see Figure 5).[87]

[86] See, for example, the red-figure figure vase by Sotades dating to 500–450, now in Munich (Antikensammlungen 6203; *ARV*² 765.1); the red-figure stemless cup by the Phiale Painter dating to 475–425, now in Verona (Museo Civico 52; *ARV*² 1023.147, 1678); and the red-figure skyphos by the Phiale Painter dating to 475–425, now in Tübingen (Eberhard-Karls-Univ., Arch. Inst. F2; *ARV*² 1023).

[87] See, for example, the red-figure bell krater by the Bendis Painter dating to 380–370, now in the Louvre (G 515); the terracotta figurine

Thus, during the period in which the *Aristonautes naiskos* was constructed, the quintessential Thracian figure in Attica wore headgear strikingly similar to that worn by Aristonautes.

Another wealthy Athenian, roughly a contemporary of Aristonautes, is also depicted with this type of helmet (but lacking any sign of cheekpieces) on a grave stele found at Eleusis.[88] The stele, dating to the second half of the fourth century, depicts a bearded warrior equipped with the same type of cuirass and shield as Aristonautes. He grasps a tiara-like helmet with his left hand as it is presented to him by a nude attendant, who appears to be a child. The identity of the warrior has not been preserved. That two fourth-century Athenians prominent enough to be memorialized by expensive stelai should be equipped with iconographically Thracian helmets is intriguing. Did these warriors have contact with Thracians – or perhaps campaign in Thracian lands?

Scholars have suggested that the nautical resonances in the names of Aristonautes and his father, Archenautes, combined with the coastal location of their deme, Halai, might indicate that the family had extensive maritime interests.[89] Perhaps seaborne trading ventures brought them into contact with Thrace and the Thracians, but such a connection is tenuous at best. Perhaps Aristonautes and his unnamed contemporary were adopting a particular Thracian attribute as a testament to their social status, much like the figures in vase-painting and sculpture already discussed. This notion finds support in another element of Aristonautes' grave plot. Nearly a century ago, von Salis implied that the statues of two oriental or Scythian archers, found in the general vicinity of Aristonautes' grave, originally flanked the naiskos.[90] Ridgeway argues that

from Tanagra, dating to around 350, also in the Louvre (CA 159); and most famously the votive stele depicting Bendis and her worshippers found near the Bendideion in the Piraeus, dating to 400–375, now in the British Museum (GR 1895.10–28.1).

[88] Athens National Museum 834; see Dintsis 1986: 31, and pl. 13.5.

[89] Ridgeway 1992: 271.

[90] Von Salis 1926: 26–28.

these archers, now also on display in the National Museum at Athens (nos. 823, 824), provided the monument with an appropriate mourning context, just as lyre-playing sirens and slave women do for other Attic grave monuments.[91] The archers, however, are clearly crouching in a position of attack, drawing the strings on their (now missing) bows. For his part, von Salis interpreted the archers as attendants following an Attic soldier to battle.[92] The tiara-like helmet in conjunction with barbarian archers could indicate that Aristonautes took part in Alexander's campaigns in the East, as proposed by Ridgeway.[93] Whether or not he took part in Alexander's invasion of Persia, it seems likely that Aristonautes, and by extension the deceased honored at Eleusis, did serve as a soldier abroad, specifically in the north where he had contact with Thracians and Scythians to an extent that he adopted a Thracian helmet and was memorialized as flanked by Scythian allies. Another possibility, by no means exclusive of the others, is that the barbarian archers served to heroize Aristonautes. There are many examples in vase-painting, particularly black-figure, of Homeric heroes accompanied by Scythian attendants.[94] In this case, the

[91] Ridgeway (1992: 273–272n18), referring to the mourning sirens found in conjunction with the famous Kerameikos plot of Dexileos and two slave women from Acharnae, now in Berlin.

[92] Von Salis 1926: 26–27.

[93] Ridgeway 1992: 274.

[94] See, for instance, a late sixth-century black-figure amphora from Rhodes that depicts three hoplites marching to battle, each accompanied by what looks to be a Scythian archer (Rhodes, Archaeological Museum, 12329; J. D. Beazley, *Attic Black-Figure Vase-Painters* (Oxford, 1956), 288.17). Exactly what is signified by the presence of these archers is much debated. Some see them as evidence of a barbarian archer corps in Athens, even in the late sixth century (Vos 1963: passim; Raeck 1981: 10–21), but others think that these were Athenian archers wearing barbarian clothing (Wardman 1959: 55–56n12. More recently, several scholars have argued that these scenes should be seen in a mythological context. The Scythians, for example, might have originated as attendants of Achilles, but they came to denote generic heroic attendants (Pinney 1983: 130–31). Miller (1991) argues that just as Athenians dressed as Thracians, so too did they dress as Scythians, probably to denote an upper-class affinity for the exotic.

Thracian helmet could serve to distinguish Aristonautes further as a heroic figure.

FEASTING AND GIFT-EXCHANGE

Xenophon's firsthand account of his time at the court of Seuthes, combined with a fragment from Middle Comedy poking fun at the decadence of Iphicrates' Thracian wedding, affords us a glimpse into Thracian aristocratic dining and feasting practices. For most Greeks, Thracian dinners far outshone Athenian ones in terms of luxury, conspicuous consumption, exoticism, and even the nature of the food consumed. At Thracian feasts status objects were exchanged as gifts, primarily to glorify the Thracian host. Other gifts and enticements, ranging from valuable estates to royal marriages, were given by Thracian rulers to Greeks. Akin to the employment of Thracian clothing and equipment, some Athenians might have desired to participate in Thracian feasts and gift-exchange in order to advertise, or perhaps even establish, their status as elites.

It is worth quoting at length from Xenophon's account of the feast hosted by Seuthes, attended by Xenophon himself and other Greek commanders along with a number of notable Thracians from the area:

When they had come in for the dinner – the noblest of the Thracians who were present, the generals and the captains of the Greeks, and whatever embassy from any state was there – the dinner was served with the guests seated in a circle; then tripods were brought in for the whole company; these were full of meat, cut up into pieces, and there were great loaves of leavened bread fastened with skewers to the pieces of meat ...

... When the drinking was well under way, there came in a Thracian with a white horse, and taking a full horn he said: "I drink your health, Seuthes, and present to you this horse; on his back pursuing you shall catch whomever you choose, and retreating you shall not fear the enemy." [27] Another brought in a boy and presented him in the same way, with a health to Seuthes, while another presented clothes for his wife. Timasion also drank his health and presented to him a silver bowl and a carpet worth ten minas. [28] Then one Gnesippus, an Athenian, arose and said that it was an ancient and most excellent custom that those who had possessions should give to the king for honour's sake, and that to those who had nought the king should give, "so that," he continued, "I too may be able to bestow gifts upon you and do you honour ..."

... Up rose Seuthes, drained the horn with Xenophon, and joined him in sprinkling the last drops. After this there came in musicians blowing upon horns such as they use in giving signals, and playing upon trumpets of raw ox-hide not only measured notes, but music like that of a harp. [33] And Seuthes himself got up, raised a war-cry, and sprang aside very nimbly, as though avoiding a missile. There entered also a company of buffoons. (*Anab.* 7.3.21, 26–28, 32–33)[95]

The feast was a ritual integral to maintaining the social order in the world of the Homeric heroes. As van Wees succinctly states, Homeric feasts were key in the "creation of personal networks, the formation of groups, and the differentiation of

[95] Ἐπεὶ δὲ εἰσῆλθον ἐπὶ τὸ δεῖπνον τῶν τε Θρᾳκῶν οἱ κράτιστοι τῶν παρόντων καὶ οἱ στρατηγοὶ καὶ οἱ λοχαγοὶ τῶν Ἑλλήνων καὶ εἴ τις πρεσβεία παρῆν ἀπὸ πόλεως, τὸ δεῖπνον μὲν ἦν καθημένοις κύκλῳ ἔπειτα δὲ τρίποδες εἰσηνέχθησαν πᾶσιν· οὗτοι δ' ἦσαν κρεῶν μεστοὶ νενεμημένων, καὶ ἄρτοι ζυμῖται μεγάλοι προσπεπερονημένοι ἦσαν πρὸς τοῖς κρέασι ...

... Ἐπειδὴ δὲ προυχώρει ὁ πότος, εἰσῆλθεν ἀνὴρ Θρᾷξ ἵππον ἔχων λευκόν, καὶ λαβὼν κέρας μεστὸν εἶπε· Προπίνω σοι, ὦ Σεύθη, καὶ τὸν ἵππον τοῦτον δωροῦμαι, ἐφ' οὗ καὶ διώκων ὃν ἂν θέλῃς αἱρήσεις καὶ ἀποχωρῶν οὐ μὴ δείσῃς [27] τὸν πολέμιον. ἄλλος παῖδα εἰσάγων οὕτως ἐδωρήσατο προπίνων, καὶ ἄλλος ἱμάτια τῇ γυναικί. καὶ Τιμασίων προπίνων ἐδωρήσατο φιάλην τε ἀργυρᾶν καὶ τάπιδα ἀξίαν δέκα μνῶν. [28] Γνήσιππος δέ τις Ἀθηναῖος ἀναστὰς εἶπεν ὅτι ἀρχαῖος εἴη νόμος κάλλιστος τοὺς μὲν ἔχοντας διδόναι τῷ βασιλεῖ τιμῆς ἕνεκα, τοῖς δὲ μὴ ἔχουσι διδόναι τὸν βασιλέα, ἵνα καὶ ἐγώ, ἔφη, ἔχω σοι δωρεῖσθαι καὶ τιμᾶν ...

... ἀναστὰς ὁ Σεύθης συνεξέπιε καὶ συγκατεσκεδάσατο μετ' αὐτοῦ τὸ κέρας. μετὰ ταῦτα εἰσῆλθον κέρασί τε οἵοις σημαίνουσιν αὐλοῦντες καὶ σάλπιγξιν ὠμοβοείαις ῥυθμούς τε καὶ οἷον μαγάδι σαλπίζοντες. [33] καὶ αὐτὸς Σεύθης ἀναστὰς ἀνέκραγέ τε πολεμικὸν καὶ ἐξήλατο ὥσπερ βέλος φυλαττόμενος μάλα ἐλαφρῶς. εἰσῇσαν δὲ καὶ γελωτοποιοί. (Translated by Brownson in Brownson and Dillery 1998)

social status."[96] The host of a feast would be sure to make use of the most ornate utensils and serving vessels possible and to display his collection of valuable prestige objects in the dining hall. As such, the diners would often stand in awe at the wealth of their host (Hom. *Od.* 4.75).[97] Van Wees demonstrates that heroes would take part in a sort of cycle of invitations and counterinvitations to feasts. Feasts were a way to define one's elite status, because only members of the nobility were invited and, in turn, invited others to their own homes – *hoi polloi* were generally excluded.[98]

Seuthes' feast falls into this rubric. The most distinguished men in the region were invited to the event, including the most powerful of the Thracians, the Greek generals and commanders, and the ambassadors from various communities. Seuthes had tripods, traditionally the most lavish of status objects, brought out for the guests, and each tripod was laden with skewers of meat.[99] A notable parallel to Homeric dining is the abundance of meat, in stark contrast to the diet of Classical Greeks. In addition to Xenophon's account, there is archaeological evidence that suggests many Thracians hunted big game and regularly ate meat. Stronk notes that in several excavations of Thracian villages, bones have been discovered from large game animals that were used by the ancient residents for food.[100] In Athens, and most other Greek poleis, meat was usually reserved for special occasions, such as public festivals. Rosivach has provided figures for the price of cattle sacrificed at Athenian festivals, showing that the prices were so high as to prevent beef from being eaten on any regular basis in Athens, let alone in the quantities described by Xenophon at

[96] Van Wees 1995:148.

[97] Van Wees 1995: 150–54.

[98] See van Wees 1995: 164–77, including more detailed bibliography.

[99] For tripods as status objects for Homer's heroes, see van Wees 1995: 151.

[100] See Stronk (1995: 231), who discusses the excavation of several Thracian villages. The best evidence for the consumption of meat comes from excavated rubbish pits, which contain the bones of cattle, other farm animals, and various game.

the feast of Seuthes.[101] Homeric heroes, on the other hand, ate meat as a staple.

Seuthes and his guests consumed a copious amount of wine at the banquet, evoking notions of heroic camaraderie and the elite institution of the symposium prevalent at Athens at this time.[102] Several times nobles drained entire horns of wine as they drank to Seuthes, and the king himself emptied a horn with Xenophon. Xenophon notes that this ritualized drinking was an established Thracian custom (*Thraikos nomos*). For instance, the negotiations between Xenophon and Seuthes over the employment of the Greek soldiers were inaugurated by means of this ritual (7.2.23). After drinking at the feast, Seuthes let out a war cry and performed a dance emulating combat in order to show his own martial prowess. As if this feat of dexterity was not enough, at the end of the festivities Seuthes sprang up, showing no sign whatsoever of being drunk in spite of the large quantities of drink he had consumed.

The Thracians were stereotypically heavy drinkers. That Seuthes was able to drink so much and still appear sober suggests an affinity for alcohol. There is ample material evidence to support this notion. The Rogozen treasure, found in northern Bulgaria in 1985, contains a large number of ornate vessels made from precious metals. The objects seem to date from the end of the fifth to the mid-fourth century, and scholars have argued that the treasure was collected by a noble Thracian family over the course of several decades.[103] The vessels, many of which are inscribed with the names of known Odrysian rulers, including Cotys and his son Cersobleptes, were most likely given to the Odrysian kings as gifts or tribute payments from subject cities. The names of these cities, most of which are

---

[101] Rosivach 1994: 95–96.

[102] Van Wees (1995: 177–79) makes explicit the link between Homeric feasting and the Archaic and Classical symposium as a means of expressing social class.

[103] See Cook 1989, Fol et al. 1986, and Fol 1989 for a comprehensive study of the treasure. See Fol (1989: 140–94) for a complete catalogue. For a relatively recent study of these and similar vessels from Bulgaria, see Zournatzi 2000.

located in southeastern Thrace near the Hellespontine region, are sometimes included on the vessels.[104] The overwhelming majority of these vessels – 163 out of 165 – are drinking phialai and wine jugs. Likewise, the Panagyurishte treasure from central Bulgaria at the western end of the Thracian plain, an astonishing find consisting of several fourth-century drinking vessels totaling over 6 kilograms of pure gold, includes several *phialai* and *rhyta*, horn-shaped vessels equivalent to the *kerata* used by Seuthes and his guests.[105] Both of these treasures, and several more from Bulgaria, include objects of strikingly ornate workmanship and valuable materials that were certainly meant to showcase their owners' wealth and status. That they consist primarily of drinking vessels demonstrates the centrality of drink-ritual for the Thracian nobility. Van Wees suspects that the profusion of precious metal at the feasts described by Homer is a glamorous fiction, hardly reflected in the poet's real world.[106] It clearly was, however, a part of the world of the Thracian rulers of the fifth and fourth centuries.

The comic playwright Anaxandrides, quoted by Athenaeus, presents a colorful description of the drink-laden wedding feast to which Iphicrates was treated by his father-in-law, Cotys:

And if you follow my instructions, I'll / entertain you with a sumptuous dinner / far better than the one in Thrace / that Iphicrates got – and yet, they say, / it was a megextravaganza. / Purple carpets strewn / in the agora northwards, / filthy-haired, cow-cheese-eating Thracians / dining by the thousands, / cauldrons of bronze / bigger than 12-couch vats, / Cotys himself in an apron, / carrying soup in a golden pitcher, / tasting the wine mixtures, / drunk before his guests. / They had Antigeneides playing the pipes, / Agras singing, and on the lyre / Cephisodotus of Acharnae, / singing hymns of praise / sometimes to Sparta's wide open spaces, / sometimes to Thebes' seven gates, / always changing his tune. / As dowry gifts he got two herds / of bay horses and a herd of goats, / a sack of spun

[104] Fol 1989: 8–11.
[105] For this treasure, see Vendikov 1961.
[106] van Wees 1995: 150.

gold / <...> and a limpet-shaped bowl, / a jugful of snow, a pitful of millet, a twelve-cubit jar of bulbs / and a hecatomb of octopuses. / That's how they say Cotys arranged it / in Thrace, the wedding for Iphicrates. (F 42 K-A)[107]

Allowing for comic exaggeration, Iphicrates' wedding feast might have looked very much like the description given by Anaxandrides. Nothing is out of keeping with Xenophon's portrayal of Seuthes' lavish banquet or with the material evidence discovered. The valuable vessels used, the gifts presented, and the centrality of the king as host are all entirely plausible elements.

Athenaeus includes this quotation from Anaxandrides in the context of describing other sumptuous dinners in order to emphasize the sparseness of meals at Athens itself (4.131–37). Judging from this section of Athenaeus and from other passages from comedy, the luxuriousness of foreign feasts in comparison to the light fare at Athens was a common comic theme. In the *Acharnians* of Aristophanes, the envoy to the Persians is ridiculed by Dicaeopolis for describing entire oxen being roasted whole to be served to the Great King (84–87).[108] For Dicaeopolis and Aristophanes' audience, such extravagance

---

[107] κἂν ταῦτα ποιῆθ᾽ ὥσπερ φράζω, / λαμπροῖς δείπνοις δεξόμεθ᾽ ὑμᾶς, / οὐδὲν ὁμοίοις τοῖς Ἰφικράτους / τοῖς ἐν Θρᾴκῃ· καίτοι φασὶν / βουβαυκαλόσαυλα γενέσθαι. / κατὰ τὴν ἀγορὰν μὲν ὑπεστρῶσθαι / στρώμαθ᾽ ἁλουργῆ μέχρι τῆς ἄρκτου· / δειπνεῖν δ᾽ ἄνδρας βουτυροφάγας, / αὐχμηροκόμας μυριοπληθεῖς· / τοὺς δὲ λέβητας χαλκοῦς εἶναι, / μείζους λάκκων δωδεκακλίνων· / αὐτὸν δὲ Κότυν περιεζῶσθαι / ζωμόν τε φέρειν ἐν χοῖ χρυσῇ, / καὶ γευόμενον τῶν κρατήρων / πρότερον μεθύειν τῶν πινόντων / αὐλεῖν δ᾽ αὐτοῖς Ἀντιγενείδαν, / Ἀργᾶν δ᾽ ᾄδειν καὶ κιθαρίζειν / Κηφισόδοτον τὸν Ἀχαρνῆθεν, / μέλπειν δ᾽ ᾠδαῖς / τοτὲ μὲν Σπάρτην τὴν εὐρύχορον, / τοτὲ δ᾽ αὖ Θήβας τὰς ἑπταπύλους / τὰς ἁρμονίας μεταβάλλειν. / φερνάς τε λαβεῖν δύο μὲν ξανθῶν / ἵππων ἀγέλας, αἰγῶν τ᾽ ἀγέλην, / χρυσοῦν τε σάκος / ... φιάλην τε λεπαστήν, / Χίου τε πρόχουν, κέρχνων τε χύτραν, / βολβῶν τε σιρὸν δωδεκάπηχυν / καὶ πουλυπόδων ἑκατόμβην. / ταῦτα μὲν οὕτως φασὶ ποιῆσαι / Κότυν ἐν Θρᾴκῃ, γάμον Ἰφικράτει. (Translated by Rusten in Rusten et al. 2011)

[108] See the commentary on this passage in Olson (2002: 98–99), who provides more examples of foreign dining excess.

was beyond the means of anyone living at Athens and beyond the bounds of acceptable social practice.

Archibald discusses the phenomenon of Thracian gift-exchange, which occurred at all levels of Odrysian society. In contrast to the Persians, who gave gifts to facilitate the smooth running of the empire by granting parcels of land to ensure loyalty, for example, Archibald argues, notable Odrysians received gifts in recognition of their own superiority.[109] This Odrysian custom is reminiscent of that practiced by Homer's heroes.[110] Great warriors such as Achilles could expect to be given the choicest spoils as a reflection of their greatness. Prestige objects, such as those given to Seuthes by his distinguished guests, were for Homeric heroes the necessary outward symbol of their *geras*, the prerogative conferred upon the nobility. Heroes also vied with one another in outgiving their rivals, the principle being that the grandest leader is able to give the grandest gifts. The exchange of gifts was crucial for the demarcation of social rank and prestige in Homeric society, as it seemed to be for many Thracians. For notable Greeks such as Alcibiades, Xenophon, and Iphicrates, the similarity to the world of epic would have been obvious. It matters little whether rulers such as Seuthes and Cotys were aware of Homeric precedent, though I see no reason why they would not have happily equated themselves with the most prestigious figures of Greek mythology.

---

[109] Archibald 1998: 148–50. See also Testard and Brunaux (2004), who argue based on this passage of Xenophon that Thracian gift-exchange, namely, the flow of gifts from the poorer to the richer, is the exact inverse of the practice as it existed in most "primitive" societies.

[110] It will be recalled that the destructive conflict that arose between Achilles and Agamemnon in the first book of the *Iliad* was a result of the latter's claim upon Achilles' prize, Briseis. Though Agamemnon had taken no part in the action by which Briseis had been acquired, his position as the more powerful king entitled him to the pick of the spoils. For a concise discussion of Homeric gift-exchange, see Finley 2002 [1954]: 46–70. See also Donlan 1982; 1989; Jones 1999. Contra, see Hooker (1989), who argues that there was no formal institution of gift-exchange as such.

Seuthes tempted Xenophon and other members of the Ten Thousand with promises of lavish gifts, including horses, estates, and even women (7.2.2, 38; 7.5.8). He declared that Xenophon and two of his comrades would be made brothers of the king, sharing in his seat of power and taking a portion of the kingdom's acquisitions. Xenophon himself was offered Seuthes' daughter in marriage along with the lovely port of Bisanthe and two other estates (7.2.38; 7.5.8). Iphicrates was also offered a royal Thracian bride and extensive property, most notably Drys, in return for his service on behalf of Seuthes and Cotys, a proposition he accepted. Harpocration, quoting Theopompus as his source, says that Drys was settled (*katoikizomai*) by Iphicrates (s.v. Δρῦς). As Pritchett points out, in Ptolemaic Egypt *katoikoi* – the nominal form of the verb used for Iphicrates' settlement – were foreigners settled on the land in return for military service. Polybius has a similar definition (5.65.10). Pritchett goes on to argue that in the case of Iphicrates, Harpocration is merely referring to a free citizen settled in a foreign land.[111] If one takes into account the parallel examples of Alcibiades and Xenophon, however, one is left with the impression that Iphicrates owned these settlements outright. The verb *katoikizomai* implies that Iphicrates actively colonized the site, perhaps with his own veterans. In any case, it was regular practice for Odrysian kings to reward foreign generals with valuable property that was sizable enough to allow for many settlers. Such estates generated a great amount of wealth. That Iphicrates fled to Drys and remained for several years after he fell out with Cotys indicates that the Athenian had considerable autonomy while on his estate. If Drys was settled with Iphicrates' own soldiers, Cotys' inability to threaten him there, even though it was located in Odrysian lands, would be explained.

Seuthes himself received valuable gifts as emblems of his royal authority. Xenophon describes how Seuthes' Greek agent, Heraclides of Maronea, made a circuit around the Greek camp

---

[111] Pritchett 1974–1991: vol. 2, 67.

trying to extort gifts for his patron, accosting Xenophon specifically and saying that the greater the gifts Xenophon should
give, the greater would be Seuthes' support (7.3.16–20). In the
feast that followed, hosted by Seuthes, distinguished guests
vied with one another in presenting their gifts, which included
ornate vessels, horses, and even clothes for the king's wife.

At the court of Thracian rulers, Greeks could be treated as
de facto royalty. They were offered the daughters of kings in
marriage, feted with lavish feasts, and granted valuable gifts of
livestock, precious metals, and lucrative property. They could
immerse themselves in a world that to an educated Greek would
have resembled that of Homer's *basileis*. Status was determined
by ostentatious wealth and military prowess, both of which
Greek Thracophiles often possessed in abundance thanks to
their own talents and the favor shown by the Thracian kings.

Throughout his speech against Aristocrates, delivered in
352/1, Demosthenes contrasts the society of Thrace with the
civilized world of the Greek polis. For example, Charidemus
of Oreus, Iphicrates' successor at the Odrysian court, did not
dwell in any civilized polity, or polis, but rather fought on
behalf of a Thracian king and exploited his patron's royal
authority to mistreat many (23.138). Earlier in the speech,
Demosthenes ponders what the consequences would be if
Charidemus were to leave Thrace to settle in a civilized Greek
polis while continuing to commit the many crimes that were
permitted to him by the authority and license (*exousia*) available in Thrace (23.57). Though Charidemus is particularly sin-
gled out, his mentor Iphicrates is also said to have fought a sea
battle against Athens on behalf of Cotys (23.130). The situation
of the two men was quite similar. Both opted for the license
of barbarous Thrace and for the royal authority of a powerful
foreign patron, spurning the confines of the polis. Charidemus
eventually became connected by marriage to Cersobleptes in
the same way Iphicrates had been to Cotys (Dem. 23.129).
Demosthenes certainly had a motive to portray Charidemus in
the worst possible light, because the aim of this speech was
to censure Aristocrates for proposing that Charidemus should

be inviolable.[112] However, the picture of the Odrysian court we are given by Xenophon and Anaxandrides, substantiated by material finds, fits Demosthenes' characterization. As many Athenians discovered and exploited to their advantage, Thrace afforded the unscrupulously ambitious ample opportunity for material enrichment and the display of regal pomp.

RELIGION AND CULT

When the elder Miltiades died he received special honors from the inhabitants of the Chersonese, including sacrifices and athletic competitions, both gymnastic and equestrian. Owing to his conflict with Lampsacus, no one from that city was allowed to take part, implying that athletes from several cities in the area competed in these games (Hdt. 6.38.1). This passage has been held by many scholars to portray an archetype for founder-cults that existed in poleis throughout the Greek world, for which evidence is otherwise sparse. Key to this idea is the standard interpretation of Herodotus' comment that such is the usual custom (*nomos*) for city-founders. However, Malkin, who has written the most comprehensive monograph on Greek colonization and religion and who believes that this passage implies the universality of the ancient founder-cult, can only provide a very few additional examples of such a cult being celebrated in honor of historical persons. Two of these are from Thrace.[113] It is possible, then, that the type of founder-cult exemplified by that celebrated in honor of Miltiades was far from a universal phenomenon. Furthermore, such a cult appears to be linked to Thrace. Accordingly, the precise meaning of Herodotus' comment must be reevaluated.

Malkin begins his survey of founder-cults by discussing the special oracular tomb associated with the king Battus at Cyrene, followed by the supposed cult of Phalanthus, founder of Taras

---

[112] As Kelly (1990: 103–4) points out, Charidemus was honored at Athens because he had performed valuable services for the Athenians, which Demosthenes wished to downplay.

[113] Malkin 1987: 189–203, 204–40.

(Tarentum), who was of dubious historicity and seems to have been overshadowed by the legendary hero Taras himself. A few late Classical and Hellenistic cases are mentioned, as are the honors bestowed upon some of the Sicilian tyrants as recorded in Diodorus. The remaining historical figures who received known cultic honors were Timesius, who was honored at Abdera; Hagnon and later Brasidas at Amphipolis; and Themistocles, who may have been treated as a founder in Magnesia. In all of these examples, the "heroic honors" are not specified as they are for Miltiades, save for Brasidas, who was honored with annual sacrifices and games, and the exceptional case of the Sicilian Timoleon, who received a yearly festival complete with athletic and musical competitions after his death in 336.

Timesius, as it is related by Herodotus (1.168), was given heroic honors by the Teian colonists of Abdera, though Timesius himself was a Clazomenian. He had attempted to found the site a hundred years prior to the Teian colony but was driven out by the local Thracians. Why should the Teians have honored Timesius with such a cult? Even though Timesius had attempted to establish a colony, he was neither Teian nor a successful founder. Malkin rejects the possibility that there was a preexisting cult to Timesius that the Teians simply adopted for themselves.[114] Yet, as Owen demonstrates, it was a regular practice of Greeks in the north Aegean to make use of and adapt preexisting Thracian cult centers. These were often linked to monumental structures, such as tombs.[115] Perhaps the Teians were confronted with the local cult of a legendary Thracian and its accompanying structures and adapted it to include Timesius, a well-known Greek who had strong connections with the site. The activities of Timesius and his status as a noble man (*anēr agathos*) are mentioned in several later sources, attesting to his renown in antiquity.[116] This famous figure would have been ideally suited for incorporation as a hero into a preexisting Thracian cult center.

[114] Malkin 1987: 222.
[115] Owen 2000.
[116] For the accounts of Timesios, see Isaac 1986: 78–79.

Thucydides tells us that after the final defeat of the Athenians at Amphipolis at the hands of Brasidas, the residents of the polis destroyed the monuments or buildings of the Athenian Hagnon and made Brasidas their new official founder, honoring him as a hero with annual sacrifices and games (Thuc. 5.11.1).[117] This looks very much like the cult granted to Miltiades. Yet, it seems Hagnon had been afforded these honors while he was still alive. The transfer of the cult occurred in 422, and Hagnon lived long enough to be appointed to the office of *proboulos* at Athens in 413 (Lys. 12.65; Xen. *Hell.* 2.3.30). To be sure, the text of Thucydides does not say explicitly that the new honors granted to the dead Brasidas had been previously bestowed upon Hagnon. Rather, it merely states that structures connected to Hagnon were torn down and the title of founder was transferred. Malkin, however, is right in asserting that Thucydides does imply equivalence between the new honors granted to Brasidas and those now denied Hagnon.[118] That Hagnon enjoyed an active cult while still living is not out of the question, but it would seem to be unique among the Greeks until the honors granted to the Spartan Lysander two decades later.

It is generally agreed that the Greek settlers in Amphipolis incorporated elements from local Thracian cults into their own religious practices. For example, coins and several inscriptions from the area demonstrate the worship of Artemis Tauropolos, who is to be identified with the Thracian goddess Bendis. Additionally, the cult of Rhesus that was practiced at Amphipolis was most likely a Greek adaptation of the worship of a Thracian god or hero. The Greeks probably made use of this particular cult to demonstrate an affinity with the indigenous population.[119] The Greeks who settled nearby Thasos made use of preexisting Thracian religious structures, and likely also Thracian deities, in the practice of their own rites.

[117] See Malkin 1987: 228–32.
[118] Malkin 1987: 230–32.
[119] Isaac 1986: 55–58; Archibald 1998: 101.

The evidence suggests that the Cave of Pan on the acropolis of Thasos was originally a Thracian rock-cut tomb, associated with ritual feasting and connected to Thracian hero- or ancestor-cult. The worship of Pan at this site by Greek settlers in the Classical period indicates that not only was the structure itself respected and utilized but perhaps also the earlier Thracian cult practices themselves were adapted to fit into Greek ritual.[120] We can reasonably conclude that, rather than abandoning local non-Greek religion, Greek newcomers to the north Aegean regularly respected and adopted Thracian cults. The unique honors granted to Hagnon and later to Brasidas can perhaps be best explained in the context of Thracian religious practices.

Another historical figure to whom Malkin attributes a proper founder-cult is Themistocles. He was given power by the Persians over several cities in Asia Minor after his expulsion from Athens. These cities included Magnesia and Myous, both in southern Ionia near Miletus, and Lampsacus on the Hellespont (Thuc. 1.138.5). Malkin does argue that Themistocles received heroic worship specifically at Magnesia, but he admits that there is no direct evidence of this.[121] The only indication that Themistocles received honors akin to those given Miltiades comes from a decree, dated to around 200 from Lampsacus, which affords an unknown recipient the same honors that were given to Themistocles' son, namely, the good things (*agatha*) associated with a festival.[122] Presumably, this festival would have included athletic contests and the like. Although this decree proves little, it is interesting that the only hint of heroic honors granted to Themistocles is connected to a city in Thrace rather than any of the other areas over which the great Athenian was given dominion.

The universality of the founder-cult is far from certain. That nearly all of the unambiguous references to such a cult in our

---

[120] Owen 2000: 139–43.
[121] Malkin 1987: 224.
[122] Malkin 1987: 226.

sources can be situated within a Thracian milieu is striking. The Chersonesitai who celebrated the rites in honor of Miltiades surely included both Thracian inhabitants of the Chersonese, because they were the ones who had initially invited Miltiades and benefited from the security he was able to provide, and the Greeks who had been settled in the region. Yet, rather than this being a noteworthy case of foreigners participating in Greek rites, as most scholars have assumed, perhaps it was the Greeks who were taking part in local Thracian cult practices.[123] Thus, Herodotus' statement that the sacrifices, and by extension the other rites, were carried out in accordance with the customary honors due a city-founder might imply a Thracian, rather than Greek, custom.

In his discussion of Thracian customs at the beginning of book 5, Herodotus outlines the funeral rites held after the death of prominent Thracians. These rites include feasting after the ritual slaughter and sacrifice of many different victims, and every sort of athletic competition (Hdt. 5.8). That such rites were uniquely Thracian is evinced by their inclusion in a passage of Herodotus meant to highlight the strange customs of the Thracians.[124] Moreover, the feasting held in honor of the dead might be connected to the ritual feasting archaeologists have associated with Thracian tombs in southern Thrace, including the Thasian Cave of Pan.[125] Xenophon partially corroborates this image when he describes Odrysian Thracians from the northern shore of the Hellespont burying their war dead and then honoring them with copious drinking and horse-racing competitions (*Hell.* 3.2.5). The literary evidence, therefore, suggests that the Thracians, quite independently

[123] See Malkin (1987: 192) for a discussion of the identity of the participants and the phenomenon of barbarians worshipping along with Greeks.

[124] For this passage and Herodotus' ethnological treatment of the Thracians, see Asheri 1990: 131–63. Asheri emphasizes that Herodotus was primarily interested in marvellous things (*thōmata*) in his study of Thrace.

[125] See Owen (2000: 141–43) for further bibliography on Thracian burial practices and ritual.

of the Greeks, celebrated their prominent dead much as the inhabitants of the Chersonese did for Miltiades.

Herodotus' language may also indicate the non-Greek nature of the sacrifices for Miltiades. The verb *thuō* is used in the context of Miltiades' honors, implying sacrifices in honor of a god instead of a hero, which would not be in accordance with the Greek *nomos* for hero-cults. Earlier in his work, Herodotus uses the example of the divine versus heroic Heracles to clearly distinguish between the sacrifices made for an Olympian god (*thuō*) and those made for a hero (*enagizō*, 2.44.5). Though there are exceptions to this rule, as has been noted by several scholars, Herodotus has chosen to comment on the distinction.[126] The other notable founder to be given sacrifices in this manner (*thusiai*) was none other than Brasidas, and perhaps by analogy Hagnon (Thuc. 5.11.1). This naturally has been offered as proof of the connection between *thusiai* and Greek founder-cult.[127] Yet, it could reflect the non-Greek elements of Brasidas' cult.

Malkin remarks on the lack of musical contests – apparently a central element in typical Greek hero-cults – in the games held for Miltiades. Otherwise, Miltiades' festival seemed to be completely regular.[128] Habicht, cited by Malkin, enumerates the types of contests (*agōnes*) held in conjunction with hero worship, which include gymnastic, equestrian, and musical competitions. Yet, the examples Habicht furnishes are all connected with Hellenistic ruler-cult, such as that held in the Ptolemeia in Alexandria. The only exception is the festival for

---

[126] See Malkin 1987: 193; McQueen (2000: 115) notes the two exceptions to this rule in Herodotus, namely, the sacrifices in honor of Onesilos at 5.114.2 and Artachaites at 7.117.2. It should be noted that the latter case may prove the rule rather than the other way around. Artachaites was a physically stunning Persian and a member of the Achaemenid family. He died at Akanthos, a city north of the Athos peninsula and thus in the vicinity of Thrace, and was given a lavish funeral and burial mound by Xerxes and the Persians. Herodotus does say that the people of Akanthos offered sacrifice (*thuein*) on the advice of an oracle, but it seems plausible that they were influenced in this decision by the Persians or even the local traditions of their region.

[127] Malkin 1987: 193, 228–32.

[128] Malkin 1987: 193n22.

Timoleon, which is, strictly speaking, late Classical.[129] The lack of musical competition in the case of Miltiades, and also of Brasidas, possibly reflects the non-Greek aspect of these honors. The sacrifices performed and the gymnastic and equestrian contests held are perfectly in line with the particularly Thracian practices as described by Herodotus and Xenophon.

If this new interpretation of the founder-cult of the elder Miltiades is correct, we must reexamine the nature of Greek founder-cults in general. Malkin himself concludes: "The cults of founders of cities which in later periods also served as a basis for the ruler-cults in the Hellenistic and Roman periods – seem to have been the creation of Greek colonies."[130] If such practices stemmed from Thracian rites, even a Greek reinterpretation and adaptation of Thracian cults, the Thracians thus had a profound influence on Greek religion. Furthermore, if mortal men such as Miltiades could expect to receive even the semblance of divine honors, the appeal of Thrace for ambitious Athenian aristocrats is made even more apparent. Hagnon, for example, might have preceded Lysander by decades in the receipt of heroic honors while he was yet alive.

THE AGŌN

In the late seventh century, a group of Athenians set out from home and captured the site of Sigeum in the Troad from the Mytileneans, thereby gaining a foothold on the Asiatic shore of the Hellespont.[131] The leader of this early Athenian expedition was a man named Phrynon, an Olympic victor in the *pankration* described as a massive man of great strength (Plut.

---

[129] Habicht 1956:150–53.

[130] Malkin 1987: 266.

[131] See Hdt. 5.94–95 for the ongoing disputes between Athens and Mytilene over possession of this site. See also the attendant commentary in How and Wells (1912: vol. 2, 56) for the chronological problems in Herodotus' account. For the history of settlement of Sigeum, see Diog. Laert. 1.74; Str. 13.1.38. Isaac (1986: 162–66) offers a comprehensive account of Athenian activities in the region. For Sigeum as part of Thrace, see Chapter 1 in this book.

Mor. 858b).[132] Phrynon the pankratiast, skilled at hand-to-hand combat, relished any chance to engage in a duel of champions (*monomachia*) and win glory for himself. Accordingly, in a subsequent dispute with Mytilene over control of the territory, he issued a challenge to anyone willing to fight him. In spite of the Athenian's intimidating stature and renowned proficiency, a famous figure by the name of Pittacus, one of the so-called Seven Sages of Greece, rose to the challenge. During the duel, Pittacus ensnared Phrynon with a net he had concealed under his shield and ran him through. Thus killing his opponent, Pittacus took back control of Sigeum for Mytilene (Plut. *Mor.* 858a–b; Diod. 9.12.1; Diog. Laert. 1.74). In recognition of this feat he became sole ruler of the Mytileneans (Diog. Laert. 1.74–81).[133]

Diogenes tells us that Pittacus' father was a Thracian (1.74), and indeed the name is shared by a king of the Edonian Thracians mentioned by Thucydides (Thuc. 4.107).[134] As Herodotus says in his ethnological account of the Thracians at the beginning of his fifth book, the Thracians considered warfare to be the most honorable way of life, and in the lavish funeral games they held for their dead, they awarded the highest prize to the victor in single combat (*monomachia*, 5.8). Even in the late Roman Republic, the Thracian was a type of gladiator (*monomachos* in Greek), and the most famous gladiator of all, Spartacus, was from Thrace.[135] Indicative of the popular Greek perception of the inhabitants of Thrace, the most notorious fighter in Greek

[132] Eusebius' list of Olympic victors places Phrynon in 636/5 (1.199).

[133] Though Herodotus makes no mention of this story, it had a strong tradition in antiquity. For the ancient sources, see Isaac 1986: 162. See Bowen (1992: 112–13) for a discussion of Plutarch's treatment of the story. As Bowen argues, Plutarch probably visited Sigeum himself, and he may have used Hellanicus of Lesbos as his source. For Diogenes Laertius' use of earlier sources, see Mejer (1978: 7–59), who aims to show that, however flawed, Diogenes was an honest compiler of material (14).

[134] For the name, see Dechev 1957: 371. The Edonians lived mainly in the Strymon valley.

[135] See Strauss 2009: 13–28. Spartacus, though, was a *murmillo*-type gladiator.

mythology, Amycus, was the king of the Bebrycians, who lived on the southern shore of the Black Sea and in the northern parts of the Troad, not far from Sigeum.[136] As told by Apollonius of Rhodes and Theocritus, the towering and arrogant Amycus demanded that every foreigner who came to his land fight him in hand-to-hand combat. Polydeuces finally silenced this bully by defeating him in a vicious boxing match (Ap. Rhod. *Argon.* 2.1–98; Theoc. *Id.* 22). Among such a people, Phrynon, who had received the highest known accolade among the Greeks in the sport of no-holds-barred fighting, would have felt right at home. That Pittacus was himself of Thracian stock and that he was able to defeat Phrynon with a cunning trick implies that he too was experienced in such combat.

Competition among the elite, though not necessarily in the form of combat to the death, was an important feature of Greek society. Jacob Burckhardt famously emphasized the importance of the *agōn*, including its manifestation in sport, for the Archaic Greeks:

[A]ristocratic states had an abundance of privileged individuals who as a group constituted the ideal of Greek life within their centuries: a common government in the state, skill in warfare, *splendor in competitive sports*, and noble leisure for all these. With them, there began that agonistic mentality, that spirit of competition among equals, which in countless ways permeated all thought and action of the Hellenes.[137]

In more recent years, the pervasiveness of the agonistic ethos has been called into question. Ian Morris, for example, argues that such a mentality was more a feature of an elite that set itself against the prevailing middling ideology emphasizing equality among the population of normal citizens. In such a climate, the elite ideology was the dominant position only in that it reinforced solidarity *within* a would-be aristocracy. Morris himself concedes, however, that the *agōn* as a

---

[136] The scholiast for Apollonius (2.2) places the Bebrycians specifically near Lampsacus on the southern shore of the Hellespont.

[137] Burckhardt and Hilty 1963: 54. Emphasis mine.

determiner of status still held an important place in Archaic society, and democratic forms of government only became possible at the end of the period with the collapse of elite ideology. The beginnings of this collapse can be seen already in the poetry of Tyrtaeus, Xenophanes, and Solon, who all rejected the agonistic ideal of the athlete in favor of more useful types of citizens.[138] In post-Solonian Athens, there continued to exist aristocratic citizens who possessed all the wealth, talent, and military/athletic skill that by all rights should have ensured them a position of dominance as victors in an intraelite *agōn*. Yet, Athens was becoming ever more egalitarian in its division of political power, and the ascendancy of the Pisistratids all but eliminated the meaningful benefits of competition among the elite.

In his infamous speech before the launching of the Sicilian Expedition, Thucydides' Alcibiades conveys, albeit rather baldly, an attitude that had once been pervasive among upper-class Athenians. Rather than skirting the issue of his wealth and extravagance, because of which he had aroused the suspicion of the Athenian populace, he tries to turn it to his advantage. His ostentation, or so he argues, is a credit to his ancestors and a benefit to his city. As his prime example, he cites a celebrated victory at the Olympic Games in which he personally entered seven chariot teams – more than any private individual had ever done – and secured the first, second, and fourth prizes. In such a way, the wider Greek world, expecting Athens to be thoroughly wrecked by the long war, was shown a clear example of Athens' continued power and greatness. Alcibiades insists he should not be censured because of such qualities but, rather, that he has every right and privilege to assume a haughty demeanor. Thus Alcibiades justifies his manner of living, his arrogance, and also his fitness to lead (Thuc. 6.16). There is no greater testament to the agonistic ethos of Greek aristocrats than the importance they placed on athletic accomplishment, especially in the Archaic period.

---

[138] Morris 2000: 156, 185–87.

The centrality of Olympic victories to the early Athenian colonizing efforts on the Hellespont is striking. The elder Miltiades
was an Olympic victor. His preferred event was the four-horse
chariot race (Hdt. 6.36.1), as it was for his half-brother, Cimon,
father of the younger Miltiades (6.103.2).[139] As Herodotus
relates, Cimon won his first Olympic victory after he had been
expelled from Athens by Pisistratus. Cimon won again at the
next games with the same team of horses, but this time relin-
quished his victory in favor of Pisistratus. Thus he was allowed
by the tyrant to return to Athens, a fact that highlights the
political importance of such prestigious athletic accomplish-
ments. Cimon later won an astonishing third victory with these
horses, a feat previously achieved only once, but this time he
was soon murdered at the instigation of the sons of Pisistratus
(Hdt. 6.103.3). As this story implies, his third Olympic triumph made him dangerously popular at Athens and therefore
a threat to the tyrants.[140] Pseudo-Andocides (4.33) says that
the younger Miltiades and his son Cimon also won Olympic
victories, presumably in the chariot competition, and an aside
by Pausanias (6.10.8) indicates that Miltiades subsequently
dedicated sculptures of horses and chariots at Delphi.[141] A
black-figure pyxis found near Brauron and dating to about 540
depicts a series of grooms leading horses, along with a slave
pulling a chariot. A youth draped in a himation and holding a
branch leads the procession. The artist has identified the youth
as Stesagoras, probably the son of Cimon who would succeed
the elder Miltiades as tyrant in the Chersonese. The prominence of horses and the chariot in the scene fit in well with the
family's propensity for chariot racing.[142]

It is well known that a large part of the prestige associated
with chariot racing was the sheer expense required to raise

---

[139] The dates of these victories, and their implications for the chronology
of settlement in the Chersonese, are disputed. See Hammond 1956:
114–19; Davies 1971: 299–300.

[140] Hammond 1956: 117.

[141] Hammond 1956: 119n4.

[142] Immerwahr 1972: 181–86.

horses.[143] As a comic take on this idea, Aristophanes begins his *Clouds* with Strepsiades lamenting the debt he has accumulated because of his son's passion for horses (12–24). It is therefore unsurprising that many of Athens' most eminent men were victors in the chariot race – few others could afford even to enter such a competition. As the son of Alcibiades says, the raising of horses is only for the most fortunate (Isoc. 16.33). Alcibiades' horse breeding and chariot victories were legendary, as is attested in several sources. The fame he won from his Olympic victories was unmatched in that he accomplished a more spectacular victory than any private individual or even king had before him (Plut. *Alc.* 11). The elite nature of the sport is brought out by Alcibiades' son, who says that his father – though inferior to no one in terms of physical ability – chose to spurn the gymnastic competitions because many of the athletes in such sports were from insignificant cities and of low birth (Isoc. 16.33).

In the late fifth century, Alcibiades thought that a peerless victory at the Olympic Games in the quintessentially noble sport entitled him to political power, even in a broadly based democracy. As the fate of the elder Cimon illustrates, Olympic victories were often crucial to one wishing to attain power in the Archaic period. If an aristocrat could afford to raise horses, the prestige and influence that could be acquired ensured that the expense was a worthwhile investment.[144] Herodotus seems to connect political power closely with the ability to raise horses, indicated by his introduction to the elder Miltiades: "Miltiades the son of Cypselus was also powerful in Athens, having a household that raced four-horse chariots."[145] The younger Miltiades, who eventually assumed leadership over the Chersonese, evidently wanted to exploit his family's prestigious victories. Herodotus says that along with Cimon

[143] For a discussion of the financial implications of raising race-horses, see Scott 2005: 513–21.
[144] McQueen 2000: 111.
[145] ἀτὰρ ἐδυνάστευε καὶ Μιλτιάδης ὁ Κυψέλου, ἐὼν οἰκίης τεθριπποτρόφου (6.35.1).

were buried the four horses that had won him the victories (6.103.3), and Aelian says Miltiades himself saw to the burial of the horses in a prestigious plot in the Kerameikos (*Hist. An.* 12.40). The ostentatious burial of the horses that had won Cimon three Olympic victories, and caused him to run afoul of the Pisistratids, made an unmistakable political statement. Miltiades avoided his father's fate despite such a public affront to the rulers of Athens. He was made eponymous archon in 524/3 by the Pisistratids, which suggests that they wished to avoid alienating the powerful Philaid family any further.

From the time of Homer, the Thracians were legendary for their horsemanship. In the *Iliad* the Thracians are called "horse herders" (*hippopoloi*, 13.4; 14.227) and "horse warriors" (*hippokorystai*, 16.287). Dolon describes the horses of Rhesus as the largest and most splendid he had ever seen, snow-white and pulling a chariot adorned with gold and silver, fitting spoils for Odysseus and Diomedes (10.435–40). Euripides describes the villainous Polymestor as king of the horse-loving people that sow crops in the fertile Chersonese (*Hec.* 7–9). The material evidence suggests that such descriptions are not without merit.[146] There are also several references to Thracian horse racing. As we have seen, Xenophon describes the Odrysians, after being defeated by the Bithynians, as holding horse-racing competitions in honor of their dead, much as the elder Miltiades was honored after his death by the inhabitants of the Chersonese. The famous fourth-century tomb of a Thracian noble at Kazanlak in central Bulgaria depicts lavish four-horse chariots and chariot races.[147] From the Early Iron Age horses became an important part of elite Thracian burials as a way to emphasize the martial prowess and wealth of their owner.[148] This practice resembles, and might have provided the inspiration for, the elder Cimon's burial with his prize-winning chariot team.

---

[146] See the discussion in Archibald 1998: 94.
[147] Zhivkova 1973: pls. 1, 11–12, 22–23.
[148] Archibald 1998: 69; Kouzmanov 2005.

Is it mere coincidence that the horse-loving Philaids were drawn to Thrace? Alcibiades grew weary of the many other Olympic contests, which included increasing numbers of competitors of low birth and dubious social status. He then focused entirely on horse racing because of its exclusive nature. Although horse racing remained prestigious in Greece well into the Classical period and beyond, it seems that Alcibiades was unable to gain the political power to which he felt his victories entitled him. Once he fell out with the Athenians for the final time, he opted to go to Thrace. Under Pisistratus, the elder Miltiades was forced to play a subordinate role in spite of his standing as an aristocrat and Olympic victor. Cimon's Olympic victories may have actually led to his political murder. The younger Miltiades flaunted his father's Olympic triumph in Athens and managed to secure the archonship, but he achieved his greatest political power when he went to Thrace to assume leadership of the family dynasty. There is every indication that the type of nobility epitomized by horse breeding and chariot racing held much more sway in Thrace than it did in an Athens controlled by the Pisistratids or under a democratic constitution.

CONCLUSION

When it comes to the cultural attractions Thrace held for certain Athenians, we can engage only in plausible speculation. Did the horse-loving Philaids feel at home among the people of the Chersonese, who were themselves fond of horse racing and skilled at mounted warfare? Did the vain and pompous Alcibiades fit in well with the Thracians, who expected their leaders to be ostentatious? And did Iphicrates appreciate the feasts to which he was treated by the Odrysians, especially in contrast to the apparent sparseness of dinners at Athens? In short, did Athenian leaders who were prone to what the Athenians might have viewed as personal excess find a cultural outlet in Thrace? I think the answer is yes, but it is impossible to say to what extent such cultural factors were involved in attracting these Athenians to Thrace.

CONCLUSION

Certain Athenians, especially members of the *hippeis*, found Thracian attributes to be an appropriate expression of their social status. From black- and red-figure vase-painting to the sculptural reliefs on the Parthenon, Athenian horsemen were regularly portrayed with Thracian clothing and equipment. To be sure, the peltast was often depicted as the antithesis of the heroic hoplite, and Thracians were associated with emblems of the barbarian other and foreign excess. But there is no mistaking that the Athenians had a fascination for the Thracians, one which seems to have been exploited by some members of the upper classes.

Maybe some truly did find Thracian culture to be a better expression of their aristocratic ideals, ideals that were out of fashion within the Athenian democracy. Also, many aspects of traditional elite training and education were out of step with the assembly-driven polis. Horsemanship, athletic prowess, and even martial skill and courage did not guarantee that political power would be granted by the demos. Alcibiades felt entitled to rule partly because he had won resplendent victories at Olympia. Other aristocrats probably felt the same. To Athenian eyes at least, the Thracians continued to revere brave warriors, whom they sometimes buried with their beloved horses. The Thracian ruler derived legitimacy from his martial prowess, his wealth, and his ability to reward his friends. He could also expect to be honored by his subjects with lavish gifts reminiscent of the symbols of *geras* so coveted by Homer's *basileis*.

In the end, Thrace made several Athenians rich and powerful. Part of this power certainly derived from their ability to appropriate Thracian cultural practices. Among Thracian dynasts the custom was to feast and exchange valuable gifts. Iphicrates, therefore, happily accepted the gifts given to him by his father-in-law along with lavish feasts and the other trappings of Thracian power. The Philaids hardly discouraged the honoring of the elder Miltiades with a cult, because this cult only enhanced their own claims to power. And so forth. Sensible political actors are able to work within the prevailing ethos, regardless of their own beliefs.

The question of the divinity of Alexander the Great may provide a useful parallel. Throughout the course of his conquest of Asia, Alexander appropriated elements of the god-king model typical of the Persian rulers who preceded him. For example, he encouraged his Iranian subjects to honor him by *proskynesis*, the kneeling homage traditionally paid to the Persian king (Arr. *Anab. Alex.* 4.10; Curt. 8.5). As his reign progressed, he promoted the idea of his divinity ever more explicitly, establishing the model for the cults of Hellenistic monarchs.[149] Was his assumption of divine honors simply a means to win over his new subjects? Or did he actually believe he was divine? Both were probably true to a certain extent. Alexander could have been an insightful political and cultural manipulator while at the same time gratifying his own predispositions.[150] The analogy can be stretched further if we consider that though these activities might have appealed to Alexander's Iranian subjects, they incensed the Macedonians. In the same way, Thrace-haunters were routinely subjected to censure and even prosecution at home because of their affinity for barbarians.

With the Thrace-haunters, careful political calculation need not have been divorced from an attraction to Thracian cultural practices. Demosthenes' suggestion that a desire for *exousia* was a prime motivation in turning to Thrace rings true (23.57). At the same time, we should not dismiss out of hand Theopompus' charge that Chabrias and other generals were too

---

[149] See Bosworth (2006 [1988]: 278–90) for a full treatment of Alexander's divinity.

[150] See, for example, Edmunds (1971), who argues that Alexander's religiosity went well beyond the requirements of his office or the purposes of propaganda. There is considerable debate concerning the extent to which Alexander pursued a deliberate policy of cultural and political fusion between Macedonians and Asians, of which his adoption of Persian customs might have been part. Long ago, Berve (1938) suggested that Alexander followed a careful, predetermined policy, but more recently Bosworth (1980) has argued that Alexander reacted as necessary to the various challenges of governing an empire filled with disparate peoples, making up policy decisions, such as integration of Iranian troops and adoption of foreign customs, as he went along.

profligate and ostentatious for Athenian society (*FGrHist* 115 F 105). Such sentiment had indeed become a well-worn topos in the fourth century, but many of those Athenians who turned to Thrace seemed genuinely dissatisfied with the restraints of Athenian society. In Thrace power and wealth could be coupled with a pseudoheroic lifestyle. This added to the appeal.

@@ @@ @@ @@

CHAPTER SIX

THRACE AS MILITARY
ACADEMY

INTRODUCTION

Many scholars have recognized that Thracian-style infantry
tactics were instrumental to Greek military developments
in the fourth century.[1] The hoplite phalanx, for so long the
primary arm of Greek militaries, came more and more to be
supplemented by a variety of different troop types, especially
light- and medium-armed skirmishers known as peltasts –
originally a type of Thracian soldier characterized by a small
crescent-shaped shield known as the *peltē* and an array of missile weapons, primarily javelins. Philip and Alexander took
the next logical step by combining several different arms,
namely, heavy and light infantry and heavy and light cavalry, into an unstoppable war machine. Most scholars have
emphasized the changing military dynamics of the fourth century, but these developments probably started considerably
earlier. In a seminal study, Best persuasively argues that the
peltast played a role in Greek armies in the fifth century also,
especially during the Peloponnesian War, and perhaps even as
early as the time of Pisistratus.[2] Military historians, including

---

[1] Lippelt (1910) is foundational. See also the classic studies of Parke
(1933); Griffith (1935; 1981); and Anderson (1970). For a popular general introduction to Thracian warfare, see Webber 2011.
[2] Best 1969.

Best, however, largely neglects the important role played by the special connection between Athens and Thrace in the introduction and integration of Thracian tactics. For many of Athens' most important military figures, Thrace served as a training ground.

Those inhabiting the Greek settlements in the Thraceward region were among the first to recognize the effectiveness of Thracian styles of warfare and adopt Thracian tactics themselves, perhaps the inevitable result of proximity to the Thracians. In the same way, Athens played a decisive role in pioneering the use of Thracian soldiers precisely because so many elite Athenians had personal ties with Thrace. Athens itself was also a geographic neighbor to the Thracians, if we consider the Thracian Chersonese to be Athenian territory, which was controlled and inhabited by Athenians through much of the period covered by this study. Places in the north Aegean such as Thasos were under Athenian suzerainty at various times. This connection, through which many prominent Athenian military leaders gained extensive experience with Thracians, was important for the introduction to mainland Greece of the peltast and possibly several other military practices that have gone unnoticed by previous scholars.

It is unlikely that proximity to and experience with Thracians were the only factors that led to such significant military change. The peltast was an important new technology – or perhaps more accurately a pre-hoplite survival reclaiming a measure of relevance – for the Greeks, but it is unclear to what extent new technologies are an impetus for reform.[3] Politics, society, and culture clearly play important roles too, both in the adoption of new ways of fighting and the retention of old. Many Athenian

[3] For a concise look at this problem, see Raaflaub's comments on the "hoplite revolution" (1999: 129–41). Raaflaub challenges the long-held notion that the development of hoplite weaponry gave rise to the hoplite phalanx. Rather, it seems that hoplite equipment was developed to complement an already existing style of massed-infantry battle.

Thracophiles were innovators who were unconstrained by traditional military norms. In their hands, the new technology learned from the Thracians could be put to optimum use.

Many studies have addressed nontechnological aspects of Greek warfare, especially how Greek tactics were intertwined with the nature of the polis. In an influential article, Vidal-Naquet insisted that the Classical hoplite phalanx, especially that of Athens, was an artificial reflection of the polis itself. Even the organizational structure of the Athenian phalanx was based on the political division of Attica wrought by Cleisthenes' reforms.[4] Hanson has argued that citizen hoplites, who were primarily middling farmers, dictated the predominance of the decisive phalanx battle until at least the Peloponnesian War. For Hanson, it was in the interest of the landowning hoplites to settle disputes as quickly as possible in order both to defend their property and to ensure that lengthy campaigns did not keep them from their crops. Once military power was in the hands of these middling farmers, they demanded their fair share of political power, which led to the community of citizens that was the Classical polis.[5] Strauss has provided similar analyses with respect to the Athenian navy, the predominance of which in the fifth century led to a more broadly based democracy with full participation of the thetic class of rowers.[6] As Strauss succinctly states, "military tactics are rarely simply a matter of military efficiency; they reflect politics, society, and culture."[7]

Recently, Lendon has focused on the cultural dimension of ancient military practices, arguing that both the Greeks and Romans found military inspiration in looking to the past, especially the mythological and epic past.[8] The Greeks were most

---

[4] Vidal-Naquet 1999 [1968].

[5] Hanson 1995; 1998; 2000. Hanson (1996) also argues that hoplite ideology was embraced by the Athenian democracy of the Classical period as a means of enforcing solidarity among the mass of citizens. Athenian hoplites in turn embraced the democracy. For more on the ideology of the hoplite, see also Osborne 1987b: 137–64.

[6] Strauss 1996; 2000.

[7] Strauss 2000: 316.

[8] Lendon 2005.

of all concerned with emulating Homeric precedent and tailored their infantry tactics accordingly. Lendon suggests that the increasing presence of the peltast in the fourth century, along with Iphicrates' reforms, was made possible not so much because the peltast mode of fighting – by charging out and hurling javelins – was tactically effective, but because it resembled Homeric warfare more than did the hoplite phalanx.[9] In the end, Iphicrates probably did not care whether his troops had epic legitimacy, and the peltast still did not replace the hoplite as the primary element of Greek armies. But Lendon's suggestion that culture plays an important part in tactics is a good one. Certainly something had to overcome the cultural and social stigma attached to non-hoplite troops.

Ferrill addresses this issue in his general survey of ancient warfare. He argues that there were two distinct strains of military development in antiquity, that of the Greeks and that of the Near East.[10] By Ferrill's model, change gradually came about in Greece because large numbers of Greek mercenaries served in the East in the late fifth and throughout the fourth centuries and brought back their experience with light-armed troops and other supposedly Eastern elements. The Greek ideological commitment to hoplite battle, however, ensured a slow rate of change. Because the Macedonians had never been fully part of the hoplite culture, Philip was finally able to merge the two strains of development in creating his invincible war machine. As a Macedonian, Philip enjoyed a relatively free hand to innovate.[11] Ferrill overstates his case in insisting that virtually all Greek military innovation was from Persian influence.[12] He rightly, though, emphasizes the conservatism of the Greek hoplite as compared to the innovative genius of Philip.[13]

[9] Lendon 2005: 93–98.
[10] Ferrill 1997: 149–86.
[11] Ferrill 1997: 150.
[12] Ferrill 1997: 180.
[13] For yet another angle from which to analyze the use of different types of military forces, see Hunt's survey of Greek military forces (2007).

Like Philip, the Athenians tied to Thrace were less bound by the hoplite ethos. Figures such as Dieitrephes and Iphicrates were all too happy to work beyond the confines of the phalanx. They were placed in charge of foreign and irregular troops and received their commands by special appointment, circumventing the regular channels, such as popular election to the generalship, the *stratēgia*. They were uninterested in the supposedly ritualized conventions of hoplite warfare and were instead willing to employ any and every device to achieve victory, to the point of unleashing bands of soldiers on defenseless towns. Many of those attracted to Thrace were also wealthy aristocrats, expert horsemen who probably felt little loyalty to the hoplite phalanx in either an ethical or political sense. The Philaids, for example, were famous horse breeders in Attica, and many members of the family, including the elder and younger Miltiades, were victors in the Olympic chariot race. Why should wealthy, talented, and ambitious descendants of the aristocracy of old, the *eupatridai*, adhere to the phalanx and its attendant values of military and political equality? This freedom to experiment beyond the regular forms of warfare was a major factor in effecting military change in Greece. Let us explore how several Athenians applied the lessons of Thrace to Greek warfare.

THRACE AND THE HERO OF MARATHON

To talk of Marathon is to tread on hallowed ground. Give or take a few days, I wrote the first draft of this section exactly 2,500 years after the Athenians and their Plataean allies defeated the Persian army in one of the greatest upsets in all of history. Because of this anniversary, there is much talk of Marathon about, and three books have appeared recently that

Hunt compellingly presents evidence that the Greeks employed, adopted, and abandoned certain types of military forces based on a cost-benefit analysis. Philip's nearly unlimited wealth enabled him to overcome issues of cost-effectiveness and therefore annihilate the mostly hoplite and amateur forces of Athens and Thebes.

offer a fresh look at this most evocative of battles.[14] The overwhelming weight of tradition – from the painted mural of the Stoa Poikile in the Athenian Agora to Herodotus and Classical authors of the next several centuries – ascribes the cause of the Athenians' victory to one man: the younger Miltiades. Before he took the field at Marathon, Miltiades had spent over two decades in the Thracian Chersonese being schooled in the ways of war, particularly how to fight the types of soldiers that composed the army of Darius' generals in 490. Could Miltiades' experiences in Thrace have played a role in the battle?

In the mid-sixth century, Thracians of the Dolonkoi tribe, inhabitants of the Chersonese, sought Delphi's advice in handling their hostile Thracian neighbors. The elder Miltiades, uncle of the hero of Marathon, along with hundreds of Athenians, accompanied the Dolonkoi back to their homeland. He was evidently successful in defending them from their enemies. His first act upon arriving in the Chersonese as city-founder and being installed as tyrant was to wall off the entire peninsula at its isthmus in order to prevent the destructive plundering raids habitually undertaken by the Thracian Apsinthioi. This wall, according to Herodotus, was 36 stades long (just over 7 kilometers) (6.36.2).[15] Miltiades was able to end the raids in this way, literally pushing the Apsinthioi out of his territory. With this threat alleviated, he felt confident enough to initiate a war with Lampsacus, a rival Greek settlement on the Asian shore of the Hellespont (Hdt. 6.37.1). The precise locations for the settlement of the several hundred Athenians who had accompanied him to Thrace were part of Miltiades' overall fortification strategy. These Athenians were carefully established at sites near the barrier wall, such as Cardia, Agora, and Pactye. These measures effectively controlled access to the Chersonese.[16] Nepos corroborates this picture, saying that Miltiades – though it is difficult to tell whether the elder

---

[14] See Billows 2010; Krentz 2010; and Buraselis and Meidani 2010.

[15] For the length, see How and Wells 1912: vol. 2, 76. For the location, which is still uncertain, see Scott 2005: 171.

[16] Isaac 1986: 166–67.

or younger is meant – scattered his enemies, barricaded the
Chersonese with fortifications, settled his fellow Athenians,
and enriched them by leading frequent raids into enemy territory (*Milt.* 2.1). The wall was rebuilt several times throughout
antiquity, demonstrating the effectiveness of this strategy.[17]

Miltiades was brought in to lend his own military mettle
to the Dolonkoi, but it seems that he himself learned from
the experience. In particular, he was forced to contend with a
type of enemy much different from that typically faced by Late
Archaic Athenians. How does one defend territory from hostile neighbors prone to raiding and pillaging rather than any
sort of "regular" warfare as epitomized by pitched battle?[18]
Miltiades' answer was his fortification wall, manned by inhabitants of the adjacent poleis. Later in antiquity, such a wall was
dubbed a *diateichisma*, the technical term applied to a barrier
intended to close off an entire region. The strategy of fortifying
an area by means of a barrier wall was employed several times
in antiquity. Examples include the wall across the Dema Gap
in Attica, Hadrian's Wall in Britain, Constantine's long wall in
Thrace, Justinian's long wall at Thermopylae, and, of course,
the wall across the Isthmus of Corinth that was attempted
at several periods, beginning with Xerxes' invasion of
480–479.[19] The wall across the Chersonese is the first such

---

[17] Rebuilt by Pericles, who brought additional settlers around 447 (Plut.
Per. 19.1); Dercyllidas the Spartan in 398 (Xen. *Hell.* 3.2.8–10; Diod.
14.38.7); by Justinian in Late Antiquity (Procopius *De Aed.* 4.10.5).
No physical remains of any of these walls have been found.

[18] For the norms of Archaic Greek warfare, see Hanson 2000: 27–39; but,
see Krentz (2000), who argues that trickery and deception were a much
larger part of Archaic warfare than is generally acknowledged. For the
effectiveness of hoplite troops against other arms, see Holladay (1982),
who argues that hoplites were the best all-around troops for the majority of Greek military purposes. The situation in the Chersonese, however, was decidedly outside the typical Greek military experience.

[19] For the strategy of blocking off an entire region, see Lawrence 1979:
167–72; Gregory 1993: 128. For the Isthmus of Corinth, see Wiseman
1978: 59–63; Gregory 1993: 4–6. For the Dema Wall, see Munn
1993: esp. 3–33, for a theoretical study of the purposes of various
fortifications.

Greek fortification mentioned in our sources.[20] Importantly, Miltiades recognized that in order for a fortification wall, no matter how imposing, to be effective, it had to be adequately manned. He accordingly settled his Athenians in its vicinity. In this vein, later barrier walls were built with forts interspersed along their entire length.[21] The wall across the Chersonese may have directly inspired the wall the Peloponnesians attempted at the Isthmus of Corinth a few decades later, and by extension other similar fortifications built throughout the Classical world.[22]

The offensive raids into Thracian territory described by Nepos fulfilled a function beyond enriching Miltiades' men. Essentially, such raids harried and weakened the Apsinthioi, rendering them less able to attack Miltiades' interests in the Chersonese. The Apsinthioi hardly faced hundreds of Athenian hoplites, supplemented by allied Dolonkoi, in pitched battle. Thus, in order to take the offensive, Miltiades and his Philaid

---

[20] There is some evidence of a Mycenaean wall on the Isthmus of Corinth from the Late Bronze Age, but most archaeologists now believe that the remaining stones represent terracing for a road rather than a fortification, and in any case there is no evidence that this structure spanned the entire isthmus. See Broneer 1966; 1968; Gregory 1993: 4–5. One might object that the so-called Phocian Wall at Thermopylae, mentioned by Herodotus (7.176), is an earlier example, but this structure is of uncertain date; see Pritchett 1958: 212–13. In any case, Herodotus says that the Phocians built the wall to keep out the Thessalians, who likely fought very much like the Thracians threatening Miltiades' territory, hence the need for such a fortification.

[21] See, for example, Gregory (1993: 129–32), who discusses the use of fortresses along the Late Antique Hexamilion Wall across the Isthmus of Corinth.

[22] In 338–335, a wall was built across the Dema Gap in Attica, lying between Mt. Parnes and Mt. Aegaleus. This defensive work was designed with special sally ports interspersed along its length that allowed light-armed troops to dart out against the enemy and fall back again to the safety of the wall. See Jones et al. 1957; Anderson 1970: 134–35; Lawrence 1979: 170–71; Ober 1985: 150; Munn 1993: 47–57. Such a fortification was ideally suited to Thracian-style troops, and it was probably inspired by the increasing use of light troops by Athens in the late fourth century. Did Miltiades' wall have a similar feature to take full advantage of Dolonkoi soldiers?

successors adopted the tactics of the enemy for themselves.[23]
Many scholars have commented on the Greeks' inability to
fight in a non-hoplite fashion and their general ineffective-
ness against light-armed troops, yet Miltiades and his men
seem to have fared quite well against Thracian fighters by pioneering the use of a barrier wall and employing local tactics.[24]
Coexistence and cooperation among Athenian settlers and
Thracian Dolonkoi in the Chersonese resulted in the two peoples learning from one another and developing military practices accordingly.

Perhaps the *Miltiades kalos* plate depicting a mounted archer
in barbarian costume implies that Greeks in the Chersonese
actually fought in the manner of Scythian or Thracian mounted
archers. As discussed in the previous chapter, any interpretation of this plate and its actual relation to Miltiades is specula-
tive. Athenian *hippeis*, however, are depicted with Thracian
equipment often enough to indicate that they esteemed the
skill of the Thracian horseman. The unusual strength of cavalry units in Greek cities of the Thraceward region, polities
well acquainted with Thracian horsemen as enemies and allies,
is attested by several ancient sources.[25] Isaac notes especially
Pindar's Second Paean, which describes the pivotal role of the
cavalry in protecting the Greek settlement of Abdera from the
local Thracians. Such cavalry units, a rarity in southern Greece,
were a necessity for Greeks struggling to secure their position
among horse-loving Thracians.[26] The younger Miltiades, the

[23] Herodotus says that all Thracians esteemed the living gained from
warfare, and specifically this type of plundering raid, above all else
(5.6.2).
[24] See Anderson (1970: 11–140) for a discussion of how hoplite armies in
the fourth century adapted to incorporate and combat different types
of troops, especially the Thracian peltast. Miltiades' campaigns in
Thrace took place a full century and a half before most of the innovations described by Anderson.
[25] See the discussions in Best (1969: 13) and Isaac (1986: 85–86).
[26] For Greek cavalry in general, see Spence (1993), who argues that most
Greek poleis did not maintain regular forces of cavalry until at least
the late fifth century.

scion of a family replete with avid horse breeders, relished the chance to fight on horseback along with the native inhabitants of his territory. Even if Greeks in the Chersonese did not fight in this way themselves, they became familiar with this style of warfare through constant contact with their non-Greek neighbors, and presumably they found a way to fight alongside and against mounted archers and other lightly armed and mobile troops. More than a century later, Xenophon demonstrated the value of his experience with different types of troops by devising an ingenious staggered march to prevent his hoplites being separated from the Thracian cavalry and peltasts of his ally Seuthes during a night maneuver.

A fragment of a cup by the artist Onesimus, now in the Getty Museum, displays an image so far unique in vase-painting.[27] What remains of the interior of the cup depicts the upper torso and head of a lone hoplite, holding a shield and engaged in combat with an unseen enemy to the right. The warrior's helmet is topped with a scalp still wearing a laurel wreath. The Scythians were famous for scalping their enemies, as Herodotus demonstrates (4.64–65), and the Greek verb for scalping was aptly *aposkythizō*, "to act like a Scythian." As one scholar suggests, this cup, dated to the later 490s, might be a reflection of the upsurge in knowledge about Scythians following the return of Miltiades to Athens in 493. Perhaps Miltiades and his men not only learned of this Scythian practice but even adopted it to a certain extent themselves, much like the Europeans who encountered scalping among the Native Americans.[28] We do not know whether the Thracians living more in the immediate vicinity of the Chersonese engaged in such activities, but the Apsinthioi were considered particularly savage. For example, in 479 they sacrificed the Persian leader Oeobazus alive to one of their gods, in accordance with their custom (Hdt. 9.119.1).

In 493, a mere three years before the Battle of Marathon, the younger Miltiades and four triremes full of Athenian settlers

---

[27] Malibu, J. Paul Getty Museum 86.AE.311; Williams 1991: 47, fig. 7a.

[28] As argued by Williams 1991: 47.

returned to Athens, having spent over two decades working with and fighting against Thracian and other foreign fighters in the Chersonese. Despite facing a charge of tyranny, Miltiades was popular enough with the Athenians to be named a general in 490. When a Persian army under the command of Datis and Artaphernes arrived at Marathon in northeastern Attica, fresh from crushing Athens' ally Eretria on Euboea, Miltiades in the assembly urged his fellow Athenians to take up arms against the enemy (Arist. *Rhet.* 1411a9–10; Dem. 19.303; Plut. *Mor.* 628e; Schol. ad. Ael. Arist. 2.219). Once the Athenians set out for the plain of Marathon, Miltiades' presence in the camp and on the field of battle outshone all nine of his colleagues in the generalship. He is remembered by posterity as the leader who spearheaded the Athenian victory.[29] How did he do it?

The Persians might have been largely done in by the Greek charge at Marathon. Herodotus' insistence that fully equipped hoplites charged the Persians for nearly a mile has vexed students of the battle for decades (Hdt. 6.112.1). Whereas most scholars do not think the Greeks could have covered the entire distance of around 1,500 meters at a full run, Herodotus' emphatic repetition of *dromōi* makes it difficult to argue that the hoplites did not advance at a significantly faster pace than normal. They certainly proceeded at a full run for the final part of the advance.[30] Several physiological tests have shown that few men with upwards of 70 pounds of hoplite equipment could have run the entire distance, but a run for the last few hundred meters was perfectly feasible.[31] In his new book on the battle, however, Peter Krentz convincingly argues that

---

[29] Aside from the accounts in Herodotus and Nepos, Pausanias describes Miltiades' prominent presence in the commemorative painting of the battle in the Stoa Poikile (1.15.3), and the monument to Miltiades in the plain itself (1.32).

[30] For the charge, see Hammond (1968: 28–29), who argues that the facts as stated by Herodotus are unimpeachable, including the supposed charge of the Greek hoplites. How and Wells (1912: vol. 2, 112) and others had previously argued that no hoplite army could have performed such a charge.

[31] The tests are cited by Scott 2006: 624.

hoplites in 490 carried less than 50 pounds of equipment – usually substantially less – thus allowing a charge of 1,500 meters.[32]

Krentz goes on to argue that the Greeks closed with the Persians so quickly to join battle before the Persian cavalry could become engaged. A reference in the Suda (under χωρὶς ἱππεῖς, "the cavalry is away") states in no uncertain terms that the cavalry was not involved at Marathon, but Krentz – along with many modern scholars – dismisses the evidence from the Suda as stemming from an erroneous later tradition.[33] It is indeed strange that no earlier source mentions the conspicuous absence of the cavalry. But, if the cavalry were present at Marathon, it would be equally strange that Herodotus fails to mention it at any point in the battle. Why did the cavalry fail to join the battle at a later stage, even if they had been prevented from taking part in the very first clash of forces? It is still a possibility that the Greeks, unsupported by sizable or well-trained contingents of cavalry and archers, needed to reduce the effectiveness of the deadly Persian archers by quickly closing the gap between the two forces. Scholars have argued that the presence of many Persian arrowheads in and around the Soros – the Athenian burial mound, which has been excavated on the Marathon plain – proves that the Persians had and employed archers in the battle.[34] Krentz raises serious doubt that any actual Persian arrows were found on the plain, because no arrowheads were yielded by the systematic excavations of the Soros. The evidence for any Persian arrowheads comes primarily from the testimony of early visitors to

[32] Krentz 2010: 45–50, 143–52.

[33] Krentz 2010: 139–42.

[34] Hammond (1968: 28–29) brings to bear the evidence of many Persian arrows found at the site, which indicate that the Persian barrage was intense for the last 150 meters or so of the Greek advance. For the arrowheads being of distinctly Eastern types, see Forsdyke 1919. Storch (2001) has argued that the Persians did not shoot their arrows at Marathon, because no arrows are depicted on the Stoa Poikile, nor are arrows mentioned in the literary sources. He does not, however, engage with the material evidence of arrows on the plain.

the site.[35] Regardless, archers made up the primary offensive arm of the Persian army in this period, and there is no reason to doubt that they were a prominent feature of the Persian force at Marathon.[36]

Miltiades had spent many years in the Chersonese among peoples who made extensive use of archers, and cavalry for that matter. He served in Darius' force during the Persian invasion of Scythia, which brought him into contact with Scythians and Persians (Hdt. 4.137.1). And, of course, he fought with the Thracian inhabitants of the Chersonese against their enemies, including other Thracians from the adjoining regions. The extent to which he was actually in control of troop movements at Marathon is unclear at best, but the tradition does give Miltiades a key role in masterminding the battle and urging his fellow generals to fight. Though perhaps corrupted by the weight of tradition, a scholiast attributes the very clear command "charge them!" to Miltiades at Marathon (Schol. ad Ael. Arist. 174.1). Faced with commanding an army of heavy infantrymen with little in the way of cavalry or archer support, Miltiades might have applied his experiences in the north in advising the Greeks to close ranks quickly with the Persians.[37] Where else but Thrace, where his family had ruled for half century, would he have learned military tactics? Herodotus is adamant that the Athenians at Marathon were the first Greeks, "so far as we know," to charge at a run.[38] For their part, the Persians thought the Athenians were mad

---

[35] Krentz 2010: 126–29. The collection of arrowheads purported to be from the Marathon plain, now in the British Museum, do appear to be Persian in form and material (see Forsdyke 1919), but they admittedly lack any firm archaeological context. We must rely upon the word of those who reportedly found them on the Marathon plain.

[36] See Krentz's own account of the Persian army in 490, including a detailed discussion of Persian archers (2010: 23–35).

[37] Scott (2005: 388) thinks it unlikely that Athenians could have fielded a cavalry force at this date even if they wanted to.

[38] Van Wees (2004: 180) says that running into battle was actually an established custom at this time, but, as Scott (2005: 389) points out, van Wees bases this conclusion on artistic evidence rather than any descriptions of specific battles.

in attacking without adequate light-armed and mounted support (Hdt. 6.112.2–3).

There was another intriguing first at Marathon, one Herodotus fails to mention.[39] In his description of the Marathon plain, Pausanias identifies two different burial mounds, one for the Athenian dead, which has been identified as the Soros in the middle of the plain, and another for the Plataeans and the slaves, about 2 kilometers to the west (1.32.3).[40] Pausanias says that the Battle of Marathon was the first time slaves fought beside their masters. Elsewhere, he attributes this innovation to Miltiades, who had passed a decree freeing the slaves before the battle (7.15.7). The evidence suggests that, by the late fifth century at least, hoplites were regularly attended on campaign by a personal slave, though the duties of these slaves did not usually involve fighting.[41] Why the innovation to involve slaves in the battle? A shortage of Athenian manpower in the face of a large Persian army does not suffice as an explanation. As Hunt observes, the thousands of Athenians of the thetic class were not mobilized, perhaps out of fears that they would derive too much political power from participation in the army.[42] But if the Athenians really were desperately outnumbered, facing a threat to their very survival as a polis, it seems that they would have called upon the thetes regardless of potential political repercussions.

What role did the slaves play in the fighting? Most scholars have assumed they fought as hoplites, just as their masters.[43] Some, though, have speculated that they served as light troops, possibly to cover the Athenian flanks.[44] The latter seems

---

[39] Evans (1993: 279) gives the best reason for Herodotus' silence, namely, that in the later fifth century Marathon had come to symbolize the ideal hoplite battle, especially in contrast to the naval mob's victory at Salamis.

[40] See Hammond (1992: 147–50) for the second mound's location and contents. See Marinatos (1970) for the fullest excavation report.

[41] For slave attendants, see Pritchett 1974–1991: vol. 1, 49–51.

[42] Hunt 1998: 27.

[43] See, for instance, Hammond 1992: 150.

[44] Delbrück 1975: 77, 81n3; Lazenby 1993: 64; Doenges 1998: 7.

much more likely, because such inexperienced and probably ill-equipped troops would have been a liability within the closely packed phalanx itself. The Athenians were clearly afraid of being outflanked, hence the famous thinning of their center in order to lengthen the line (Hdt. 6.111). Placing light troops on the flanks added further insurance against a longer Persian line. Even newly freed slaves inexperienced in combat were better than nothing, and they made good use of the terrain as the ground rose sharply on either side of the Athenian phalanx.[45] If the slaves were used as light troops, this would be a very early example of a combined-arms force, however ad hoc, which prefigured the tactics of later influential generals from Demosthenes to Iphicrates. After Marathon, the Athenians seemed to gain an appreciation for light troops – there was a corps of citizen archers at Plataea in 479 that played no small part in the battle (Hdt. 9.22, 60).[46]

Spending so much time in the Chersonese, facing threats from local Thracians and Greeks alike, the elder Miltiades and his nephew were forced to innovate in their ways of fighting. They had considerable latitude to work outside the confines of the phalanx while leading the Dolonkoi along with Athenian settlers. Necessity played a considerable role in encouraging changes in tactics. The younger Miltiades might well have applied the military lessons he learned in Thrace to the Battle of Marathon, and thus the unprecedented decision to free a number of Athenian slaves in order to complement the

---

[45] There are two main schools of reconstructing the positions of the Athenian and Persian lines. For the first, which places both forces parallel to the coast, with the Greeks to the west towards Vrana and nestled between Mt. Kotroni and Mt. Agriliki, see the map in Hammond 1968: 19. For the second, which places both forces at right angles to the coast, with the Greeks to the south towards Nea Makri with Mt. Agriliki on their left and the sea on their right, see Vanderpool 1966: 103–5. In either case, there was high ground on at least one flank, which could have been utilized by light troops.

[46] For the Athenian archers at Plataea, and the notion that the Athenians might have learned the usefulness of archers from the experience of Marathon, see Wardman 1959: 55–56, and note 12.

citizen hoplites. Many of these Attic slaves were most likely Thracians themselves, or at least from other lands familiar with light-armed warfare.[47] Their military value in the battle might have been minimal, but the Athenians had to make the most of what they had on hand. Herodotus neglects their presence because Marathon had come to represent the glory of the Athenian hoplite class. But at the time, in 490, the slaves who had fought along with their hoplite masters were accorded a singular honor: burial on the battlefield itself.[48]

We should consider one further factor in the battle, namely, that Miltiades and his fellow settlers of the Chersonese were a sizable group of hardened veterans. Herodotus tells us that in 493, five triremes' worth of people and property accompanied Miltiades from Thrace (6.41). One of these ships, commanded by Miltiades' son Metiochus, was captured by the pursuing Persians. Therefore, as many as 800 people returned to Athens with Miltiades. Subtracting women, children, and property, we can speculate that perhaps fifty men of fighting age sailed with each ship. This means that the Athenian army in 490 was supplemented by a corps of around 200 warriors experienced in fighting alongside and against the types of soldiers that composed the Persian army of Datis and Artaphernes. Once the disposition of the battle lines had been set, once the mile-long charge had begun, once Greek spear met Persian shield, it all came down to the Athenians outmatching the well-trained Persian regulars. It is difficult to overestimate the importance of a large number of rough-and-ready exemplars to spur on the less experienced – and surely frightened – Athenian hoplites. After all, the Theban army of the later Classical period was

---

[47] For the prevalence of Thracian slaves at Athens at this time, see Rosivach 1999: 155–56. It is interesting that in the Late Archaic period, precisely when the Philaids were in the Chersonese, not only do Thracians begin to appear on Attic pottery but so too do barbarian archers. These archers are often shown paired with a hoplite, working as a duo.

[48] Thucydides (2.34.5) says that the Athenian war dead were traditionally buried in the same spot on the outskirts of Athens, except for the warriors of Marathon, who were buried where they fell.

esteemed and feared largely because of the 300 elite warriors of its Sacred Band, a small but vitally important part of the overall army.

A Bad Day at Mycalessus

By taking a closer look at the massacre perpetrated at Mycalessus, we can gain an idea of what types of Thracian soldiers were employed by Athens, and how such soldiers were used in the field. Additionally, in tracing how the Dioi – the tribe that attacked Mycalessus – and others like them came to be in Athenian service, we can also see how the military lessons of Thrace were passed on by a continuous succession of Athenians.

In 413, Dieitrephes had been instructed to inflict as much damage as he could while sailing with the Dioi up the Boeotian coast. The use of Thracian mercenaries to ravage Boeotia might have been a strategy planned by the Athenians for quite some time. In Aristophanes' *Acharnians*, performed in 425, the Athenian envoy to Thrace suggests that if the Athenians pay his group of Thracian soldiers 2 drachmas per day, they will "thoroughly peltast (*katapeltasontai*)" all of Boeotia (159–60). Dieitrephes' first action was to lead his troops against the territory of Tanagra, which suffered only a quick raid and the loss of plunder, according to Thucydides. Plundering raids and the destruction of crops were common offensive operations during the Peloponnesian War, employed by Archidamus in the early years of the conflict and central to Athens' strategy in Messenia.[49] The city of Tanagra itself, like Mycalessus without effective walls, was situated several kilometers from the sea.[50] Between the city and the sea was a large flat area suited to agricultural activity, and Tanagra is known to have had extensive extramural habitation in so-called suburbs

[49] See, for example, Thuc. 2.19–20, 4.41.
[50] Tanagra's walls were destroyed by Athens in 458/7 (Thuc. 1.108.2) and not rebuilt until probably after the Peace of Antalcidas. See Roller 1974.

(*proasteia*).[51] Presumably, the broad plain in Tanagra's territory, widely settled and lying next to the sea, afforded both ample material for plunder and ease of access for seaborne invaders. This at least partially explains the sparing of the city itself. Nevertheless, the settlers on the plain suffered from the raid, perhaps in lives, and at least in terms of property and livelihood. The city as a whole surely felt the economic sting.

After leisurely ravaging these lowlands on the coast, the Thracians continued in their ships to Chalcis on Euboea. After nightfall, Dieitrephes led them across the Euripus Strait, and they spent the night about 3 kilometers from Mycalessus, at a certain temple of Hermes. As noted by Thucydides, the inhabitants of Mycalessus did not expect any attack from the sea because their city lay apparently safely inland. Though actually quite close to the Euripus, Mycalessus was separated from the sea by a high range of mountains that effectively formed the border between Boeotia and the territory of Chalcis. The temple of Hermes was most likely situated on the Anephorites Pass, which affords access over the mountain barrier, and may have demarcated the official boundary of Boeotia.[52] The pass, though the low point over the mountain ridge, is still around 300 meters higher than sea level, where the mercenaries began their nighttime march from Chalcis. The mountains must have been formidable enough to lull the people of Mycalessus into a false sense of security. The Thracians' nocturnal ascent to a pass 5 kilometers or so from the sea therefore indicates a high level of skill and familiarity with mountainous terrain.

From this elevated situation, Dieitrephes and his troops looked down on Mycalessus below, corresponding to the modern village of Ritsona. At daybreak, the Thracians stormed down from the heights and quickly crossed the few kilometers to the unsuspecting town. Two low knolls are visible from

[51] Hansen 2006: 45–46. For a complete topographical study of the region around Tanagra, including its rich agricultural areas, see Fossey 1988: 43–99.

[52] Burrows and Ure (1907–1908: 232–42) provide a good topographical discussion of the area. See also Bakhuizen 1970; Fossey 1988: 80–85.

the pass, and the ancient town occupied either one, or perhaps both, of these.[53] Mycalessus was situated in the midst of a fertile basin, which fits in well with Homer's epithet for the site in the Catalogue of Ships: spacious Mycalessus (*euruchoros Mycalēssos, Il.* 2.498).[54] Although most readings of Thucydides imply that the town was small (*ou megalē*, 7.29.3), nearly all manuscripts omit the negative particle *ou*, and the excavated necropolis of the town extends for the better part of a kilometer.[55] Ulrichs in the mid-eighteenth century noted that the area was covered with ancient stones and tile, and today the fields are full of substantial building blocks brought to the surface by modern agricultural plowing.[56] A sizable settlement may be indicated.[57]

Ultimately, it is impossible to determine the exact number of casualties. According to Pausanias, although other Boeotian towns that had been destroyed in the past had been reoccupied by survivors, Mycalessus remained deserted, implying that the entire population had been wiped out (1.23.3). That the town declined significantly in the years after the attack is confirmed by archaeological evidence, primarily in the form of graves, which virtually disappear in the late fifth century.[58] As for the

---

[53] See Burrows and Ure (1907–1908: 235) for a discussion concerning the size of the town.

[54] Fossey 1988: 83.

[55] Burrows and Ure 1907–1908: 235. It is true that most editors of Thucydides follow the Vatican manuscript B in including the negative particle, and this would appear to fit better in the text. Yet the possibility remains that the town was of a substantial size.

[56] Fossey 1988: 81–82.

[57] No one attempts to calculate the exact population of Mycalessus itself. Hansen provides the most up-to-date study of Greek demographics, wherein he argues that all of Boeotia (including Thebes) had around 200,000–250 000 people (2006: 84–92). The territory of Mycalessus was considerable, probably at least 50 km^2 and perhaps closer to 100 km^2 (Hansen and Nielsen 2004: 446).

[58] The vast majority of the graves date to the sixth century, with a few in the fifth century. Although there are Hellenistic remains in the cemetery, nothing from the intervening period (i.e., late fifth through fourth centuries) has been found, and the site itself was a ruin by Hellenistic and Roman times. See Burrows and Ure 1907–1908; Bakhuizen 1970: 18–31.

numbers present at the ill-fated boys' school, we are equally in the dark. Thucydides says that it was the largest in the area (7.29.5). This either means that Mycalessus itself had several schools, further indication of a settlement of substantial size, or that the school served children from the surrounding countryside and villages along with the town proper. We only have two figures for schools in the fifth century, one from Herodotus who describes 119 out of 120 boys dying in Chios when their school collapsed (6.27.1), and another from Pausanias, who relates the story of an enraged Olympic boxer on the tiny island of Astypalaea slaughtering sixty children as they were learning letters (6.9.6–7). It would be reasonable to guess that at least several dozen children were killed at Mycalessus.

The Dioi were known to be bloodthirsty yet highly skilled warriors. While describing the huge force accompanying the Thracian king Sitalces in his expedition against Macedon in 429/8, Thucydides calls the Dioi the most warlike (*machimōtatoi*) of the Thracians. By means of a *men ... de* clause used to establish a contrast, Thucydides makes a sharp distinction between the Dioi and the rest of the jumbled horde (*homilos xymmeiktos*) that was fearsome only because of sheer numbers (2.98.4). This is a morally dubious distinction to say the least, but the reader is left with no doubt as to the sheer ferocity and military prowess of the tribe. A further indication of this tribe's bellicosity is that whereas Sitalces needed to persuade some of them to join the expedition by offering them pay as mercenaries, others came of their own free will (Thuc. 2.96.2).[59] Best explains this desire to join in the expedition as rooted in the prospect of plunder. The Dioi, he argues, suffered in extreme poverty and thus jumped at the chance to enrich themselves through the loot of a military campaign.[60] We should not, however, rule out as a source of motivation a fondness for warfare and all its attendant adventure and pillaging. Otherwise, why did many of the Dioi not hold out for wages also? Presumably

[59] καὶ τοὺς μὲν μισθῷ ἔπειθεν, οἱ δ' ἐθελονταὶ ξυνηκολούθουν.
[60] Best 1969: 133.

those paid by Sitalces would have had just as much opportunity for plunder as those volunteering for service.

In Thucydides, the Dioi are further distinguished as sword bearers, *machairophoroi* (2.96.2; 7.27.1). A Thracian *machaira* can be best described as an inverted scimitar, that is, a curved sword suited for slashing and hacking, a truly terrible weapon of which several survive and are on display in Bulgarian museums.[61] The Dioi, however, were perfectly capable of fighting in the peltast manner too. While they were retreating from Mycalessus, Thucydides describes the Thracians employing the tactics of their native land against the Theban cavalry, namely, swarming out in detachments and then falling back into mass, presumably with javelins (7.30.2). By utilizing these tactics, which are exactly those employed by peltasts, the Dioi performed quite well against the Thebans, losing but a few men. It would appear that in rampaging through the town, encountering men, women, and children helpless and unawares, the Dioi opted to use the weapon for which they were famed and undoubtedly feared, hacking and slashing their way through Mycalessus with ease, and ready to employ more suitable weapons and tactics against the Theban cavalry.

Thucydides seems impressed with the martial skill of the Dioi. Most of the 250 Thracians who were killed were struck down while trying to embark on their ships, because they did not know how to swim – those manning the ships had anchored them out of bowshot. Others were killed owing to their negligence while looting the town (7.30.2). Those who did stand and fight, utilizing coordinated peltast tactics, lost only a few of their own men while killing several Theban hoplites and horsemen, including one of the Boeotarchs. The expression

---

[61] Archibald (1998: 202) argues that in the Classical period, a Thracian *machaira* referred to the curved dagger native to the region, significantly smaller than a slashing sword. I doubt that such a small weapon could have served as the primary offensive arm, as indicated by the epithet *machairophoroi*, and that the dagger, common kit among many Thracian peoples, would have so distinguished the Dioi from other Thracians. See Best (1969: pl. 5) for a Thracian *machaira*.

Thucydides employs to describe the Thracians' performance in the orderly retreat is *ouk atopōs*, "not in an unaccustomed manner," which is clarified by the historian's account of the tactics of their native land. The translations of this passage typically render *ouk atopōs* as "very creditably" (Warner), "a respectable defense" (Crawley), and "a very fair defense" (Jowett).[62] The scholiast to this passage explains *ouk atopōs* as *ouk akosmōs*, "not in a disorderly way."

These renderings miss an important nuance in Thucydides' intended meaning. The LSJ, citing this specific passage, defines *atopōs* as "marvelously" or "absurdly," but we can arrive at a more specific definition in this case. The Mycalessus episode provides the only adverbial use of the word in Thucydides, but there are four instances of the adjective. *Atopon* is used to describe the strange or unnatural breath of sufferers of the plague (2.49.2). Continuing the description of the plague, Thucydides says he will pass over the peculiarities, *atopias*, of individual cases (2.51.1). During the Mytilenian Debate *tōn atopōn*, "newfangled" or "unaccustomed" things, are contrasted with *tōn eiōthotōn*, or "customary" and "usual" things (3.38.5). And finally, in his horrific description of the *stasis* at Corcyra and the effect it had on the rest of the Greek world, Thucydides notes that people seeking revenge contrived ever more novel devices, *technēsei ... atopiai*, to use against their foes (3.82.4). Thus, Thucydides employs this word to denote something strange, unaccustomed, or unusual.

In the context of the Thracians' retreat at 7.30.2, we should render *ouk atopōs* as follows: "In the rest of the retreat, the Thracians fought in a *not unaccustomed* manner," in other words, they fought *exactly how one would expect them to*. The way Thucydides expected them to fight is explained by the description of their native tactics and by the loss of only a few fighters. Those killed while looting the town and trying to embark on their ships are the exception rather than the rule. As in the use of the adjective *machimōtatoi*, Thucydides

62 Warner and Finley 1972 [1954]; Crawley 1903; Jowett 1900.

is again passing favorable judgment on, at the very least, the formidable martial *skill* of the Dioi. The Dioi were selected to serve with the Athenians in 413 precisely because they were excessively fond of, and therefore skilled in, fighting.

There are very few references in our sources to the Dioi, and more fieldwork needs to be done in the Rhodope range to shed light on settlements there. Several sources mention two other important tribes inhabiting the same area, namely, the Satrai and Bessoi, with whom the Dioi were likely connected.[63] In any case, the Dioi probably shared many characteristics with their better-known mountain-dwelling neighbors. The Satrai appear in Hecateaus (*FGrHist* 1 F 157) and also figure prominently in Herodotus' description of Xerxes' invasion route (7.110–13). Herodotus says that the Satrai were the only tribe of the Thracians that Xerxes was unable to subject to himself, adding that they remained to his own day the only Thracians who had never been subject to anyone. The reason for this is the nature of their home terrain, namely, thickly wooded and snow-covered mountains. Also, they are said by the historian to be surpassing in the arts of war. The similarity to Thucydides' description of the Dioi is manifest. Seemingly at odds with their designation as ferocious inhabitants of the mountains, the Satrai are also said by Herodotus to have been the most prominent tribe in exploiting the gold and silver mines of Pangaeum.

Herodotus says that the Bessoi, according to him a branch of Satrai, were responsible for an oracle of Dionysus, located on the highest of their mountains. Herodotus' description indicates that this oracle was well known to the Greeks.[64] Strabo mentions the Bessoi as an independent tribe inhabiting the region from the Rhodope range to the Illyrian frontier (7.5). He says that the tribes in this region are of all peoples the most prone to brigandage, but that the Bessoi are called brigands

---

[63] Archibald (1998: 109) notes the attestation of the tribal name "Diobessoi." See Plin. *Nat. Hist.* 4.40.

[64] How and Wells 1912: vol. 2, 168.

even by the other brigands. Strabo rounds out his description with the detail that the Bessoi live in huts (*kalubitai*) and lead a wretched life. Aeschylus, in the *Persae* (869–70), calls the dwellings of the Thracians *epauloi*. An *epaulos* usually describes a fold for cattle, whereas *epaulis* can denote a farm building, crude country dwelling, an army camp, or even an open unfortified village. A crude dwelling of some sort seems to be implied. The Vetren-Pistiros inscription mentions *epaulistai*, a hapax that may mean either "encamping soldiers" or "hut dwellers."[65] It is clear that the Thracians, especially those living in mountainous regions, lived in rough structures. Finally, these rugged mountain men were said by Valerius Flaccus to be massive in stature (2.229).

Scholars have suggested that the Dioi, along with the Satrai, Bessoi, and other mountain tribes, had common customs, shared the worship of Dionysus, and most of all discouraged foreign influences.[66] How did Athens come to acquire the services of these autonomous and lawless fighters in 413? Who made the necessary arrangements? In truth, several prominent figures, most notably Hagnon, had gained experience with such troops and could have acted as liaisons between Athens and those providing mercenary services. Hagnon was immensely successful at Amphipolis, so much so that he was chosen as a commander for Sitalces' invasion of Macedon in 429/8. Hagnon likely passed on to a succeeding generation of Athenians the military lessons he learned in Thrace.

Why did Hagnon succeed at Amphipolis when so many had failed before him? Archibald argues that he must have come to some sort of arrangement with the neighboring Edonians to prevent attacks against the city. Previous ventures had

---

[65] Domaradzka 2002: 341.

[66] As Archibald (1998: 110) points out, the Satrai's dominance of the mines at Pangaeum, coupled with the distribution of both Greek and Thracian coins throughout the Rhodope range and beyond, suggests some sort of interaction with the Greeks. The coins, of course, could be as much from raiding and theft as from legitimate economic contacts with the Greek world.

been viewed by the area's Thracians as hostile incursions, and Hagnon sought to remedy that.[67] One way this could have been accomplished was by seeking common cultural and religious ground with the local population. Isaac and Archibald both insist that the worship of Rhesus by the Greeks at Amphipolis was a way to do just that.[68] Polyaenus says that it was Hagnon who established the cult, bringing the bones of Rhesus to Amphipolis from the Troad (6.53). Shrewd diplomacy probably played a role in cementing alliances with the Thracians. Cimon had made inroads nearby, and several Athenians such as Thucydides had connections in the area.[69] Many local Thracians eventually became allies of Athens, such as the Edonian king in Myrcinus, Pittacus, who had to be murdered before his city was handed over to Brasidas (Thuc. 4.107). Hagnon's military mettle, though, was equally important to his success. Thucydides' emphasis is on Hagnon driving the Edonians from the region and encircling the city with fortifications. In the case of the bones of Rhesus too, Polyaenus describes Hagnon as tricking the Thracians into a brief truce that let him cross the river with the bones and also construct his defensive works.[70] This hardly indicates that relations with the locals were always amicable.

By any measure, Amphipolis' defenses were impressive. Because the city sits upon a hill surrounded on the north, west, and south by a bend in the Strymon, many scholars have attempted to reconstruct the plan of the long wall mentioned by Thucydides as essentially forming a 2,500-meter arc from north to south, totally closing the city off from the land to the east towards Pangaeum.[71] This seems to suit Thucydides' description. Pritchett, investigating the remains of the wall

[67] Archibald 1998: 117.
[68] Isaac 1986: 55–58; Archibald 1998: 101.
[69] See Isaac (1986: 31–33) for Athens' influence in the area even after the defeat at Drabscus.
[70] See Pesely (1989: 196–97), who sees no reason to doubt the story in its essentials.
[71] For the standard reconstruction of the fortifications, see Gomme et al. 1945–1981: vol. 3, 574, and map facing 654.

excavated in the 1970s by Lazaridis and drawing extensively on Thucydides' text, suggests that Hagnon had intended to encircle the city and construct a long wall that extended out from the enclosure wall and down to the river. But the planned long wall was not completed when Brasidas attacked in 424, and the city was defended only by a 2,220-meter inner enclosure wall. To be sure, this enclosure was rather extensive and impressive in its own right.[72] The excavator Lazaridis argues that the material evidence indicates the city was encircled on all sides by a massive set of enclosure walls even in Hagnon's time. According to Lazaridis' plan, the wall circuit was about 7,450 meters long, with a smaller enclosure for the citadel of 2,220 meters. He compares the enclosure at Amphipolis to the massive areas within the fourth-century fortifications at Messene and Megalopolis. According to Lazaridis, Amphipolis was thus extensively fortified to protect the resources of the region, including much of the arable land outside of the citadel proper, and to enforce a unity among the disparate inhabitants of the new colony.[73]

In spite of the discrepancies in the various reconstructions of the Hagnonian fortifications, it remains clear that the city's founder envisioned comprehensive fortifications and that the result was impressive. In addition to being a skilled leader of soldiers, evinced by his ability to expel the Thracians from the region and by his special appointment to lead Sitalces' troops in 429/8, Hagnon protected Amphipolis with defensive works of nearly unparalleled scale. In doing so, he seems to have safeguarded not only the city itself but also much of its territory. In this way, he kept the Edonians at bay, and even Brasidas was only able to take the city through the treachery of the non-Athenian inhabitants (4.106). Emulating the strategy of the elder Miltiades, Hagnon relied on extensive fortifications to safeguard his gains on the Strymon from attacks of

---

[72] Pritchett 1965–1992: vol. 3, 304–14.

[73] Lazaridis 1986. For his plan of the walls, showing the excavated sections and his reconstructions, see Lazaridis 1997: 22–23.

the Edonians and other Thracians. His military skill, certainly coupled with a sharp instinct for diplomacy, enabled Hagnon to deal with the Thracians dwelling near Amphipolis more effectively than his predecessors had.

Because Hagnon enjoyed such military success in Thrace, he was chosen as a leader in Sitalces' expedition of 429/8. This expedition included the Dioi as its most fearsome members. It is attractive to see Hagnon as the connection through which the Athenians acquired the services of these mercenaries in later years. Hagnon had demonstrated an ability to command Thracian troops, and also in turn to fight against them and keep hostile incursions at bay. We may conjecture that he imparted some of his acquired tactical sense to his fellow Athenian commanders, namely, Demosthenes and Dieitrephes.

Thucydides tells us that the Dioi who arrived in Athens in 413 were originally intended to serve with Demosthenes in Sicily. This general had used light-armed troops, including Thracians, before and was keenly aware of their usefulness. His tactical ingenuity is widely acknowledged by scholars.[74] He seems to have developed his talents in response to a crushing defeat at the hands of light-armed Aetolians in 427/6 (Thuc. 3.94–98). For his renowned victory at Pylos in 425, in which he captured around 300 Spartans on the island of Sphacteria, he employed hundreds of peltasts, archers, and slingers, troops that utterly confounded the Spartan hoplites (Thuc. 4.32–33). It was Cleon who had brought these troops from Athens to reinforce Demosthenes. Thucydides tells us that Cleon's force consisted of soldiers of unspecified type from Imbros and Lemnos, peltasts from Aenus, and 400 archers from other

[74] Best (1969: 17–29) gives Demosthenes pride of place as the leader who singlehandedly introduced peltast tactics to the Athenians. Best does not seem to think that Pisistratus' Thracians or any of the Athenians who had contact with Thrace during the period between Pisistratus' tyranny and Demosthenes' generalships had any measurable impact on Athenian military practices. For a comprehensive treatment of Demosthenes' use of ambush and surprise, see Roisman (1993), who, I should note, is not overly impressed with his generalship and use of light troops at Sphacteria (39–40).

locations (4.28). Imbros and Lemnos had been captured and granted to Athens by the younger Miltiades while he was in the Chersonese (Hdt. 6.141), and Aenus seems to have served as a mustering point for Thracian mercenaries entering the service of Athens.[75] Cleon deliberately selected Demosthenes as his fellow commander (4.29), and many scholars have conjectured that Demosthenes and Cleon were working together to effect a prearranged plan to use light troops in the battle against the Spartans.[76] In the capable and experienced hands of Demosthenes, the fearsome Dioi could have been very effective in Sicily in 413.

Cleon himself might have had Thracian ties through one Theorus. In the *Acharnians*, Aristophanes portrays Theorus as an Athenian envoy to Thrace leading a group of Odomantoi to Athens (153–56). Theorus proudly declares his group of Thracians to be the most warlike of all (*machimōtaton*). We learn from Herodotus that they mined Pangaeum along with the Satrai (7.112). Although it is implied in the play that the Odomantoi were subject to Sitalces, Thucydides says they were an independent tribe dwelling beyond the Strymon in the plains (2.101.3).[77] Archibald, following Hammond, locates them in the southernmost foothills of the Rhodope range.[78] This places them very near the home of the Dioi and other mountain tribes, and their designation as independent and

---

[75] For Lemnos and Imbros, see Scott 2005: 452–54. For Aenus, see Isaac 1986: 153. Gomme et al. (1945–1981: vol. 3, 469) believe that the manuscript reading for this passage of Thucydides (4.28.4) cannot be retained, and after ἔκ τε Αἴνου we should understand a lacuna of the type καὶ τῆς ἄλλης Θρᾴκης. If this emendation is right, other Thracian suppliers of troops are indicated.

[76] For the notion that Demosthenes planned his entire strategy at Pylos around the use of light-armed troops, see Woodcock 1928: 101; Stahl 1966: 151; Best 1969: 21; Hunter 1973: 72; Hornblower 1991–2008: vol. 2, 189. That Demosthenes and Cleon worked together on a prearranged plan, see Gomme et al. 1945–1981: vol. 3, 486; Kagan 1974: 242; van de Maele 1980: 121–24; Rhodes 1998: 229; Lazenby 2004: 75.

[77] Olson 2002: 120.

[78] Archibald 1998: 85–86n35.

warlike indicates a similarity in character to Dieitrephes' men. Perhaps Theorus was among the Athenian ambassadors who took part in Sitalces' invasion of 429/8, a mere three years before *Acharnians* was produced.

Aristophanes portrays Theorus in several passages, especially throughout the *Wasps*, as a close political associate of Cleon and a fellow demagogue.[79] We know little about Theorus outside of these two plays, but there is no reason to suspect his connection to the Odomantoi or to Cleon. In 422, Cleon, perhaps relying on his connection to Theorus, made a special appeal to the Odomantian king Polles for mercenaries to help in retaking Amphipolis from Brasidas (Thuc. 5.6.2). Unfortunately for Cleon, the issue was forced before these mercenary troops arrived. The Athenians were defeated by Brasidas, and Cleon himself was killed by one of the Spartan's mercenary peltasts (Thuc. 5.10.9). In spite of Thucydides' derogatory portrayal of Cleon's activities surrounding the Pylos affair in 425 and the undignified manner of his death in 422, Cleon certainly seems to have had an appreciation for Thracian-style light troops.[80]

Finally, in 423, an Athenian expedition, which included 1,000 Thracian mercenaries and an undisclosed number of peltasts from various allies, was sent against the Thraceward cities of Mende and Scione. As we have seen, in command of this force was Nicias and one Nicostratus, the son of a Dieitrephes,

---

[79] Olson 2002: 114

[80] Best (1969: 29–35), in discussing Cleon's campaign to retake Amphipolis from Brasidas, argues that Cleon might have been inspired by Demosthenes' use of light troops, but that he was himself an inferior leader unable to take full advantage of this new type of soldier. Though Cleon might have been inferior to Demosthenes in terms of skill, he did have Thracian ties in his own right and might have been instrumental in securing light troops for Demosthenes in 425. In the end, Best goes too far in arguing that Demosthenes and his appreciation for light-armed troops existed in a vacuum. For Thucydides' unfair treatment of Cleon, see Woodhead 1960; but see also Spence (1995), who argues that Cleon might have been as much a failure as Thucydides portrays him to be. In either case, he understood the usefulness of Thracian mercenaries, though he might have failed to use them to their full effect.

and therefore probably the father, or at least the uncle, of the Dieitrephes who commanded the Dioi in 413 (Thuc. 4.129.2). Dieitrephes almost certainly had a family connection to Thrace and Thracian mercenaries. The evidence, then, indicates that Hagnon, Demosthenes, Cleon, and Dieitrephes' close relative Nicostratus had all led Thracian troops during the Peloponnesian War before 413. Some of these troops were Dioi, and others were very similar to the Dioi in fighting style and geographic origin. Dieitrephes could have learned from any or all of these Athenian leaders the particular advantages – and dangers – of such Thracian fighters.

Dieitrephes was not the first and certainly not the only Greek to deal with the Dioi and others like them. Though Thucydides says little about Dieitprephes' role in the actual attack on Mycalessus, he does say explicitly that Dieitrephes himself led the mercenaries against the town (7.29.2). Because of his knowledge of Thracians, gained from his own family's ties to Thrace and his connections to other leading Athenian Thracophiles, Dieitrephes commanded his men in such a way as to complement their particular style of warfare. The Dioi were probably specifically selected because of their fearsome reputation. It is difficult to believe that Dieitrephes – let alone a good number of Athenians – was unaware of their propensity for rapine and slaughter and the implications this would have had for the town of Mycalessus.

THRACIAN BARBARIANS SAVE ATHENIAN DEMOCRACY!

By the time he led the fight to restore democracy in 404–403, Thrasybulus had had extensive experience campaigning in Thracian lands. A close examination of his struggle against the Thirty Tyrants reveals that he probably utilized his Thracian connections in securing troops to deploy against the forces of the Thirty and their formidable Spartan allies. It seems also that, like other Athenian leaders, Thrasybulus learned from his experiences in Thrace and knew well how to use Thracian soldiers. Thracians might have played such an important role in 404–403 that one could reasonably conclude Thracian barbarians had saved Athenian democracy, a notion as surprising to us as it was awkward for many Athenians.

Middleton argues that Thrasybulus relied heavily on Thracian fighters in the battles against the forces of the Thirty and the Spartans that took place in the Piraeus.[81] Middleton bases his argument on three things: the location of the Battle of Munichia, which was in the vicinity of the shrine of the Thracian goddess Bendis; the names of some of the foreigners involved in the struggle; and the fighting style of the troops with Thrasybulus. Xenophon describes a large number of light-armed troops that fought with the democratic forces in the Piraeus. These fighters included peltasts and light-armed javelin throwers, along with stone throwers or slingers (Xen. *Hell.* 2.4.12). Thrace was of course well known for such light-armed fighters, especially peltasts and javelin throwers. As Middleton suggests, Athens' use of Thracian troops during the course of the Peloponnesian War, and Thrasybulus' own activities in Thrace from 411 to 407, make it all but certain that a sizable number of these light troops were Thracians.

Why did the Thracians in the Piraeus fight for Thrasybulus on behalf of democracy? Middleton argues that metics, including those of Thracian origin, were well treated under the democracy, and they participated in the struggle in the hope of winning even more rights.[82] Thrasybulus could have made personal appeals to the Thracians of the Piraeus too, because he had spent a great deal of time in Thrace. Middleton insists that the location of the battle was decided largely by proximity to the shrine of Bendis, and therefore to the local Thracian population. This argument hinges on Xenophon's comment that the light troops lived in that very district. Xenophon's wording, however, need only mean that the third group of light troops,

[81] Middleton 1982.
[82] Middleton 1982: 303.

that is, the slingers, lived in the immediate vicinity.[83] Instead, many of the Thracian fighters could have been mercenary soldiers, hired by supporters of the democracy and under the personal command of Thrasybulus.

The orator Lysias paid for at least 300 and as many as 500 mercenaries for the democratic forces. He also persuaded his guest-friend Thrasydaeus of Elis to contribute 2 talents, presumably also to pay for mercenaries (Plut. *Mor.* 835f; Just. 5.9.9; Oros. 2.17.9).[84] Lysias implies that there were many others who supported the men from Phyle with money and materiel (Lys. 31.15), and some of this support could have gone to fund mercenaries too. Because we have no explicit record of the activities of these troops during any part of the struggle, we ought to assume their presence in the Piraeus battles in which many light-armed mercenary-style fighters participated.[85] Thrasybulus had many Thracian connections with which to secure mercenaries, enlisting the help of his contacts in the north to supply him with the appropriate troops. Thrasybulus could very well have commanded a skilled group of Thracian fighters in Athens.

After democracy had been restored, Thrasybulus proposed rewards for his supporters, including full Athenian citizenship. This motion was opposed by Archinus of Coele, who charged Thrasybulus with introducing an unlawful motion (*graphē paranomōn*) on the grounds that several of those to whom he wanted to grant citizenship were slaves (*Ath. Pol.* 40.2). Strauss suggests that Archinus might have been motivated less by a principled aversion to granting citizenship to slaves and foreigners than by a fear that his political rival Thrasybulus

---

[83] *Hell.* 2.4.12: ἐτάχθησαν μέντοι ἐπ' αὐτοῖς πελτοφόροι τε καὶ ψιλοὶ ἀκοντισταί, ἐπὶ δὲ τούτοις οἱ πετροβόλοι. οὗτοι μέντοι συχνοὶ ἦσαν· καὶ γὰρ αὐτόθεν προσεγένοντο. The οὗτοι of the last sentence need only refer to the latter group of the three mentioned.

[84] See Buck (1998: 73–74) for Lysias' contributions. Although the sources are late, they were probably relying on now lost testimony from Lysias himself.

[85] As argued by Buck 1998: 77.

would gain more than 1,000 new supporters.[86] In any case, Xenophon's account of the democratic uprising and a surviving inscription indicate that many of Thrasybulus' troops were eventually granted the lesser honor of *isoteleia* (*IG* ii² 10).[87]

Although the Athenians granted citizenship to slaves and foreign allies in exceptional circumstances, such as after the Battle of Arginusae (Aristoph. *Frogs* 693–694 and the scholiast to this passage), it was a regular practice for certain foreign powers to offer mercenaries lands on which to settle as a reward for services rendered.[88] Many Greeks, including most notably Xenophon and Iphicrates, were offered such perks by Thracian kings. During the Peloponnesian War, Athens had granted citizenship to influential Thracians in return for military alliance. Sadocus, the son of Athens' Odrysian ally Sitalces, dwelt in Athens and was made a citizen in 431 (Thuc. 2.29.5; Aristoph. *Ach.* 145–49). Philip's *Letter to the Athenians*, contained in the Demosthenic corpus, indicates that in the mid-fourth century the Thracian rulers Teres and Cersobleptes had been made Athenian citizens ([Dem.] 12.8). The mercenary captain Charidemus was granted Athenian citizenship and sundry other honors in 357 for helping Athens regain the Thracian Chersonese through his mediation with Cersobleptes (Dem. 23.23, 65, 89, 145, 185, 188). The Thracians were given special property rights at Athens from the time of the Peloponnesian War, and they evidently returned the favor. Beyond seeking

---

[86] Strauss 1987: 96, 116n26.
[87] Xenophon (*Hell.* 2.4.25) records that oaths were exchanged that promised *isoteleia* to the non-Athenians present. For the numbers of foreign supporters and the decree granting *isoteleia* instead of citizenship, see Krentz 1980. Although many of the specific honors given, including possibly *isoteleia*, are missing from the extant fragments of the inscription, leading many scholars to conclude that Thrasybulus' abortive citizenship grant is depicted, Krentz persuasively argues that a failed motion would not have been recorded on stone, and that the telltale language of citizenship is absent.
[88] See, for example, Pritchett (1974–1991: vol. 2, 67), who discusses the practice in the context of Ptolemaic Egypt. See also Hdt. 2.152–54 for an account of Greek mercenaries settled by Psammetichus in Egypt in the seventh century.

to grant citizenship and other rewards to metics who already lived in the Piraeus, perhaps Thrasybulus intended to reward his Thracian mercenaries, or at least their commanders, according to the custom practiced by the Thracians themselves and by the Athenians in the case of some of their more important Thracian friends.[89]

Archinus' opposition to these rewards is especially interesting in light of a decree mentioned by Aeschines (3.187–90) and corroborated on stone in which Archinus himself honored around a hundred supporters of Thrasybulus with laurel crowns and a sum of less than 10 drachmas apiece. Based on the surviving fragments of the decree's inscription, Raubitschek first proposed that, in addition to Athenians, many foreigners were honored in this decree, albeit in a second list of names now lost. Recently, Taylor has provided further evidence and analysis in support of these conclusions, particularly noting that the current list of slightly more than fifty names does not account for the hundred or so implied by Aeschines, and that the stele itself would have been large enough to list many more honorands, specifically foreigners.[90] Taylor convincingly argues that those honored, both Athenians and foreigners, were the earliest participants in Thrasybulus' rebellion against the Thirty, namely, the small band that withstood the Thirty's brief siege of Phyle in the opening days of the occupation of the fort (Xen. *Hell.* 2.4.2–3). Krentz has argued that the decree honored the much larger number of those who defeated the Thirty and their Spartan allies in a subsequent battle in northern Attica, probably in the plain towards Acharnae, which lies only a few miles from Phyle (Xen. *Hell.* 2.4.4–7; Diod. 14.33.1). Accordingly, the small number of names listed in the decree

---

[89] Osborne (1981: vol. 4, 142–45) argues that Pericles' 451 law on citizenship included the provision that citizenship be granted solely for good services rendered to the Athenian people. See also Lape (2010: 254–62) for a discussion of wartime cases of naturalization. For Lape, the stresses of war provided the perfect opportunity for reassessing the conventional boundaries barring citizenship to foreigners.

[90] Raubitschek 1941; Taylor 2002.

denotes the entire Athenian contribution to the battle, leaving out what would have amounted to several hundred foreigners, indeed the vast majority of the fighters.[91] Taylor, however, convincingly demonstrates that foreigners were probably listed in the decree and that Aeschines more accurately describes the siege of Phyle rather than the later battle.[92] If this is the case, it follows that Archinus had no objection to honoring foreigners per se, in spite of his strident opposition to Thrasybulus' proposal. We must ask, then, why he chose to honor only those few early supporters of Thrasybulus rather than the larger number of fighters who defeated the Thirty in later battles in northern Attica and the Piraeus.

Perhaps Archinus carefully honored only the earliest participants in the resistance because Thrasybulus' later force consisted not only of an increasingly large portion of foreign troops but also significant numbers of Thracian mercenaries in particular. Though our sources are not explicit about the makeup of the democratic forces, especially prior to the battles in the Piraeus, it is plausible that Thracians were involved even at Phyle. As already mentioned, many hundreds of mercenaries were supplied to Thrasybulus, paid for by Lysias and other wealthy opponents of the Thirty. In the battle on Munichia Hill, the democrats had with them many peltasts and javelin throwers, who were very effective against the Thirty. Following the battle, Xenophon says that members of Thrasybulus' growing army needed to equip themselves with arms by making shields out of wood or wickerwork (*Hell.* 2.4.25). The soldiers who fought at Munichia appear to have been fully equipped already, thus it follows that they had accompanied Thrasybulus from Phyle. The Thirty had, after all, rushed out to confront Thrasybulus immediately upon his arrival in the Piraeus (Xen. *Hell.* 2.4.10). The peltasts and javelin throwers in question, then, may not only have been Thracians, but even part of the mercenary forces supplied by

[91] Krentz 1982: 82–84.
[92] Taylor 2002: 382–86.

Thrasybulus' supporters who joined the struggle while the democrats were still at Phyle.

After the Thirty had been rebuffed by a snowstorm in their attempt to besiege Phyle very early on in the conflict, they were worried that Thrasybulus' men would be able to plunder the nearby fields. Accordingly, they sent a large force, including nearly the entire Spartan garrison and two divisions of cavalry, to keep watch over the fields (Xen. *Hell.* 2.4.4). Although Xenophon says that they encamped only 3 kilometers or so from Phyle, this appears to denote the distance from the center of the deme itself rather than the fort.[93] The fort lies high on the slopes of Mount Parnes, at an elevation of over 650 meters and several kilometers into the mountain, whereas the forces of the Thirty were positioned so as to protect the lower-lying fields. Diodorus says that they were close to Acharnae, lying on an open plain about 10 kilometers from the fort itself and at an elevation of approximately 150–175 meters (14.33.1). This situated the Thirty and their Spartan allies to protect the fields in terrain ideal for their cavalry forces. Both Xenophon and Diodorus say that Thrasybulus and his forces, numbered at 700 and 1,200, respectively, descended from the fort by night and made a surprise attack against their enemies.[94] Not only is the fort of Phyle at a considerable elevation but it is also surrounded by sheer cliffs and extremely rugged terrain, perfect for the fort's purpose as providing a strong defensive position. Remains of a retaining wall have been found for an ancient road extending from the fort in the direction of Athens, but the route was arduous nevertheless, especially at night.[95] Because night maneuvers were a specialty of highly skilled Thracian fighters, it is attractive to conceive of this operation as spearheaded by Thrasybulus' Thracians. Citizen volunteers, most

---

[93] The location of the deme itself is currently unknown. For the position of the fort, see Ober 1985: 145–47.

[94] Xen. *Hell.* 2.4.5: καταβαίνει τῆς νυκτός; Diod. 14.33.1: νυκτὸς ἀπροσδοκήτως.

[95] For the route and the remains of an ancient road, see Ober 1985: 116–17.

familiar with hoplite warfare, would have found a nocturnal descent over several kilometers and a 500-meter drop in elevation very difficult.[96]

Xenophon vividly describes the attack itself (Hell. 2.4.6–7). Shortly before dawn, Thrasybulus led his troops at a full run (dromōi) against the unsuspecting oligarchs. Thrasybulus' forces straightaway killed some of the enemy and put the rest to flight, pursuing them for the better part of a mile. They killed more than 120 of the enemy hoplites and, notably, three of the cavalry commanders, who were caught still in their beds. Xenophon's phrasing suggests that most of the hoplite casualties resulted from the lengthy chase.[97] Thracian peltasts, relatively lightly armed, were well suited for such a pursuit, and that they were able to kill so many of the enemy bespeaks their deadly effectiveness at a run. Furthermore, the verb used to describe the initial killing of some of the men in the camp, kataballō – a compound form of ballō, meaning to throw or hurl – is strongly evocative of a missile attack. In fact, of the instances of this verb in Xenophon's corpus that denote killing, all but one describe killing by ranged weapons, such as javelins, arrows, and stones, including at the hands of Thracian peltasts. In most cases, the verb is accompanied by a participle of either akontizō ("to hurl a javelin"), toxeuō ("to shoot an arrow"), or both.[98] The one exception is used in the context of

---

[96] For the rarity of hoplites engaging in night maneuvers, see Roisman's (1993: 52–70) account of the general Demosthenes' disastrous night attack against Epipolae at Syracuse. A few examples of hoplite night maneuvers do exist, but I can think of no examples of such maneuvers taking place over mountainous terrain.

[97] καὶ ἔστι μὲν οὓς αὐτῶν κατέβαλον, πάντας δὲ τρεψάμενοι ἐδίωξαν ἓξ ἢ ἑπτὰ στάδια, καὶ ἀπέκτειναν τῶν μὲν ὁπλιτῶν πλέον ἢ εἴκοσι καὶ ἑκατόν, τῶν δὲ ἱππέων Νικόστρατόν τε τὸν καλὸν ἐπικαλούμενον, καὶ ἄλλους δὲ δύο, ἔτι καταλαβόντες ἐν ταῖς εὐναῖς. Note the μὲν ... δὲ clause in the first part of the sentence that contrasts the few killed initially with the many killed in the subsequent rout.

[98] See Hell. 3.2.4 (Thracian peltasts killing Greeks); 4.1.19 (Persian cavalry and chariots, units that primarily used the bow, killing Greeks); Cyr. 1.3.14; 1.4.8; 4.6.3; 4.6.4 (all describing the hunting of game with ranged weapons).

Spartans pursuing and killing Locrians, who incidentally had first attacked the Spartans with stones and javelins and were fleeing through a dense wood.[99] Thus, Xenophon describes the forces of the Thirty as being struck down by missile weapons of the sort used by Thracians.

We know that by 404 Thrasybulus had spent several years in Thrace, crushing revolts and exacting funds by any and every means. A good use of the monetary support given him by his supporters was to pay for Thracian mercenaries, supplied through his northern contacts. He had seen firsthand the effectiveness of Thracian fighters, and his actions in 404–403 demonstrate that he knew how to apply their strengths, from complicated nighttime maneuvers over mountainous terrain to nimble assaults with ranged weapons. In this way, Thrasybulus prefigured the genius of Iphicrates and the innovations of Xenophon in the use of light troops. Several months had probably passed between the initial siege of Phyle and the battle in the plain, more than enough time for soldiers to have arrived from the north.[100] These mercenaries accompanied Thrasybulus to the Piraeus and were instrumental in defeating the Thirty and the Spartans at Munichia and in subsequent engagements. Middleton is right in asserting that many Thracians lived in the Piraeus. If Thrasybulus had arrived in their neighborhood with hundreds of Thracians in tow, those Thracians dwelling in the area would have been quick to take up arms for Thrasybulus and alongside their countrymen. Perhaps it was the Piraeus Thracians who picked up sling stones with which to pelt the Thirty and later set about improvising light shields out of wood and wickerwork, from which *peltai* and other light shields were typically made.

Strauss argues that Archinus proposed subtle honors to the hundred or so heroes of Phyle, of which he was one, in order to deemphasize their achievements and in turn deemphasize

---

[99] See *Hell*. 4.3.22. The other uses of the verb range from cutting down trees to dismounting from horseback.
[100] For the date, see Buck 1998: 75; Taylor 2002: 382.

the villainy of their opponents, namely, the Thirty. In this way, Archinus played the role of a reconciler, though his sympathies were more in line with the few than the many.[101] On the other hand, the epigram affiliated with Archinus' decree, quoted by Aeschines and partially surviving on stone, praises those who placed themselves in mortal danger in order to lead the fight against "the men ruling the city with unjust laws."[102] The epigram does not whitewash the reign of the Thirty, nor does it offer subtle praise of the democratic forces from Phyle. Furthermore, Thrasybulus himself was instrumental in bringing about the reconciliation between the democrats and oligarchs, including the famous amnesty law (Xen. *Hell.* 2.4.40–43), and was reckoned by the Oxyrhynchus historian as a member of the few (*Hell. Oxy.* 1.2–3). Strauss does allow that the ideological differences between Archinus and Thrasybulus were probably not great and that the opposition to Thrasybulus' decree was based at least as much on political rivalry as principle.[103]

Archinus' uneasiness with Thrasybulus' later supports is in line with Strauss' description of the factional opposition between the two men. Archinus might have disapproved of the involvement of so many Thracian soldiers, especially if they were personally tied to Thrasybulus. Striving for political power in his own right, Archinus was wary of such a powerful military force in the hands of a rival, all the more so if substantial civic rewards were thrown into the mix. Also, rather than deemphasizing the crimes of the Thirty or the achievements of the democratic opposition, Archinus wished to acknowledge

---

[101] Strauss 1987: 96–97.

[102] Aesch. 3.190:

Τούσδ' ἀρετῆς ἕνεκα στεφάνοις ἐγέραιρε παλαίχθων
    δῆμος Ἀθηναίων, οἵ ποτε τοὺς ἀδίκοις
θεσμοῖς ἄρξαντας πόλιος πρῶτοι καταπαύειν
    ἦρξαν, κίνδυνον σώμασιν ἀράμενοι.

For the partial preservation of the epigram on the inscription itself, which adds further credibility to Aeschines' description of the decree, see Taylor 2002: 378.

[103] Strauss 1987: 96, 98.

the role of Athenian citizens such as himself and those early foreigners who lent assistance, namely, distinguished Greek metics and citizens of Thebes. Thrasybulus' Thracians were to be excluded if at all possible. In the factional competition among the elite at Athens, a private foreign army and a large bloc of loyal new citizens in the hands of any one politician was too much of a threat to the balance of power. After brilliantly employing the Thracians in combat against the Thirty, perhaps Thrasybulus overplayed his hand and made himself vulnerable to Archinus' charge.

IPHICRATES AND THE IDEAL INFANTRYMAN

Iphicrates is perhaps Greek antiquity's most famous mercenary commander. His prodigious tactical sense was so legendary that Polyaenus attributes to him sixty-four stratagems, by far the largest number given to any man, eclipsing even Julius Caesar (*Strat.* 3.9). In the field he was an able experimenter, unconfined by traditional Greek military practice and ever ready to adapt the tactics and equipment of his soldiers to suit the needs of the campaign and more effectively combat the enemy. Thracian warfare provided the inspiration for many of his innovations, and the unusual experience of almost continuous campaigning with unconventional auxiliary troops provided the ideal forum for honing his craft, leaving an indelible mark on Greek military history. Iphicrates' demonstrated facility with the staples of unconventional warfare, including ambush and deception, were perfectly complemented by the Thracian peltast and the Thracian habits of brigandage and raiding.

The Persian satrap Pharnabazus and Conon, his Athenian ally, had raised a force of mercenaries while liberating the Asian cities after the Battle of Cnidus in 394. These mercenaries were acquired in the region around the Hellespont (*Hell.* 4.8.7). It is reasonable to assume that these mercenaries were the famous corps later stationed at Corinth under the command of Iphicrates. This is especially likely because the force at Corinth consisted largely of javelin-wielding peltasts, a type of soldier readily available from the area around the Hellespont. This implies a sizable Thracian presence at Corinth.[104] Still, there is debate among scholars as to the exact makeup and origin of the mercenary force. Best argues that Greeks from the Hellespont made up most of the force, supplemented with peltasts from Athens' allies in central Greece, such as the Acarnanians.[105] Pritchett supposes the force was a mixture of Greeks and Asians recruited by Conon and Pharnabazus.[106] It is most likely that the mercenary force at Corinth consisted of foreign mercenaries from the Hellespont supplemented by Greek citizen fighters. But the extent to which these Hellespontines were Thracians, Greeks, or a mixture of both remains unclear.

Citizens of Greek cities in the Thraceward area adopted Thracian military practices at an earlier date and to a greater extent than cities farther south.[107] The formation of citizen cavalry and peltast units by poleis such as Abdera and Aenus is hardly surprising. Parke believes that the peltasts in the service of Olynthus were citizens because they are described as part of the regular army.[108] Peltasts from Olynthus and the surrounding area had bested Athenian troops in the Chalcidice early in the Peloponnesian War (Thuc. 2.79). A coin from Abdera dating to the third quarter of the fifth century shows a naked peltast, which Isaac takes as proof that Abdera had a corps of citizen peltasts. Others, though, suggest this peltast represents a soldier in Sitalces' Thracian army.[109] Arrian, describing Alexander's campaigns in Thrace, says that the autonomous Thracians of Mount Haemus banded together with many armed Greek merchants to oppose Alexander from the heights (*Anab. Alex.* 1.1.6–7). Along with their non-Greek neighbors, these

[104] As persuasively argued by Parke (1933: 50–52). For their use of javelins, see Xen. *Hell.* 4.4.16–17.
[105] Best 1969: 85–97.
[106] Pritchett 1974–1991: vol. 2, 118.
[107] See, for example, Best 1969: 12–13; Isaac 1986: 85–86, 103–4.
[108] Parke 1933: 84n3.
[109] Isaac 1968: 103–4. For the peltast being a Thracian in Sitalces' service, see Mattingly 1977: 93.

merchants exploited the mountainous terrain to their advantage in a typically Thracian fashion.

Regular contact with Thracians required soldiers suited to dealing with the threats specific to the region. Also, the inherent tactical effectiveness of these non-hoplite arms was readily apparent to those Greeks who had witnessed them in action time and again. The innovations of Athenian commanders, such as the elder and younger Miltiades, Hagnon, and Demosthenes, largely came from extended contact with lightly armed foreign fighters. Greeks living on the edge of the Thracian world could hardly afford the luxury of maintaining affected hoplite snobbery.[110]

Though peltasts are frequently listed as coming from northern allies, Greek peltasts are by no means always meant.[111] As Isaac argues, the Greek city of Aenus probably acted as a mustering point for peltasts, both native Thracians and Greeks, in the service of Athens.[112] Isaac posits that Aenus was also likely a hub of the Thracian slave trade, collecting slaves destined to mainland Greek cities. He continues this line of reasoning to assert that Pisistratus recruited his own Thracian mercenaries in the sixth century from Aegean Greek cities.[113] In the fifth and fourth centuries, Thracian mercenaries were of necessity regularly recruited from Greek cities in the northern Aegean. How else would a Greek commander come into contact with Thracian soldiers-for-hire? Thus, when the sources tell us that a particular mercenary force originated in Aenus, such as that accompanying Cleon to Pylos in 425 (Thuc. 4.28.4), or from the Hellespont, as was the case with the force recruited by Conon

---

[110] For the hoplite ethos, see Hanson 2000, and his concise discussion in 1991: 3–6. For Hanson, during the period of the hoplite (ca. 650–450), only the owners of small farms, the "wearers of bronze armor," had any reason to enter the battlefield, and then only to defend their land from other Greeks (1991: 5). This, of course, would not apply to Greeks needing to defend themselves against the incursions of Thracian marauders.

[111] For the opposite view, see Best (1969: 13n72).

[112] Isaac 1986: 152–53.

[113] Isaac 1986: 145–46.

(Xen. *Hell.* 4.8.7), there is reason to believe that a majority of the fighters were Thracians who had been mustered in Greek cities.

In the years preceding the recruitment of the force for Corinth, Thracian mercenaries from the Hellespont were active under Greek commanders. While Alcibiades was in the area he commanded large numbers of Thracian troops, whose support he offered the Athenians at Aegospotami (Plut. *Alc.* 30.4–5; 36.3; 37.2; Diod. 13.105.3–4). Plutarch says that these Thracian soldiers were numerous and zealous in their service for Alcibiades because of the affection they had for him (*Alc.* 30.4–5). The Spartan Clearchus had recruited a large force of mercenaries in the Hellespont. Xenophon tells us that when he joined Cyrus for the expedition against Artaxerxes, Clearchus brought 1,000 hoplites, 800 Thracian peltasts, and 200 Cretan bowmen (*Anab.* 1.2.9). Note that the mercenary hoplites might have been Greek, but the peltasts were Thracian.

In many ways, Iphicrates' position as commander of the mercenary force at Corinth resembles Dieitrephes' leadership over the Dioi in 413. Both men seem to have exploited the opportunity of a special command over a group of Thracians in order to circumvent the confines of the *stratēgia*. Iphicrates was appointed to positions of leadership before reaching the age traditionally required to be a *stratēgos*, and both men were given commands without being elected by the demos as *stratēgoi*. Long ago, Rehdantz speculated that Iphicrates owed his appointment at Corinth to preexisting ties to Thrace, but there is no firm evidence of this.[114]

Iphicrates put his time with mercenary peltasts to good use. In 390, after several years of campaigning, he and his peltasts put to rout an entire *mora* of Spartan hoplites – that is, 600 of Greece's most fearsome heavy infantrymen – near Corinth's port at Lechaeum (Xen. *Hell.* 4.5).[115] The Spartans, arrogantly

---

[114] Rehdantz 1845. This is followed by Parke (1933: 52) and Best (1969: 86).

[115] See Konecny 2001 for a comprehensive account of the battle. Scholars have variously suggested anywhere between 1,200 and 4,000 (!) for

confident in their own invincibility – and no doubt in the fear they inspired in their enemies – proceeded to march past Corinth without adequate light-armed and cavalry support. Iphicrates and his peltasts sprang into action, and they made full use of their mobility and training. The peltasts repeatedly approached the Spartans to hurl javelins, after which they retreated with ease. Many Spartans were enticed to pursue the peltasts only then to be separated from the phalanx and rendered even more vulnerable to attack. Harried and cut down in great numbers, the heavily armed Spartans were forced to retreat in humiliation. This feat brought Iphicrates nearly unparalleled renown in antiquity because it shattered the myth of Spartan invincibility, much as Demosthenes' victory at Pylos had. Good Greek hoplites, let alone the Spartan warrior elite, simply were not supposed to be bested by light-armed troops, especially ignoble Thracian soldiers for hire.

Although Iphicrates has often been credited with making peltasts a prominent feature of Greek armies, he was not the first to realize the usefulness of light-armed Thracian troops and exploit them to great effect.[116] The light infantry tactics of the Thracians certainly had a profound and lasting effect on Greek military practice, but peltasts had been used by the Athenians in many engagements before the Corinthian War, including at Pylos in 425, and with Xenophon in the expedition of Cyrus and subsequent return to the Aegean at the turn of the fourth century. In fact, Xenophon's experience showcases how valuable extended campaigning with Thracians could be to military innovation.

Xenophon's familiarity with Thracian tactics probably began earlier than most have realized. Born into an equestrian family, he likely fought on behalf of the Thirty as a member

the size of Iphicrates' peltast force, but Konecny estimates around 1,500, which seems reasonable. See also Best 1969: 87–88; Anderson (1970: 123–26), who emphasizes the importance of the hoplite support of the peltasts in this battle; and Lendon 2005: 93–94.

[116] As Best (1969: 47, 102–10) conclusively shows.

of the cavalry in 404–403.[117] Thus, he probably took part in the battles against Thrasybulus in the Piraeus and elsewhere. Xenophon gives a vivid account of Thrasybulus' use of light-armed troops in these battles, troops that likely included mercenary and metic Thracians. Xenophon's account seems to be that of an eyewitness and participant in the events. As a very young man, not much more than eighteen years old, Xenophon probably took part in Thrasyllus' expedition to Asia in 409.[118] Thrasyllus eventually wound up on the Hellespont where he joined his forces with those of Alcibiades as they raided the territory of Pharnabazus (Xen. *Hell.* 1.2.13). Xenophon tells us that Thrasyllus equipped 5,000 of his sailors as peltasts before he set out from Athens (Xen. *Hell.* 1.2.1). Xenophon's phrasing implies that these ad hoc peltasts were to serve with a contingent of peltasts – perhaps Thracian mercenaries – that was already part of the expedition.[119] At 1.2.2–3, Xenophon seems to distinguish between the Athenian light troops – *psiloi*, a term Xenophon often uses interchangeably with peltasts – and other peltasts. The former seems to designate the improvised peltast-sailors, and the latter denotes Thracian mercenaries. Finally, Thracian mercenaries were an important part of Cyrus' expedition of 401 and fought at Cunaxa, a battle in which Xenophon himself participated (Xen. *Anab.* 1.10.6).

Because of his familiarity with Thracian fighters, Xenophon had no fears about living in Thracian territory, as his desire to

---

[117] This was first proposed by Schwartz 1889, who sees Xenophon's account of the battles between Thrasybulus and the oligarchs in 404–403 as bearing the marks of an eyewitness. Xenophon seems to have been an admirer of Theramenes and his more moderate oligarchic tendencies, and he has fairly high praise for the democratic champion Thrasybulus. Anderson (1974: 47–48) argues that Xenophon was a rather reluctant supporter of the Thirty.

[118] The account of this campaign seems to be given from an eyewitness perspective. See Stronk 1995: 4.

[119] The OCT text of this passage shows that despite the agreement of the manuscripts, one editor has deleted the line about the preexisting peltasts (ὡς ἅμα καὶ πελτασταῖς ἐσομένοις). Presumably the editor felt this line to be redundant, unnecessarily so given that two different peltast contingents would explain the line perfectly well.

settle the harbor at Calpe demonstrates. Xenophon highlights his own fitness to lead such a colony in his detailed description of the rescue of a fellow Greek contingent that had fallen under threat from the natives. The lightly armed Bithynians, in defense of their homes, had slaughtered great numbers of plundering Arcadian hoplites, who had proven unable to defend themselves because of their unwieldy armament. As the Arcadians huddled together on a hilltop to spend the night, the Bithynians called out to each other in the dark – a terrifying cacophony to the Greeks – and skillfully mustered greater forces. The next day, many Greeks were again cut down. As Xenophon heard of the plight of his fellow Greeks, he marched his own contingent to their position by night, shrewdly placing his light troops on the flanks and upon the heights to provide cover, while setting much of the area ablaze to give the impression of a huge army. The plan worked: by daybreak the Bithynians had all fled (*Anab.* 6.3). Where the Arcadian hoplites failed, Xenophon and his competent use of a combined-arms force succeeded. Implicitly, Xenophon tells us that he was not only willing to found a settlement in barbarian lands but was also the perfect leader for the job.

Once in European Thrace, the Greek hoplite force under Xenophon served as the perfect complement to the light-armed infantry and cavalry of Seuthes. When the Greeks had first arrived in Seuthes' territory, they fared poorly against the local Thracians because of their lack of cavalry and light-armed troops (6.3.7). But Xenophon and Seuthes eventually worked out a way to integrate their two types of soldiers to great effect, and they overcame the mountain-dwelling tribes that had been harassing them (7.3.37–4.24). As an example of Xenophon's tactical acumen, he ordered his troops to stagger their march through the night, with the slower hoplites given a head start. This ensured that the faster units did not outpace the slower, and in the morning the entire force was still together in the appropriate order (*Anab.* 7.3.37–39). Because of his experience with light-armed Thracian troops, Xenophon was able to showcase the effectiveness of a combined-arms force. In this way, he and his younger contemporary Iphicrates were part of a longstanding tradition of military innovation among Athenian disciples of Thrace, from Miltiades to Demosthenes.

One must not discount Iphicrates' own military talent. His victory over the Spartans at Lechaeum was a tour de force. Although only peltasts were involved in the actual fighting as described by Xenophon, the Athenian general Callias marshaled the Athenian hoplites during the battle and advanced toward the Spartans once they had already been badly thrashed by Iphicrates' men. It was this hoplite threat that finally caused the Spartans to withdraw (*Hell.* 4.5.14–17). This is an example of the type of coordination between hoplites and peltasts that had been utilized by Xenophon a decade earlier. Iphicrates recognized that versatility of arms was paramount for an effective army. Polyaenus says that Iphicrates likened an army to a human body: the phalanx was the chest, the light-armed troops the hands, and the cavalry the feet. Without any of these parts, the army, like a body, would cease to function to its full potential (*Strat.* 3.9.22). His singular achievement at Corinth was to take full advantage of the extended time in the field. By the use of his legendarily strict discipline and constant drill, he honed the skills of his mercenaries to levels rarely achieved in the Greek world.[120] Iphicrates' talent as a commander and as an enforcer of discipline, plus his prodigious resourcefulness, made him a valuable addition to the Athenians and also to the Odrysian court. He was the perfect man to make the best use of Thracian tribesmen, who, though fierce, were likely unaccustomed to such rigorous drill and maneuver.

Whether or not he had connections with Thrace prior to his command of the mercenaries at Corinth, Iphicrates demonstrated a penchant for Thracian-style warfare, including far more than the use of peltasts. In particular, he was adept at

[120] Thus Pritchett 1974–1991: vol. 2, 123–25. Anderson (1970: 121) emphasizes Iphicrates' innovation in marshaling peltasts so skillfully that they became accustomed to fighting in formation when the situation demanded it. This was no small feat for troops accustomed to fighting loosely as individuals.

plundering raids and probably began raiding enemy territory while part of Conon's expedition after Cnidus. Beginning in the Hellespont, Conon and Pharnabazus laid waste to Spartan possessions near Sestus and Abydos and then ravaged Spartan territory itself, doing as much damage as possible (Xen. *Hell.* 4.8.6–11). While stationed at Corinth, Iphicrates led many raids against the adjacent territories, attacking Phlius and plundering its territory (Xen. *Hell.* 4.4.15). He also attacked Arcadia, assaulting walled towns and seizing plunder. The Arcadian hoplites did nothing to prevent this because they were terrified of the peltasts (Xen. *Hell.* 4.4.16). Thrace was a natural haven for a commander prone to this style of warfare.

Iphicrates also demonstrated an ability to attack under cover of darkness and to make effective use of trickery and ambush. At Phlius, he ambushed the men of the city when they came out to defend themselves and killed a great many of them (Xen. *Hell.* 4.4.15). In the Hellespont, he slaughtered Anaxibius along with hundreds of his soldiers after springing a trap (Xen. *Hell.* 4.8.35–39). Polyaenus' enumeration of Iphicrates' stratagems includes many instances of trickery, ambush, and night operations (3.9). As we have seen, night maneuvers, even over rough terrain, were a specialty of many Thracians. The similarity of the speed, mobility, and trickery inherent in Thracian warfare to the maxims prescribed by modern guerrilla leaders, such as Mao, has been noted by Best.[121]

While in Thrace, Iphicrates was a close advisor to Cotys on many matters in addition to providing military expertise. There are several references in our sources to Iphicrates' talent for finding money with which to pay his troops. From Xenophon's account of his activities in the Hellespont in 388, we learn that it was the Athenian commander's customary practice to sail up and down the straits in order to exact financial contributions from the local people (*Hell.* 4.8.35–39). It is difficult to imagine that such contributions were made entirely willingly. Both Anaxibius and Iphicrates initially carried on their conflict

[121] Best 1969: 25–26.

with one another by conducting plundering raids against their respective holdings. The resulting booty helped to pay the troops. Years later, when appointed to lead an expedition to Corcyra, Iphicrates made many raids along the way, including capturing several Sicilian ships, in order to raise funds (Diod. 15.47.7; Xen. *Hell.* 6.2.35, 38). In Corcyra, he instructed his troops to work the land in order to make money, and his force was also hired as mercenaries by allied mainland states (Xen. *Hell.* 6.2.37). These and other similar means of acquiring funds with which to maintain an army were required by the difficult financial straits faced by the Greek cities in the fourth century.[122] Commanders were therefore expected to conduct raids in order to raise their own money, because the city was unable to finance sizable military expeditions through the regular channels.

Iphicrates, then, had a penchant for devising novel ways of raising funds. His particular military experiences were instrumental in developing these talents. Polyaenus tells us of three episodes that demonstrate Iphicrates' financial savvy: marching his troops through poor lands when short of money to encourage less spending; withholding a portion of his soldiers' pay as a security against desertion; and dressing some men in Persian clothes to give the impression to the other troops that even larger sums were on their way from the Great King (3.9.35, 51, 59). This ingenuity came in handy for his patron Cotys. Pseudo-Aristotle tells us of one of Iphicrates' schemes to raise money for his father-in-law (*Econ.* 1350a30). Essentially, Iphicrates advised Cotys to demand a quantity of grain from the lands under his control, which was then sold at the local *emporia* for a huge profit, providing pay for the whole army.

Most vexing for scholars, yet seemingly most famous in antiquity, are the military reforms enacted by Iphicrates, which are outlined by both Diodorus (15.44) and Nepos (*Iph.* 1). Supposedly by these reforms Iphicrates radically modified the standard Greek infantry soldier. Both authors agree that

---

[122] As argued by Pritchett 1974–1991: vol. 2, 68–70.

the large and unwieldy hoplite shield, the *aspis*, was replaced by the smaller Thracian-style *peltē*. Allegedly because of the adoption of the *peltē*, these soldiers became known as peltasts, though clearly peltasts were around long before Iphicrates. Iphicrates increased the size of the spear, Diodorus says by half, but Nepos says the length was doubled. Also, the sword was lengthened to up to twice its original size. The soldiers were all given boots that were light and easy to untie, aptly dubbed *iphikratidai*. Finally, Nepos provides the detail that the standard mail or brass armor was replaced by a lighter linen cuirass. All of these reforms were designed to make the infantryman more maneuverable and agile, much like traditional Thracian soldiers. Diodorus places these reforms after Iphicrates' experiences as a mercenary commander in Egypt in the early 370s.

Best dismisses the reforms as spurious.[123] For a long time, the standard interpretation of these passages was that this new "Iphicratid" infantryman, a sort of hybrid soldier, became a staple throughout the fourth century and was the key military development of the time.[124] The problem with this line of argument is that there is no evidence in our sources for such an infantryman in the Classical period.[125] Also, Diodorus and Nepos seem to imply that these reforms introduced peltasts to Greek warfare, but peltasts had been used by the Greeks for decades by this point. Additionally, the reforms in question seem to point to a modification of hoplite soldiers with sturdy thrusting spears rather than a creation of new light-armed peltasts.[126] Yet, as Stylianou argues, it is doubtful whether both Nepos and Diodorus fabricated this information. Rather, it seems that they used Ephorus as a source and simply misunderstood the information he provided. Stylianou concludes that Iphicrates probably equipped some of his men in Egypt in this fashion to better combat the unwieldy heavy infantry of

---

[123] Best 1969:102–9.
[124] See, for example, Lippelt 1910: 65–67; Parke 1933: 77–83; Griffith 1935: 5, 7, 196, 239, 317.
[125] Stylianou 1998: 344.
[126] Parke 1933: 77–83; Best 1969: 102–10; Anderson 1970: 129–31.

the Egyptians, and that these reforms were only temporarily used in this specific context.[127]

Diodorus does, however, place these reforms within the context of the Egyptian campaign and claims that they applied to heavy-armed hoplite troops rather than peltasts, but they were probably inspired by Iphicrates' experiences with Thracian soldiers. The most successful type of army, especially for combating the tribesmen of Thrace, was a combined-arms force of heavy and light infantry and cavalry.

Peltasts were effective against heavy infantry unsupported by other arms but were vulnerable against a variegated force. Iphicrates chose to attack the Spartan *mora* at Lechaeum because he saw that the Spartan hoplites were largely unsupported by either cavalry or peltasts of their own (Xen. *Hell.* 4.5.13). Peltasts alone were thus able to cut down the more encumbered Spartans. Callias, however, did draw up the Athenian hoplites in case they were needed in the battle. The final blow was struck when the Athenian hoplite phalanx began to advance against the Spartans. The Spartans attempted to chase down Iphicrates' troops with what horsemen they did have, but the horsemen never drove home their pursuit because they attempted to maintain a continuous front with the hoplites (Xen. *Hell.* 4.5.16). In this way, the Spartans failed to use their cavalry support to its full potential.

Some more or less effective measures were devised by the Spartans to combat a light-armed enemy. Xenophon says that Iphicrates' peltasts were initially terrified of the Spartans because, on one occasion, the younger and more agile of the Spartan hoplites had managed to capture some retreating peltasts even over a long distance (*Hell.* 4.4.16).[128] This tactic had

---

[127] Stylianou 1998: 343–45. Another perspective is given by Griffith (1981), who thinks that Nepos and Diodorus conflated many reforms of Iphicrates, occurring over several years, into the single context of the Egyptian campaign. Griffith argues that it was only the longer spear that was introduced in Egypt.

[128] Anderson (1970: 123) argues that perhaps the Spartans learned these tactics from the Thracians themselves.

already been employed by Brasidas in 423 against lightly armed Illyrians (Thuc. 4.125). It was indeed attempted by the Spartan *mora* against Iphicrates' peltasts at Lechaeum when the polemarch ordered the men in the age classes of twenty-five to thirty to run out in pursuit of the enemy. This time, however, they were unsuccessful, primarily because the peltasts exploited the gaps formed during the pursuit and cut down many men (*Hell.* 4.5.16). It appears that Iphicrates learned from his earlier experience of this new Spartan tactic and found a way to turn it his own advantage.[129]

That his peltasts worked in conjunction with hoplites and that he noticed the Spartans were unprotected by faster troops implies Iphicrates well understood the importance of diversity of arms. During his first stay in Thrace in the service of Seuthes and Cotys during the 380s, he probably developed his tactical abilities further, much as Xenophon had a decade and a half earlier. It also seems that Iphicrates grasped the potential of having more heavily armed soldiers able to execute speedy maneuvers as the Spartans did at Lechaeum, however unsuccessfully. Polyaenus tells us that Iphicrates never allowed his troops to break formation during a pursuit, which suggests that he also learned from the Spartans' mistakes (3.9.2). His reforms, if they did take place in Egypt, were based on a combination of his prior experiences. If he had been leading primarily hoplites in Egypt, it would have been difficult to change their way of fighting completely, which would have resulted from a conversion to proper peltasts. Also, a force consisting solely of peltasts could be left vulnerable if unsupported by heavier arms, as Xenophon's mountain-dwelling enemies found out. Iphicrates' reforms, then, could have been an experiment in creating an ideally versatile soldier, capable of fighting in a dense phalanx formation with a long thrusting spear while

---

[129] Anderson (1970: 124–25) argues that it was the presence of the Athenian hoplites that prevented the Spartans from using their "running out" tactics to the fullest advantage. Xenophon's account, though, is clear in that the Spartan runners were cut down when they were returning to their lines in a disordered fashion.

light enough to harass a less mobile enemy with relative ease. Such a soldier was also able to chase after a lightly armed foe, as the Spartans had attempted, and cut him down with a long slashing sword or run him through with a thrusting spear.

We will never know why this new type of soldier is absent from our sources.[130] Such a novel fighting style could only be developed and maintained during continuous military service over a long period, which was the case in Egypt. This is in line with Pritchett's explanation as to why Iphicrates' success at Lechaeum was not repeated until the professional war machine of Philip and Alexander.[131] Once back in the service of Athens, Iphicrates had to rely on the traditional citizen-hoplite supplemented by specialized foreign troops. We are not told what types of troops he had at his disposal while in the service of Cotys, but the impressive wealth of the Odrysians enabled continuous military exercise and perhaps similar experimentation. In any case, we should accept the accounts of Iphicrates' capacity for invention and creativity presented by Nepos and Diodorus.

Iphicrates' particular talents made him a natural commander of Thracian troops. The Thracians in turn helped to inspire this most gifted of tacticians to new heights of innovation. More than that, because Iphicrates was unconstrained by the Greek

---

[130] Some have seen a prototype of this new soldier in Chabrias' famous maneuver in Boeotia in 378. Chabrias, or so the sources seem to indicate, received a charge by ordering his troops to kneel on one knee and extend their spears outward (Nep. *Chab.* 1; Diod. 15.32–33; Polyaen. 2.1.2). Parke (1933: 81) argues that this was "just the maneuver suited to a peltast in the new equipment." Burnett and Edmonson (1961) have suggested that fragments from a statue of Chabrias in the Agora indicate that a kneeling hoplite was depicted on the monument. This, however, has been adequately refuted by both Anderson (1963) and Buckler (1972), who insist that the statue fragments do not support such a reconstruction, and moreover that the literary sources are in fact muddled. In reality, it seems that Chabrias ordered his men to stand "at ease" with their shields resting against their knees and their spears standing straight up. It was their apparent contempt and nonchalance that caused the enemy army to break off the attack.

[131] Pritchett 1974–1991: vol. 2, 123–25.

hoplite ethos, he was free to innovate in ways others were not. Thracian tactics were disdained by most Greeks as ungentlemanly and base. The Spartans poured scorn upon the methods by which they were defeated at Pylos in 425 (Thuc. 4.40.2), and Thucydides also contemptuously reported the death of Cleon at the hands of a peltast near Amphipolis (Thuc. 5.10.9). Ferrill argues that Philip was able to fuse the phalanx with different troop types because the Macedonians were largely outside of the Greek hoplite ethos, a notion that has a lot of merit.[132] Another military genius, the Spartan Brasidas, seems to have introduced novel tactics for dealing with a light-armed enemy while he himself campaigned in Thrace. Perhaps he enjoyed a relatively free hand to innovate because a full 700 of his 1,700 hoplites in Illyria were helots rather than full Spartiates (Thuc. 4.80.5). The 1,000 who were not helots were probably allied soldiers from Corinth, Sicyon, and Phlius.[133] A very few, then, of Brasidas' troops were proper Spartans, the archetypical hoplite soldiers. By leading a force of foreign mercenaries and by serving in Thrace, Iphicrates too had plenty of leeway to work out his tactics as the situation demanded.

CONCLUSION

Though delayed by the dogged persistence of the hoplite phalanx, Greek tactics did evolve in the Archaic and Classical periods. Athenian contact with Thrace played no small part in this. Thrace, rather than the egalitarian armies of the polis, served as military academy for many of Athens' most important leaders. As effective as many of the innovations of Thrace's disciples were, however, they were rarely fully adopted by the poleis of the Greek mainland. As Best has shown, peltasts became a regular presence in Greek infantries from the last quarter of the fifth century on, but they never replaced the hoplite phalanx as the primary military arm of virtually every Greek

---

[132] Ferrill 1997: 150.
[133] See Gomme et al. 1945–1981: vol. 3, 532.

polis. Greeks themselves were often prized as mercenaries in the fourth century precisely because they were heavy infantrymen, a type of soldier underrepresented in the armies of the Persians and other non-Greek powers.[134]

Several factors prevented the Greeks from realizing a lasting combined-arms force. Greek poleis could not maintain professional armies for extended periods, which was essential for the intensive training and expertise required for an effective variegated force. On those occasions when Greek soldiers did take the field for years at a time, such as the March of the Ten Thousand, effective ways of integrating heavy and light infantry were developed and utilized, often to great effect. The Greeks were also constrained by their own military conventions, the predominance of the hoplite ethos in particular. Much as the Spartan hoplites at Sphacteria displayed contempt for the missile troops that forced them to surrender, so good Athenian hoplites disdained the "naval mob" that had been empowered by their role as rowers in the fleet (Thuc. 8.72.2).[135] The level of prejudice was often so great that commanders strove to fight de facto hoplite battles even at sea, privileging the hoplite soldier over the lowly rower.[136]

In the fourth century, the most important land battles were fought between opposing phalanxes, which is perhaps the greatest testimony to Greek reluctance to adopt the new tactics and embrace the measures pioneered in large part by Athenian Thracophiles. In Herodotus, the Persian general Mardonius mocks the Greek style of battle, namely, finding a level plain and fighting it out on even terms without either

[134] See Best 1969: 110–19.

[135] These sentiments are also expressed in the so-called Old Oligarch's essay on Athenian government. For a synopsis of this text, including its treatment of the naval mob, see Cartledge 2009: 140–42.

[136] Strauss (2000) argues that at the Battle of Eurymedon, Cimon modified his triremes to hold more hoplites for the political purpose of undercutting the importance of the thetic rowers. Fornara (1966) plausibly argued that the hoplite victory on the small island of Psyttaleia during the Battle of Salamis was exaggerated by Herodotus' sources in order to highlight the hoplite achievement at the expense of the navy.

side attempting to employ strategic devices or make use of advantageous terrain (7.9b). This is an exaggeration to be sure, but, so far as we can tell, even at Chaeronea in 338 the Greek forces consisted overwhelmingly of traditional citizen hoplites. They were crushed by Philip's variegated and professionally trained army.[137]

[137] This battle has been notoriously difficult to reconstruct. Our principal source is Diod. 16.85–86, supplemented with Polyaen. 4.2.2, 7. For a good reconstruction, see Hammond et al. 1972–1988: vol. 2, 596–603. Diodorus says that Philip had in addition to his infantry no less than 2,000 cavalry. The role of the cavalry in the battle is disputed. See, for example, Gaebel (2002: 154–57), who argues that, despite most scholarly reconstructions of the battle, the Macedonian cavalry could not have broken the densely packed phalanx of the Theban Sacred Band. In any case, Philip's own phalanx was expertly trained and had the advantage in technology with the longer *sarissa* that replaced the conventional hoplite spear. As the mainland Greeks – aside from the Thessalians – developed no heavy cavalry to match the Macedonians, so too did they fail to adapt to the threat posed by the Macedonian phalanx.

CHAPTER SEVEN

EPILOGUE

CHARES AND CHARIDEMUS IN A

MACEDONIAN WORLD

Nepos concludes his biography of Iphicrates' contemporary Timotheus with a grim assessment of the Athenian generalship, the *stratēgia*, in the following years: "The time of Iphicrates, Chabrias, and Timotheus was the last age of Athenian generals. After their death, there was no captain from that city worthy of remembrance" (*Timoth.* 4.4).[1] There were, however, several generals who earned considerable notoriety, especially Charidemus, Iphicrates' infamous protégé, and Chares, seen by many as the quintessential soldier of fortune. But, were the careers of these mercenary generals really so different from those of their predecessors? Athens was under increasing pressure when its allies revolted in the Social War of the 350s and when Philip began to consolidate his power over all of Thrace, starting in the west with Amphipolis and moving ever eastward until he threatened Athens' interests on the Hellespont. In such a climate, the exigencies of generalship in the service of a cash-strapped polis might have led to ever more unseemly measures to finance expeditions.[2] Decades earlier, though, even

[1] *Haec extrema fuit aetas imperatorum Atheniensium, Iphicratis, Chabriae, Timothei, neque post illorum obitum quisquam dux in illa urbe fuit dignus memoria.*

[2] See, for instance, the comment of Salmond (1996: 44): "[Chares'] elevation marks something of a turning-point in the development of the fourth-century *strategia* ... Chares demonstrated to the Athenians, if

Thrasybulus had resorted to financial exactions and plundering, and when Athens was particularly beset by financial difficulties in 413, Dieitrephes had unleashed his Thracians on Mycalessus.[3] There is little to suggest that the commanders active in the north in the mid-fourth century exceeded earlier leaders by their methods or readiness to derive advantage from the chaotic situation in the region. Eventually, Philip's total annexation of Thrace coupled with his decisive victory over the Greek poleis at Chaeronea in 338 did permanently alter the strategic environment in the Aegean. Athens was effectively prevented from ever again projecting power overseas, and individual Athenians lost Thrace as a source of refuge and personal power. The era of the Athenian disciple of Thrace had come to an end.

Iphicrates' most obvious military successor was Charidemus of Oreus. As it happens, our fullest source for his career is Demosthenes' *Against Aristocrates*, a hostile account to say the least.[4] Charidemus was originally from Euboea, and in the 370s he fought as a slinger and light infantryman for various polities before he was hired by Iphicrates as a *xenagos* (mercenary commander) for the campaign to Amphipolis from 368–364 (Dem. 23.148). As Parke suggests, Charidemus likely left the service of Athens to work for the Thracians after Timotheus replaced Iphicrates at Amphipolis.[5] Charidemus thus followed the example set by his commander, who had famously spurned Athens in favor of the Odrysian court. Charidemus later became connected by marriage to Cotys' son Cersobleptes in the same way Iphicrates had been to Cotys (Dem. 23.129). He seems to

any evidence was still needed, that if they required continued success from their *strategoi*, they had to accept that the demands of campaigning often required less than honourable solutions."

[3] See Kallet (1999; 2001: 121–46), who argues that Thucydides means to link the massacre at Mycalessus with the moral degradation of Athens brought on by troubled finances.

[4] Pritchett (1974–1991: vol. 2, 85–89) provides a useful summary of Charidemus' career, including a chart outlining the various states by which he was employed.

[5] Parke 1933: 125–26.

have campaigned on behalf of Cersobleptes against Athens for a time (Dem. 23.163–65). Eventually, though, he was granted Athenian citizenship and various other honors, including the title of benefactor (*eueregtēs*) in 357. These honors were principally owing to his role in convincing Cersobleptes to cede the Chersonese to Athens.[6] As Kelly points out, Charidemus and Cersobleptes must have rendered valuable services for the Athenians to account for so many prestigious honors, a point Demosthenes wished to downplay in his oration.[7] Later in his career Charidemus remained popular at Athens. Plutarch says that many Athenians desired to have Charidemus made their general after the Battle of Chaeronea, but Phocion was chosen instead (*Phoc.* 16.3). In recompense for his many campaigns against Macedonian interests, in 335 Alexander demanded that Charidemus be banished from Athens (Arr. *Anab. Alex.* 1.10.6). With the wreckage of Thebes smoldering just over the horizon, Athens complied.

Charidemus was a commander skilled enough to be chosen to accompany Iphicrates to Amphipolis. But it was after the death of Cotys that Charidemus revealed the extent of his talent, both military and political. In 360/59 Cotys was murdered, and his kingdom was divided among his three sons, Bersiades in the west, Medocus in the center, and Cersobleptes in the east. Demosthenes advocated a policy of keeping the Odrysian kingdom divided, thus limiting a potential threat to Athenian interests in Thrace (23.103). But Charidemus took advantage of the confusion and division, becoming essentially the court general of Cersobleptes. Demosthenes relates that Charidemus fought on Cersobleptes' behalf against the Athenians in the Chersonese and supported Cersobleptes against his two pro-Athenian brothers (23.163–68). Charidemus clearly became an important player in Thrace at this time, and because of this

---

[6] For the date and reason for the honors, see Parke 1928: 170; Davies 1971: 571; Pritchett 1974–1991: vol. 2, 86; Kelly 1990.

[7] Kelly 1990: 103–4. See also Archibald (1998: 218–22) for Athenian relations with Cotys and Cersobleptes, which were not always as dire as Demosthenes contends.

he was positioned to help or harm Athenian interests to no end. In 357, the Athenians came to an arrangement with all three kings according to which Cersobleptes granted Athens the Chersonese through Charidemus' influence (Dem. 23.173).[8] In 353/2, Cersobleptes urged the Athenians to appoint Charidemus as their general in Thrace, because he alone could recover Amphipolis. Despite Demosthenes' objections to Charidemus, in 351/50 the Athenians sent out Charidemus with ten ships, mercenaries, and lots of money (Dem. 3.5). Demosthenes' attempts to turn Athens against Charidemus had obviously failed.[9]

It is remarkable that this humble light-armed mercenary from Euboea rose to such a level of prominence. After serving with Iphicrates he became a top advisor and kinsman of Cersobleptes, and in short order a citizen and prominent general of Athens. He died while serving as a military advisor to the Persian king. He had three sons by his Thracian wife, who were counted as Athenian citizens. They were still present in Athens in 330/29 and wealthy enough to pay off their father's naval debt (IG ii² 1627.205–222).[10] Just like Iphicrates, Charidemus rose from obscurity because of his military skill and by making himself an indispensible agent to both Athens and a Thracian king. As for many Athenians, the dynastic quarrels of Thracian rulers coupled with Athenian interest in the Thracian littoral provided Charidemus with an opportunity to obtain power and influence abroad and in Athens itself.

Chares had a long and checkered career as an Athenian commander, with a reputation as utterly profligate with little regard for the wishes of the polis. Yet, as many scholars have pointed out, the ancient sources, particularly Isocrates, were unduly harsh in their portrayal of Chares.[11] Chares was

---

[8] This treaty was arranged by Chares and is preserved in an inscription: IG ii² 126 = Bengston 1962–1969: vol. 2, no. 303; Harding 1985: no. 64.

[9] See Pritchett 1974–1991: vol. 2, 86–87; Archibald 1998: 221.

[10] See Davies 1971: 571–72.

[11] See Pritchett 1974–1991: vol. 2, 77–85; Moysey 1985; 1987; Salmond 1996; Bianco 2002.

consistently popular with the demos, elected general numerous times over several decades.[12] He may have been less scrupulous than Isocrates' pupil Timotheus, but he was no less so than countless other Athenian generals who were treated positively by the sources. As Moysey argues, Isocrates and Chares occupied opposite ends of the political spectrum in the mid-fourth century, a spectrum that was much narrower than that of the fifth century. Isocratean rhetoric is largely responsible for the distorted picture of Chares we have inherited.[13]

In 355, the last year of the Social War, Chares aided the satrap Aratabazus in his revolt from the Persian king Artaxerxes, a decision made apparently without any instruction from Athens. This has led many scholars to suggest that Chares was the archetypical condottiere.[14] We are told, however, that Chares joined in the satrap's revolt because he was desperately in need of money with which to pay his troops. Athens did not seem to object to his actions until the Persians complained and threatened to bolster Athens' rebellious allies (Diod. 16.22).[15] Chares' sack of Sestus two years later, after which he slaughtered the male inhabitants and enslaved the women and children, has also been censured by scholars (Diod. 16.34).[16] Sestus' fate, however, had been inflicted by Athens on a few unfortunate cities before Chares' career. There is no indication in the sources that Chares violated any Athenian directives in this action. Despite his service abroad and his seemingly independent and self-interested campaigns, the Athenians esteemed him enough to select him as one of their two generals at the Battle of Chaeronea (Diod. 16.85).

[12] Moysey (1985: 225) calls him the "darling of the demos."

[13] Moysey 1987.

[14] Parke (1974–1991: vol. 2, 77) says that Chares is generally regarded as the condottiere par excellence.

[15] See Pritchett (1974–1991: vol. 2, 80) for the suggestion that Athens tacitly approved of Chares' support of Artabazus until threatened by Persia. This situation recalls Chabrias' service in Egypt, for which see Chapter 1.

[16] Salmond (1996: 45), who largely defends Chares, nevertheless argues that the sack of Sestus reveals Chares' lack of scruples.

As with other generals in Thrace, Chares was sure to secure his own interests while campaigning in the region. He is listed by Theopompus as the general who opted to go to Sigeum instead of remaining in Athens (*FGrHist* 115 F 105). Though we are not told when Chares first settled in the northern Troad, Arrian tells us he was living there in 335, because he came from Sigeum to crown Alexander at Illium (*Anab. Alex.* 1.12.1). Pritchett thinks that Chares retired to Sigeum only after the Battle of Chaeronea, when many prominent Athenians left the city.[17] Alexander had ordered the Athenians to surrender Chares along with Charidemus and other prominent anti-Macedonian figures, yet the Athenians only exiled Charidemus in the end. At any rate, the political situation after 338 was less than favorable for generals who had fought the forces of Philip. Besides, the loss of Athens' autonomy in foreign affairs meant that there would be a shortage of lucrative campaigns for Athenian soldiers. Iphicrates seems to have realized the same after the imposition of the King's Peace in the 380s.

We catch two snippets of Chares' career after Chaeronea. The great mercenary captain Memnon of Rhodes had captured Mytilene and the rest of the island of Lesbos from Alexander's forces, and at his death in 333 he instructed that charge of island be given to the Persians Pharnabazus and Autophradates (Arr. *Anab. Alex.* 2.1). We are told that in the following year, the island had to be surrendered back to the Macedonians, and Chares was then in command of the anti-Macedonian forces stationed there (Arr. *Anab. Alex.* 3.2). It is fitting that Chares followed in the footsteps of Memnon, though he seems not to have enjoyed equivalent success in Persian service. There is one brief reference in Plutarch to Chares acting as the commander of a mercenary force stationed at Cape Taenarum in 331 (Plut. *Mor.* 848e).[18] This force became most famous after

---

[17] Pritchett 1974–1991: vol. 2, 100.

[18] Griffith (1935: 35) thinks the mention of Chares in this passage is a mistake, and should instead be read as Leosthenes. Though it is true that Leosthenes is the only man mentioned by name in other sources

the death of Alexander, but Alexander himself had ordered vast numbers of mercenaries in Asia to disband, and many of them had made their way to Cape Taenarum to await the highest bidder (Diod. 17.108.6; 17.111; 18.21.1–2). Cape Taenarum is at the southernmost tip of the Peloponnese, on an extremely rugged and isolated peninsula known today as the Mani. Its geography has always encouraged a fierce feeling of independence among its inhabitants, which led to the Mani playing a key role in modern Greece's struggle for independence in the nineteenth century. Perhaps this was the last possible place of refuge for Chares.

No further military exploit of Chares is recorded, likely because there was none worthy of recording. We do not know when or where he died, but given his connection to Sigeum, it is reasonable to guess he died there, if not in the mercenary camp at Taenarum. The death of Charidemus, on the other hand, is afforded a vivid description by both Diodorus (17.30) and Curtius (3.2.10–19). After Charidemus had been exiled from Athens in 335 by the order of Alexander, he offered his services to Darius III. Asked for his advice before what would be the Battle of Issus in 333, he cautioned Darius against going personally to battle. Charidemus suggested that Darius choose a capable and experienced commander – surely a reference to himself – to lead the army instead. Curtius portrays Charidemus in the mold of Demaratus of Sparta, who in Herodotus (7.101–5) is made to give Xerxes sage advice about the hardiness of the Spartans and their unshakeable deference as free men to the rule of law.[19] Darius, either because he played the part of a stereotypical Eastern despot accustomed only to flattery on the part of his advisors or because Charidemus' jealous rivals brought the wily Greek's intentions into question, ordered Charidemus' throat cut. Thus the once lowly Euboean mercenary who had charmed by turns the Athenians, the kings of Thrace, and even the Great King of Persia met his end.

as a commander of the force at Taenarum (Diod. 17.111), there is no solid reason to reject the mention of Chares as a commander also.
[19] As argued by Blänsdorf 1971.

There is no doubt that both Chares and Charidemus were military adventurers, extraordinarily resourceful and willing to take whatever measures necessary to achieve their objectives and advance their own careers. Such figures could best thrive outside of the Athenian polis and even outside of Athenian service. When Athens still had a hope of securing its interests on the Hellespont, these soldiers proved valuable to the home authorities, who turned a blind eye to their pillaging and profiteering and even to mercenary service for foreign powers. Yet once Macedonian ascendancy in the northern Aegean was assured, especially after Chaeronea, Chares and Charidemus had to turn elsewhere. Neither would again enjoy the kinds of military or diplomatic successes they had while campaigning in Thrace. If there was any consistency in their careers, it was in opposition to Philip and later Alexander. Forced out of Athens by the vengeful Macedonians, they were essentially driven into Persian service. As Charidemus found out, whereas a resourceful and unscrupulous warrior could find a sufficient and relatively secure outlet in Thrace, such was not necessarily the case at the court of the Great King. And once Darius was crushed by Alexander, only the barren and windswept backwater of Cape Taenarum was safe for mercenaries like Chares – a land as far as could be from the fertile pasturage of the Chersonese, the gold mines of Pangaeum, and the decadent feasts of the Odrysian court.

BIBLIOGRAPHY

Alcock, S. E. 1991. "Tomb Cult and the Post-Classical Polis." *AJA* **95**: 447–67.

Amyx, D. A. 1958. "The Attic Stelai: Part III. Vases and Other Containers." *Hesperia* **27**: 163–254.

Amyx, D. A., and W. K. Pritchett. 1958. "The Attic Stelai: Part III. Vases and Other Containers." *Hesperia* **27**: 255–310.

Anderson, J. K. 1963. "The Statue of Chabrias." *AJA* **67**: 411–13.

1970. *Military Theory and Practice in the Age of Xenophon*. Berkeley.

1974. *Xenophon*. London.

Andrewes, A. 1953. "The Generals in the Hellespont, 410–407 B.C." *JHS* **73**: 2–9.

Antonaccio, C. M. 1995. *An Archaeology of Ancestors: Tomb Cult and Hero Cult in Early Greece*. Lanham, Md.

Archibald, Z. 1998. *The Odrysian Kingdom of Thrace: Orpheus Unmasked*. Oxford.

2000. "Space, Hierarchy, and Community in Archaic and Classical Macedonia, Thessaly, and Thrace." In R. Brock and S. Hodkinson (eds.), *Alternatives to Athens: Varieties of Political Organization and Community in Ancient Greece*. Oxford. 212–33.

Armayor, O. K. 1978. "Did Herodotus Ever Go to the Black Sea?" *HSCPh* **82**: 45–62.

Asheri, D. 1990. "Herodotus on Thracian Society and History." In W. Burkert, G. Nenci, and O. Reverdin (eds.), *Hérodote et les peuples non grecs: neuf exposés suivis de discussions*. Geneva. 131–63.

Asheri, D., A. B. Lloyd, A. Corcella, O. Murray, A. Moreno, and M. Brosius. 2007. *A Commentary on Herodotus: Books I–IV*. Oxford.

Avery, H. C. 1979. "The Three Hundred at Thasos, 411 B.C." *CPh* **74**: 234–42.

Azoulay, V. 2004. "Exchange as Entrapment: Mercenary Xenophon?" In R. Lane Fox (ed.), *The Long March: Xenophon and the Ten Thousand*. New Haven, Conn. 289–304.

Baba, K. 1990. "The Macedonian/Thracian Coastland and the Greeks in the Sixth and Fifth Centuries B.C." *Kodai* 1: 1–23.

Badian, E. 1989. "History from 'Square Brackets.'" *ZPE* 79: 59–70.

2004. "Xenophon the Athenian." In C. Tuplin (ed.), *Xenophon and His World*. Stuttgart. 33–53.

Bakhuizen, S. C. 1970. *Salganeus and the Fortifications on Its Mountains*. Groningen.

Beloch, J. 1893–1904. *Griechische Geschichte*. 3 vols. Strasbourg.

1884. *Die attische Politik seit Perikles*. Leipzig.

Bengston, H. 1962–1969. *Die Staatsverträge des Altertums*. 3 vols. Munich.

Berve, H. 1937. *Miltiades: Studien zur Geschichte des Mannes und seiner Zeit*. Berlin.

1938. "Die Verschmelzungspolitik Alexanders des Grossen." *Klio* 31: 135–68.

1967. *Die Tyrannis bei den Griechen*. Munich.

Best, J. G. P. 1969. *Thracian Peltasts and Their Influence on Greek Warfare*. Groningen.

Bianco, E. 2002. "Carete: cane del popolo?" *AncSoc* 32: 1–28.

Bichler, R. 2004. "Herodotus' Ethnography: Examples and Principles." In V. Karageorghis and I. Taifacos (eds.), *The World of Herodotus. Proceedings of an International Conference held at the Foundation Anastasios G. Leventis, Nicosia, September 18–21, 2003*. Nicosia. 91–112.

Bicknell, P. 1982. "Themistokles' Father and Mother." *Historia* 31: 161–73.

Billows, R. A. 2010. *Marathon: The Battle that Changed Western Civilization*. New York.

Blänsdorf, J. 1971. "Herodot bei Curtius Rufus." *Hermes* 99: 11–24.

Blass, F. 1887. *Die attische Beredsamkeit*. 2nd ed. Leipzig.

Blok, J., and A. P. M. Lardinois (eds.). 2006. *Solon of Athens: New Historical and Philological Approaches*. Leiden.

Bosworth, A. B. 1980. "Alexander and the Iranians." *JHS* 100: 1–21.

2006 [1988]. *Conquest and Empire: The Reign of Alexander the Great*. Cambridge.

Bottini, A. 1988. *Antike Helme: Sammlung Lipperheide und andere Bestände des Antikenmuseums Berlin*. Mainz.

Bouzek, J. 2002. "Addenda to Pistiros I." In J. Bouzek, L. Domaradzka, and Z. Archibald (eds.), *Pistiros II: Excavations and Studies*. Prague. 343–48.

Bouzek, J., L. Domaradzka, and Z. Archibald. 2002. *Pistiros II: Excavations and Studies*. Prague.

Bouzek, J., M. Domaradzki, Z. Archibald, and L. Domaradzka. 1996. *Pistiros I: Excavations and Studies*. Prague.

Bowen, A., ed. 1992. *Plutarch: The Malice of Herodotus* = De malignitate Herodoti. Warminster.

Bradeen, D. W. 1963. "The Fifth-Century Archon List." *Hesperia* 32: 187–208.

Broneer, O. 1966. "The Cyclopean Wall on the Isthmus of Corinth and Its Bearing on Late Bronze Age Chronology." *Hesperia* 35: 346–62.

1968. "The Cyclopean Wall on the Isthmus of Corinth, *Addendum*." *Hesperia* 37: 25–35.

Broodbank, C. 1993. "Ulysses without Sails: Trade, Distance, Knowledge and Power in the Early Cyclades." *World Archaeology* 24: 315–31.

Brownson, C. L., and J. Dillery. 1998. *Xenophon's Anabasis*. Cambridge, Mass.

Buck, R. J. 1978. *A History of Boeotia*. Edmonton.

———. 1998. *Thrasybulus and the Athenian Democracy: The Life of an Athenian Statesman.* Stuttgart.

Buckler, J. 1972. "A Second Look at the Monument of Chabrias." *Hesperia* 41: 466–74.

Buraselis, K., and K. Meidani, eds. 2010. Μαραθών: η μάχη και ο αρχαίος Δήμος / *Marathon: The Battle and the Ancient Deme.* Athens.

Burckhardt, J., and P. Hilty. 1963. *History of Greek Culture*. New York.

Burckhardt, L. A. 1996. *Bürger und Soldaten: Aspekte der politischen und militärischen Rolle athenischer Bürger im Kriegswesen des 4. Jahrhunderts v. Chr.* Stuttgart.

Burich, N. J. 1994. "Timotheus, Son of Conon, Prostates of the Second Athenian Confederacy." PhD diss., University of Kansas.

Burkert, W., G. Nenci, and O. Reverdin. 1990. *Hérodote et les peuples non grecs: neuf exposés suivis de discussions.* Geneva.

Burnett, A. P., and C. N. Edmonson. 1961. "The Chabrias Monument in the Athenian Agora." *Hesperia* 30: 74–91.

Burrows, R. M., and P. N. Ure. 1907–1908. "Excavations at Rhitsona in Boeotia." *BSA* 14: 226–318.

Canfora, L. 2006. "Biographical Obscurities and Problems of Composition." In A. Rengakos and A. Tsakmakis (eds.), *Brill's Companion to Thucydides*. Leiden. 3–32.

Carey, C. 1994. "Comic Ridicule and Democracy." In R. G. Osborne and S. Hornblower (eds.), *Ritual, Finance, Politics: Athenian Democratic Accounts Presented to David Lewis*. Oxford. 69–83.

Cargill, J. 1981. *The Second Athenian League: Empire or Free Alliance?* Berkeley.

Cartledge, P. 2009. *Ancient Greek Political Thought in Practice*. Cambridge.

Cawkwell, G. L. 1962. "Notes on the Social War." *C&M* 23: 34–49.

———. 1976. "The Imperialism of Thrasybulus." *CQ* 26: 270–77.

Cawkwell, G. L., and R. Warner, eds. 1978. *Xenophon: A History of My Times (Hellenica)*. Harmondsworth.

Chankowski, V., and L. Domaradzka. 1999. "Réédition de l'inscription de Pistiros et problèmes d'interprétation." *BCH* 123: 247–58.

Chankowski, V., and A. Gotzev. 2002. "Pistiros et son territoire: les premiers résultats de la prospection franco-bulgare." In J. Bouzek, L. Domaradzka, and Z. Archibald (eds.), *Pistiros II: Excavations and Studies*. Prague. 271–82.

Coldstream, J. N. 1976. "Hero-Cults in the Age of Homer." *JHS* 96: 8–17.

Cole, J. W. 1975. "Peisistratus on the Strymon." *G&R* 22: 42–44.

Connor, W. R. 1971. *The New Politicians of Fifth-Century Athens*. Princeton, N.J.

Cook, B. F., ed. 1989. *The Rogozen Treasure: Papers of the Anglo-British Conference, 12 March 1987*. London.

Cooper, C. R. 2008. *Epigraphy and the Greek Historian*. Toronto.

Costa, E. A., Jr. 1974. "Evagoras I and the Persians, ca. 411 to 391 B.C." *Historia* 23: 40–56.

Crawley, R. 1903. *Thucydides' Peloponnesian War*. London.

Danov, K. M. 1976. *Altthrakien*. Berlin.

Davies, J. K. 1971. *Athenian Propertied Families, 600–300 B.C.* Oxford.

1993. *Democracy and Classical Greece*. 2nd ed. Cambridge, Mass.

De Angelis, F. 1994. "The Foundation of Selinous: Overpopulation or Opportunities?" In G. R. Tsetskhladze and F. De Angelis (eds.), *The Archaeology of Greek Colonisation*. Oxford. 87–110.

Dechev, D. 1957. *Die thrakischen Sprachreste*. Wien.

Delbrück, H. 1975. *History of the Art of War within the Framework of Political History*. Translated by Walter J. Renfroe, Jr. Westport, Conn.

Delebecque, E. 1951. *Euripide et la guerre du Péloponnèse*. Paris.

1957. *Essai sur la vie de Xénophon*. Paris.

Develin, R. 1989. *Athenian Officials, 684–321 B.C.* Cambridge.

Dewald, C., and J. Marincola 2006. *The Cambridge Companion to Herodotus*. Cambridge.

Diesner, H. J. 1959. "Peisistratidenexkurs und Peisistratidenbild bei Thukydides." *Historia* **8**: 12–22.

Dinsmoor, W. B. 1941. *Observations on the Hephaisteion*. Baltimore.

Dintsis, P. 1986. *Hellenistische Helme*. Rome.

Doenges, N. A. 1998. "The Campaign and Battle of Marathon." *Historia* **47**: 1–17.

Domaradzka, L. 1996. "Graffiti from Pistiros." In J. Bouzek, L. Domaradzka, and Z. H. Archibald (eds.), *Pistiros I: Excavations and Studies*. Prague. 89–94.

2002. "Addenda ad Pistiros I: The Pistiros-Vetren Inscription." In J. Bouzek, L. Domaradzka, and Z. Archibald (eds.), *Pistiros II: Excavations and Studies*. Prague. 339–42.

Domaradzka, L., and V. Velkov. 1994. "Kotys I (383/2–359 av. J.-C.) et l'emporion Pistiros de Thrace." *BCH* **118**: 1–15.

Domaradzki, M. 2000. "Problèmes des emporia en Thrace." In M. Domaradzki, L. Domaradzka, J. Bouzek, and J. Rostropowicz (eds.), *Pistiros et Thasos: structures économiques dans la péninsule Balkanique aux VIIe–IIe siècles avant J.-C.* Opole. 27–38.

2002. "An Interim Report on Investigations at Vetren-Pistiros 1995–1998." In J. Bouzek, L. Domaradzka, and Z. Archibald (eds.), *Pistiros II: Excavations and Studies*. Prague. 11–30.

Donlan, W. 1982. "The Politics of Generosity in Homer." *Helios* **9**: 1–15.

1989. "The Unequal Exchange between Glaucus and Diomedes in Light of the Homeric Gift-Economy." *Phoenix* **43**: 1–15.

Dover, K. J. 1978. *Greek Homosexuality*. Cambridge.

Duff, T. 1999. *Plutarch's Lives: Exploring Virtue and Vice*. Oxford.

Dunbar, N., ed. 1995. *Aristophanes: Birds*. Oxford.

Edmunds, L. 1971. "The Religiosity of Alexander." *GRBS* **12**: 363–91.

Edson, C. 1947. "Notes on the Thracian Phoros." *CPh* **42**: 88–105.

Edwards, M., ed. 2007. *Isaeus*. Austin, Tex.

Ellis, J. R. 1967. "The Order of the Olynthiacs." *Historia* **16**: 108–11.

Evans, J. A. S. 1963. "Note on Miltiades' Capture of Lemnos." *CPh* **58**: 168–70.

1993. "Herodotus and the Battle of Marathon." *Historia* **42**: 279–307.

Fehling, D. 1989. *Herodotus and his "Sources": Citation, Invention and Narrative Art.* Liverpool.

Ferguson, W. S. 1944. "The Attic Orgeones." *HThR* **37**: 1–140.

——— 1949. "Orgeonika." *Hesperia Supplements* **8**: 130–63.

Ferrill, A. 1997. *The Origins of War: From the Stone Age to Alexander the Great.* Rev. ed. Boulder, Colo.

Finley, M. I. 2002 [1954]. *The World of Odysseus.* New York.

Fitzpatrick, D. 2001. "Sophocles' 'Tereus.'" *CQ* **51**: 90–101.

Flower, M. A. 1994. *Theopompus of Chios: History and Rhetoric in the Fourth Century B.C.* Oxford.

Fol, A., ed. 1989. *The Rogozen Treasure.* Sofia.

——— ed. 2002. *Thrace and the Aegean: Proceedings of the Eighth International Congress of Thracology, Sofia – Yambol, 25–29 September 2000.*

Fol, A., and R. Ivanova. 1993. *Der Thrakische Dionysos.* Sofia.

Fol, A., and I. Marazov. 1977. *Thrace and the Thracians.* New York.

Fol, A., B. Nikolov, and R. F. Hoddinott. 1986. *The New Thracian Treasure from Rogozen, Bulgaria.* London.

Fornara, C. W. 1966. "The Hoplite Achievement at Psyttaleia." *JHS* **86**: 51–54.

——— 1970. "ΝΙΚΟΣΤΡΑΤΟΣ ΔΙΕΙΤΡΕΦΟΥΣ ΣΚΑΜΒΩΝΙΔΗΣ." *CQ* **20**: 41.

——— 1971a. *The Athenian Board of Generals from 501 to 404.* Wiesbaden.

——— 1971b. *Herodotus: An Interpretative Essay.* Oxford.

Forsdyke, E. J. 1919. "Some Arrow-heads from the Battlefield of Marathon." *Society of Antiquaries of London* **32**: 146–58.

Forsdyke, S. 2005. *Exile, Ostracism, and Democracy: The Politics of Expulsion in Ancient Greece.* Princeton, N.J.

Fossey, J. M. 1988. *Topography and Population of Ancient Boiotia.* Chicago.

Fraser, P. M. 2009. *Greek Ethnic Terminology.* Oxford.

Frost, F. J. 1998. *Plutarch's Themistocles: A Historical Commentary.* Rev. ed. Chicago.

Funke, P. 1980. *Homonoia und arche: Athen und die griechische Staatenwelt vom Ende des peloponnesischen Krieges bis zum Königsfrieden (404/3–387/6 v. Chr.).* Wiesbaden.

Gaebel, R. E. 2002. *Cavalry Operations in the Ancient Greek World.* Norman, Okla.

Garland, R. 1992. *Introducing New Gods: The Politics of Athenian Religion.* Ithaca, N.Y.

——— 2001. *The Piraeus: From the Fifth to the First Century B.C.* 2nd ed. London.

Garnsey, P. 1985. "Grain for Athens." *History of Political Thought* **5**: 62–75.

——— 1988. *Famine and Food Supply in the Graeco-Roman World: Responses to Risk and Crisis.* Cambridge.

Gauthier, P. 1973. "A propos des clérouquies athéniennes du Ve siècle." In M. I. Finley (ed.), *Problèmes de la terre en Grèce ancienne.* Paris. 163–78.

——— 1976. *Un commentaire historique des Poroi de Xénophon.* Geneva.

Geiger, J. 1988. "Nepos and Plutarch: From Latin to Greek Political Biography." *ICS* **13**: 245–256.

Golden, M. 2000. "Demosthenes and the Social Historian." In I. Worthington (ed.), *Demosthenes: Statesman and Orator.* London. 159–80.

Gomme, A. W. with A. Andrewes and K. J. Dover. 1945–1981. *A Historical Commentary on Thucydides*. 5 vols. Oxford.

Gregory, T. E. 1993. *Isthmia V: The Hexamilion and the Fortress*. Princeton, N.J.

Griffith, G. T. 1935. *The Mercenaries of the Hellenistic World*. Cambridge.

1950. "The Union of Corinth and Argos (392–386 B.C.)." *Historia* 1: 236–56.

1981. "Peltasts, and the Origin of the Macedonian Phalanx." In H. J. Dell (ed.), *Ancient Macedonian Studies in Honor of Charles F. Edson*. Thessaloniki. 161–67.

Grote, G. 1851–1856. *A History of Greece*. 12 vols. London.

Gruen, E. S. 1970. "Stesimbrotus on Miltiades and Themistocles." *CSCA* 3: 92–98.

Guthrie, W. K. C. 1952. *Orpheus and Greek Religion; A Study of the Orphic Movement*. 2nd ed. London.

Habicht, C. 1956. *Gottmenschentum und griechische Städte*. Munich.

Hall, E. 1989. *Inventing the Barbarian: Greek Self-Definition through Tragedy*. Oxford.

Hall, J. M. 1997. *Ethnic Identity in Greek Antiquity*. Cambridge.

2005. "*Arcades his oris*: Greek Projections on the Italian Ethnoscape?" In E. S. Gruen (ed.), *Cultural Borrowings and Ethnic Appropriations in Antiquity*. Stuttgart. 259–84.

Hamilton, C. D. 1979. "On the Perils of Extraordinary Honors: The Cases of Lysander and Conon." *AncW* 2: 87–90.

Hammond, N. G. L. 1956. "The Philaids and the Chersonese." *CQ* 6: 113–29.

1968. "The Campaign and the Battle of Marathon." *JHS* 88: 13–57.

1992. "Plataea's Relations with Thebes, Sparta and Athens." *JHS* 112: 143–50.

Hammond, N. G. L. with G. T. Griffith and F. W. Walbank. 1972–1988. *A History of Macedonia*. 3 vols. Oxford.

Hansen, M. H. 2006. *The Shotgun Method: The Demography of the Ancient Greek City-state Culture*. Columbia, Mo.

Hansen, M. H., and T. H. Nielsen. 2004. *An Inventory of Archaic and Classical Poleis*. Oxford.

Hanson, V. D., ed. 1991. *Hoplites: The Classical Greek Battle Experience*. London.

1995. *The Other Greeks: The Family Farm and the Agrarian Roots of Western Civilization*. New York.

1996. "Hoplites into Democrats: The Changing Ideology of Athenian Infantry." In J. Ober and C. Hedrick (eds.), *Demokratia: A Conversation on Democracies, Ancient and Modern*. Princeton, N.J. 289–312.

1998. *Warfare and Agriculture in Classical Greece*. Rev. ed. Berkeley.

2000. *The Western Way of War: Infantry Battle in Classical Greece*. 2nd ed. Berkeley.

Harding, P., ed. 1985. *From the End of the Peloponnesian War to the Battle of Ipsus*. Cambridge.

Harris, E. M. 1988. "The Date of Apollodorus' Speech against Timotheus and Its Implications for Athenian History and Legal Procedure." *AJPh* 109: 44–52.

1989. "Iphicrates at the Court of Cotys." *AJPh* 110: 264–71.

1995. *Aeschines and Athenian Politics*. New York.

Harrison, A. R. W. 1968–1971. *The Law of Athens*. 2 vols. Oxford.

Harrison, T. 2000. *Divinity and History: The Religion of Herodotus*. Oxford.

Hartog, F. 1988 [1980]. *The Mirror of Herodotus: The Representation of the Other in the Writing of History.* Translated by J. Lloyd. Berkeley.

Hatzfeld, J. 1940. *Alcibiade: Étude sur l'histoire d'Athènes à la fin du Ve siècle.* Paris.

Helms, M. W. 1988. *Ulysses' Sail: An Ethnographic Odyssey of Power, Knowledge, and Geographical Distance.* Princeton, N.J.

Henderson, J. 1990. "The *Demos* and the Comic Competition." In J. J. Winkler and F. I. Zeitlin (eds.), *Nothing to Do with Dionysos? Athenian Drama in Its Social Context.* Princeton, N.J. 271–313.

Henry, A. 1998. "The Sigma Enigma." *ZPE* 120: 45–48.

——— 2001. "The Sigma Stigma." *ZPE* 137: 93–105.

Herman, G. 1987. *Ritualised Friendship and the Greek City.* Cambridge.

Higgins, W. E. 1977. *Xenophon the Athenian: The Problem of the Individual and the Society of the Polis.* Albany, N.Y.

Hirsch, S. W. 1985. *The Friendship of the Barbarians: Xenophon and the Persian Empire.* Hanover, N.H.

Hoddinott, R. F. 1981. *The Thracians.* London.

Hoeck, A. 1891. "Das Odrysenreich in Thrakien: Im Fünften und Vierten Jahrhundert v. Chr." *Hermes* 26: 76–117.

Holladay, A. J. 1982. "Hoplites and Heresies." *JHS* 102: 94–103.

Hooker, J. T. 1989. "Gifts in Homer." *BICS* 36: 79–90.

Hornblower, S. 1991–2008. *A Commentary on Thucydides.* 3 vols. Oxford.

Horsfall, N. 1982. "Cornelius Nepos." In E. J. Kenny (ed.), *The Cambridge History of Classical Literature. Vol. 2, Latin Literature.* Cambridge. 290–92.

How, W. W., and J. Wells. 1912. *A Commentary on Herodotus.* 2 vols. Oxford.

Hunt, P. 1998. *Slaves, Warfare, and Ideology in the Greek Historians.* Cambridge.

——— 2001. "The Slaves and the Generals of Arginusae." *AJPh* 122: 359–80.

——— 2007. "Military Forces." In P. Sabin, H. van Wees, and M. Whitby (eds.), *The Cambridge History of Greek and Roman Warfare,* Vol. 1: *Greece, the Hellenistic World and the Rise of Rome.* Cambridge. 108–46.

Hunter, V. J. 1973. *Thucydides: The Artful Reporter.* Toronto.

Immerwahr, H. R. 1972. "Stesagoras II." *TAPA* 103: 181–86.

Irwin E. 2007. "'What's in a Name?' and Exploring the Comparable: Onomastics, Ethnography, and *Kratos* in Thrace." In E. Irwin and E. Greenwood (eds.), *Reading Herodotus: A Study of the Logoi in Book 5 of Herodotus' Histories.* Cambridge. 41–87.

Isaac, B. H. 1986. *The Greek Settlements in Thrace until the Macedonian Conquest.* Leiden.

Jeanmaire, H. 1951. *Dionysos; histoire du culte de Bacchus: l'orgiasme dans l'antiquité et les temps modernes, origine du théâtre en Grèce, orphisme et mystique dionysiaque, évolution du dionysisme après Alexandre.* Paris.

Jones, D. W. 1999. "The Archaeology and Economy of Homeric Gift Exchange." *Opuscula Atheniensia* 24: 11–24.

Jones, J. E., L. H. Sackett, and C. W. Eliot 1957. "τὸ Δέμα: A Survey of the Aigaleos-Parnes Wall." *BSA* 52: 152–89.

Jordan, B. 1970. "A Note on the Athenian Strategia." *TAPA* 101: 229–39.

Jowett, B. 1900. *Thucydides, Translated into English, to which is Prefixed an Essay on Inscriptions and a Note on the Geography of Thucydides.* Oxford.

Kagan, D. 1974. *The Archidamian War.* Ithaca, N.Y.

——— 1987. *The Fall of the Athenian Empire.* Ithaca, N.Y.

Kallet, L. 1983. "Iphikrates, Timotheos, and Athens, 371–360 B.C." *GRBS* **24**: 239–52.

——— 1999. "The Diseased Body Politic, Athenian Public Finance, and the Massacre at Mykalessos (Thucydides 7.27–29)." *AJPh* **120**: 223–44.

——— 2001. *Money and the Corrosion of Power in Thucydides: The Sicilian Expedition and Its Aftermath.* Berkeley.

Keaveney, A. 2003. *The Life and Journey of Athenian Statesman Themistocles (524–460 B.C.?) as a Refugee in Persia.* Lewiston, N.Y.

Keen, A. G. 2000. "'Grain for Athens': The Importance of the Hellespontine Route in Athenian Foreign Policy before the Peloponnesian War." In G. J. Oliver, R. Brock, T. J. Cornell, and S. Hodkinson (eds.), *The Sea in Antiquity.* Oxford. 63–73.

Keesling, C. M. 2004. "The Hermolykos/Kresilas Base and the Date of Kresilas of Kydonia." *ZPE* **147**: 79–91.

Kelly, D. 1990. "Charidemos's Citizenship: The Problem of *IG* ii² 207." *ZPE* **83**: 96–109.

Kinzl, K. H. 1968. *Miltiades-Forschungen.* Vienna.

Kirchner, J. 1901. *Prosopographia attica.* 2 vols. Berolini.

Knigge, U. 1991. *The Athenian Kerameikos: History, Monuments, Excavations.* Athens.

Kolarova, V. 1996. "Study on the Section of the Emporion's Fortification, As Discovered by the End of 1994." In J. Bouzek, L. Domaradzka, and Z. Archibald (eds.), *Pistiros I: Excavations and Studies.* Prague. 35–42.

Konecny, A. 2001. "*Katekopsen ten moran Iphikrates.* Das Gefecht bei Lechaion im Frühsommer 390 v. Chr." *Chiron* **31**: 79–127.

Kouzmanov, M. 2005. "The Horse in Thracian Burial Rites." In L. D. Jan Bouzek (ed.), *The Culture of Thracians and Their Neighbors. Proceedings of the International Symposium in Memory of Prof. Mieczyslaw Domaradzki, with a Round Table "Archaeological Map of Bulgaria."* Oxford. 143–46.

Krentz, P. 1980. "Foreigners against the Thirty: 'IG' 2² 10 Again." *Phoenix* **34**: 298–306.

——— 1982. *The Thirty at Athens.* Ithaca, N.Y.

——— ed. 1989. *Xenophon, Hellenika I-II.3.10.* Warminster.

——— 2000. "Deception in Archaic and Classical Greek Warfare." In H. van Wees (ed.), *War and Violence in Ancient Greece.* Swansea. 167–200.

——— 2010. *The Battle of Marathon.* New Haven, Conn.

Lane Fox, R., ed. 2004. *The Long March: Xenophon and the Ten Thousand.* New Haven, Conn.

Lape, S. 2002. "Solon and the Institution of the 'Democratic' Family Form." *CJ* **98**: 117–39.

——— 2010. *Race and Citizen Identity in the Classical Athenian Democracy.* Cambridge.

Lateiner, D. 1977. "Pathos in Thucydides." *Antichthon* 11: 42–51.

Lavelle, B. M. 1992. "The Pisistratids and the Mines of Thrace." *GRBS* 33: 5–23.

Lawrence, A. W. 1979. *Greek Aims in Fortification*. Oxford.

Lawrence, T. E. 1991 [1926]. *Seven Pillars of Wisdom: A Triumph*. Garden City, N.Y.

Lazaridis, D. 1986. "Les fortifications d'Amphipolis." In P. Leriche and H. Tréziny (eds.), *La fortification dans l'histoire du monde grec*. Paris. 31–38.

1997. *Amphipolis*. Athens.

Lazenby, J. F. 1993. *The Defence of Greece, 490–479 B.C.* Warminster.

2004. *The Peloponnesian War: A Military Study*. London.

Lazov, G. 1996. "Clay Altars." In J. Bouzek, M. Domaradzki, and Z. Archibald (eds.), *Pistiros I: Excavations and Studies*. Prague. 63–76.

Lee, J. W. 2007. *A Greek Army on the March: Soldiers and Survival in Xenophon's Anabasis*. Cambridge.

Lendon, J. E. 2005. *Soldiers and Ghosts: A History of Battle in Classical Antiquity*. New Haven, Conn.

Lengauer, W. 1979. *Greek Commanders in the 5th and 4th Centuries B.C.: Politics and Ideology: A Study of Militarism*. Warsaw.

Lewis, D. M. 1983. "Themistocles' Mother." *Historia* 32: 245.

Lewis, D. M., and R. S. Stroud. 1979. "Athens Honors King Evagoras of Salamis." *Hesperia* 48: 180–93.

Lippelt, O. 1910. *Die griechischen Leichtbewaffneten bis auf Alexander den Grossen*. Weida.

Lissarrague, F. 1990a. *L'autre guerrier: archers, peltastes, cavaliers dans l'imagerie attique*. Paris.

1990b. *The Aesthetics of the Greek Banquet: Images of Wine and Ritual*. Princeton, N.J.

Long, T. 1986. *Barbarians in Greek Comedy*. Carbondale, Ill.

Loukopoulou, L. 2005. "Addendum on the Inscription of Vetren: Custom Duties of the Odrysians." In L. D. Jan Bouzek (ed.), *The Culture of Thracians and Their Neighbors. Proceedings of the International Symposium in Memory of Prof. Mieczyslaw Domaradzki, with a Round Table "Archaeological Map of Bulgaria."* Oxford. 13–17.

MacDowell, D. M. 1965. "Nikostratos." *CQ* 15: 41–51.

ed. 1988. *Aristophanes, Wasps*. Oxford.

ed. 2000. *Demosthenes: On the False Embassy (Oration 19)*. Oxford.

Maitland, J. 1996. "'Marcellinus' Life of Thucydides: Criticism and Criteria in the Biographical Tradition." *CQ* 46: 538–58.

Malkin, I. 1987. *Religion and Colonization in Ancient Greece*. Leiden.

1998. *The Returns of Odysseus: Colonization and Ethnicity*. Berkeley.

March, D. A. 1997. "Konon and the Great King's Fleet, 396–394." *Historia* 46: 257–69.

Marinatos, S. 1970. "ΑΝΑΣΚΦΑΙ ΜΑΡΑΘΩΝΟΣ." *Praktika*: 5–28.

Martin, R. H., and A. J. Woodman, eds. 1989. *Tacitus, Annals. Book IV*. Cambridge.

Mattingly, H. B. 1971. "Formal Dating Criteria for Fifth Century Attic Inscriptions." In *Acta of the Vth International Congress of Greek and Latin Epigraphy, Cambridge 1967*. London. 27–33.

——— 1977. "The Second Athenian Coinage Decree." *Klio* **59**: 83–100.

——— 1999. "What Are the Right Dating Criteria for Fifth-Century Attic Texts?" *ZPE* **126**: 117–22.

McKechnie, P. R., and S. J. Kern, eds. 1988. *Hellenica Oxyrhynchia*. Warminster.

McQueen, E. I. 2000. *Herodotus Book VI*. London.

Meiggs, R. 1966. "The Dating of Fifth-Century Attic Inscriptions." *JHS* **86**: 86–98.

——— 1972. *The Athenian Empire*. Oxford.

Meiggs, R., and D. Lewis. 1988. *A Selection of Greek Historical Inscriptions to the End of the Fifth Century B.C.* Rev. ed. Oxford.

Mejer, J. 1978. *Diogenes Laertius and His Hellenistic Background*. Wiesbaden.

Meritt, B. D., H. T. Wade-Gery, and M. F. McGregor. 1939–1953. *The Athenian Tribute Lists*. 4 vols. Cambridge, Mass.

Middleton, D. F. 1982. "Thrasyboulos' Thracian Support." *CQ* **32**: 298–303.

Miller, M. 1991. "Foreigners at the Greek Symposium?" In W. J. Slater (ed.), *Dining in a Classical Context*. Ann Arbor, Mich. 59–81.

——— 1997. *Athens and Persia in the Fifth Century B.C.: A Study in Cultural Receptivity*. Cambridge.

Mitchell, L. G. 1997. *Greeks Bearing Gifts: The Public Use of Private Relationships in the Greek World, 435–323 B.C.* Cambridge.

Moreno, A. 2007. *Feeding the Democracy: The Athenian Grain Supply in the Fifth and Fourth Centuries BC*. Oxford.

Morris, I. 1992. *Death-ritual and Social Structure in Classical Antiquity*. Cambridge.

——— 1996. "The Strong Principle of Equality and the Archaic Origins of Greek Democracy." In J. Ober and C. Hedrick (eds.), *Demokratia: A Conversation on Democracies, Ancient and Modern*. Princeton, N.J. 19–48.

——— 2000. *Archaeology as Cultural History: Words and Things in Iron Age Greece*. Malden, Mass.

Moysey, R. A. 1985. "Chares and Athenian Foreign Policy." *CJ* **80**: 221–27.

——— 1987. "Isokrates and Chares: A Study in the Political Spectrum of Mid-Fourth Century Athens." *AncW* **15**: 81–86.

Munn, M. H. 1993. *The Defense of Attica: The Dema Wall and the Boiotian War of 378–375 B.C.* Berkeley.

Munson, R. V. 2001. *Telling Wonders: Ethnographic and Political Discourse in the Work of Herodotus*. Ann Arbor, Mich.

Neils, J. 2001. *The Parthenon Frieze*. Cambridge.

Newell, W. R. 2009. *The Soul of a Leader: Character, Conviction, and Ten Lessons in Political Greatness*. New York.

Nilsson, M. P. 1942. "Bendis in Athen." In *From the Collections of the Ny Carlsberg Glyptothek*. Vol. 3. Copenhagen.

Nippel, W. 1990. *Griechen, Barbaren und "Wilde": alte Geschichte und Sozialanthropologie*. Frankfurt am Main.

Nouhaud, M. 1982. *L'utilisation de l'histoire par les orateurs attiques*. Paris.

Nussbaum, G. B. 1967. *The Ten Thousand: A Study in Social Organization and Action in Xenophon's Anabasis.* Leiden.

Nye, J. S. 1990. *Bound to Lead: The Changing Nature of American Power.* New York.

2004. *Soft Power: The Means to Success in World Politics.* New York.

Ober, J. 1985. *Fortress Attica: Defense of the Athenian Land Frontier, 404–322 B.C.* Leiden.

1989. *Mass and Elite in Democratic Athens: Rhetoric, Ideology, and the Power of the People.* Princeton, N.J.

1998. *Political Dissent in Democratic Athens: Intellectual Critics of Popular Rule.* Princeton, N.J.

2005. *Athenian Legacies: Essays on the Politics of Going On Together.* Princeton, N.J.

Olson, S. D., ed. 2002. *Aristophanes: Acharnians.* Oxford.

Osborne, M. J. 1981. *Naturalization in Athens.* Brussels.

Osborne, M. J., and S. G. Byrne. 1996. *The Foreign Residents of Athens: An Annex to the Lexicon of Greek Personal Names: Attica.* Louvain.

Osborne, R. 1987a. "The Viewing and Obscuring of the Parthenon Frieze." *JHS* 107: 98–105.

1987b. *Classical Landscape with Figures: The Ancient Greek City and Its Countryside.* Dobbs Ferry, N.Y.

2000. "An Other View: An Essay on Political History." In B. Cohen (ed.), *Not the Classical Ideal: Athens and the Construction of the Other in Greek Art.* Leiden. 23–42.

2010. *Athens and Athenian Democracy.* Cambridge.

Owen, S. 2000. "New Light on Thracian Thasos: A Reinterpretation of the 'Cave of Pan.'" *JHS* 120: 139–43.

2006. Mortuary Display and Cultural Contact: A Cemetery at Kastri on Thasos. *OJA* 25: 357–70.

Parissaki, M.-G. G. 2007. *Prosopography and Onomasticon of Aegean Thrace.* Athens.

Parke, H. W. 1933. *Greek Mercenary Soldiers: From the Earliest Times to the Battle of Ipsus.* Chicago.

Parker, R. 2004. "One Man's Piety: The Religious Dimension of the *Anabasis.*" In R. Lane Fox (ed.), *The Long March: Xenophon and the Ten Thousand.* New Haven, Conn. 130–53.

Pearson, L. 1941. "Historical Allusions in the Attic Orators." *CPh* 36: 209–29.

Peek, W. 1941. "Heilige Gesetze." *Mitteilungen des Deutschen Archäologischen Instituts, Athenische Abteilung* 66: 171–217.

Pelling, C. B. R. 2002. *Plutarch and History.* London.

Pemberton, E. G. 1988. "An Early Red-Figured Calyx-Krater from Ancient Corinth." *Hesperia* 57: 227–35.

Pesely, G. E. 1989. "Hagnon." *Athenaeum* 67: 191–209.

Pinney, G. 1983. "Achilles Lord of Scythia." In W. G. Moon (ed.), *Ancient Greek Art and Iconography.* Madison, Wis. 127–46.

Planeaux, C. 2000. "The Date of Bendis' Entry into Attica." *CJ* 96: 165–92.

Podlecki, A. J. 1975. *The Life of Themistocles: A Critical Survey of the Literary and Archaeological Evidence*. Montreal.

Popov, D. 1977. "Le relief de Copenhague." *Archéologie (Sofia, Académie des Sciences)* 19: 1–13.

Popović, V. 1964. "Les masques funéraires de la nécropole archaïque de Trebenište." *Archaeologia Iugoslavica* 5: 33–44.

Poulter, A. G., ed. 1983. *Ancient Bulgaria: Papers Presented to the International Symposium on the Ancient History and Archaeology of Bulgaria, University of Nottingham, 1981*. Nottingham.

Pownall, F. 2008. "Theopompos and the Public Documentation of Fifth-Century Athens." In C. R. Cooper (ed.), *Epigraphy and the Greek Historian*. Toronto. 119–28.

Pritchett, W. K. 1953. "The Attic Stelai, Part I." *Hesperia* 22: 225–99.

1958. "New Light on Thermopylai." *AJA* 62: 203–13.

1965–1992. *Studies in Ancient Greek Topography*. 8 vols. Berkeley.

1974–1991. *The Greek State at War*. 5 vols. Berkeley.

1993. *The Liar School of Herodotos*. Amsterdam.

Pritchett, W. K., and A. Pippin. 1956. "The Attic Stelai: Part II." *Hesperia* 25: 178–328.

Quinn, T. J. 1995. "Thucydides and the Massacre at Mycalessus." *Mnemosyne* 48: 571–74.

Raaflaub, K. A. 1999. "Archaic and Classical Greece." In K. A. Raaflaub and N. Rosenstein (eds.), *War and Society in the Ancient and Medieval Worlds: Asia, the Mediterranean, Europe, and Mesoamerica*. Washington, D.C. 129–61.

Raeck, W. 1981. *Zum Barbarenbild in der Kunst Athens im 6. und 5. Jahrhundert v. Chr.* Bonn.

Rahn, P. J. 1981. "The Date of Xenophon's Exile." In G. S. Shrimpton and D. J. McCargar (eds.), *Classical Contributions: Studies in Honor of Malcolm Francis McGregor*. Locust Valley, N.Y. 103–19.

Raubitschek, A. E. 1941. "The Heroes of Phyle." *Hesperia* 10: 284–95.

Ramón Palerm, V. 1992. *Plutarco y Nepote: Fuentes e interpretación del modelo biográfico plutarqueo*. Zaragoza.

Rehdantz, C. O. A. 1845. *Vitae Iphicratis, Chabriae, Timothei, Atheniensium*. Berolini.

Rhodes, P. J. 1981. *A Commentary on the Aristotelian Athenaion Politeia*. Oxford.

1998. *Thucydides, History IV.1-V.24*. Warminster.

2006. "The Reforms of Solon: An Optimistic View." In J. H. Blok and A. P. M. H. Lardinois (eds.), *Solon of Athens: New Historical and Philological Approaches*. Leiden. 248–60.

Rhodes, P. J., and R. Osborne 2003. *Greek Historical Inscriptions: 404–323 BC*. Oxford.

Ridgway, B. S. 1992. "Aristonautes' Stele, Athens Nat. Mus. 738." In H. T. Froning Heide and Mielsch Harald (eds.), *Kotinos: Festschrift für Erika Simon*. Mainz. 270–75.

Roisman, J. 1993. *The General Demosthenes and His Use of Military Surprise*. Stuttgart.

Roller, D. W. 1974. "The Date of the Walls at Tanagra." *Hesperia* **43**: 260–63.

Romm, J. S. 1998. *Herodotus*. New Haven, Conn.

Rood, T. 2006. "Herodotus and Foreign Lands." In C. Dewald and J. Marincola (eds.), *The Cambridge Companion to Herodotus*. Cambridge. 290–305.

Rosivach, V. J. 1999. "Enslaving 'Barbaroi' and the Athenian Ideology of Slavery." *Historia* **48**: 129–57.

Roy, J. 1998. "The Threat from the Piraeus." In P. Cartledge, P. Millett, and S. Von Reden (eds.), *Kosmos: Essays in Order, Conflict, and Community in Classical Athens*. Cambridge. 191–202.

Rusten, J. S., ed. 1989. *Thucydides, The Peloponnesian War, Book II*. Cambridge.

2006. "Thucydides and Comedy." In A. Rengakos and A. Tsakmakis (eds.), *Brill's Companion to Thucydides*. Leiden. 547–58.

Rusten, J. S., J. Henderson, D. Konstan, R. Rosen, and N. W. Slater. 2011. *The Birth of Comedy: Text, Documents, and Art from Athenian Comic Competitions*. Baltimore.

Sacks, K. 1990. *Diodorus Siculus and the First Century*. Princeton, N.J.

Salmond, P. D. 1996. "Sympathy for the Devil: Chares and Athenian Politics." *G&R* **43**: 43–53.

Salviat, F. 1999. "Le roi Kersobleptès, Maronée, Apollonia, Thasos, Pistiros et l'histoire d'Hérodote." *BCH* **123**: 259–73.

Scott, L. 2005. *Historical Commentary on Herodotus, Book 6*. Leiden.

Schröder, B. 1912. "Thrakische Helme." *Jahrbuch des Deutschen Archäologischen Instituts* **27**: 317–44.

Schwartz, E. 1889. "Quellenuntersuchungen zur griechischen Geschichte II." *RhM* **44**: 161–93.

Seaford, R. 1994. *Reciprocity and Ritual: Homer and Tragedy in the Developing City-State*. Oxford.

Seager, R. 1967. "Thrasybulus, Conon and Athenian Imperialism, 396–386 B.C." *JHS* **87**: 95–115.

Sealey, R. 1955. "Athens after the Social War." *JHS* **75**: 74–81.

1993. *Demosthenes and His Time: A Study in Defeat*. New York.

Sears, M. A. 2011. "The Topography of the Pylos Campaign and Thucydides' Literary Themes." *Hesperia* **80**: 157–68.

Shapiro, H. A. 2004. "Leagros the Satyr." In C. Marconi (ed.), *Greek Vases, Images, Contexts, and Controversies: Proceedings of the Conference Sponsored by the Center for the Ancient Mediterranean at Columbia University, 23–24 March 2002*. Leiden. 1–12.

Shrimpton, G. 1980. "The Persian Cavalry at Marathon." *Phoenix* **34**: 20–37.

Simms, R. 1988. "The Cult of the Thracian Goddess Bendis in Athens and Attica." *AncW* **18**: 59–76.

Slater, N. W. 1999. "The Vase as Ventriloquist: Kalos-inscriptions and the Culture of Fame." In E. A. MacKay (ed.), *Signs of Orality: The Oral Tradition and Its Influence in the Greek and Roman World*. Leiden. 143–61.

Sommerstein, A. H. 1996. "How to Avoid Being a Komodoumenos." *CQ* **46**: 327–56.

Spence, I. G. 1993. *The Cavalry of Classical Greece: A Social and Military History with Particular Reference to Athens*. Oxford.

1995. "Thucydides, Woodhead, and Kleon." *Mnemosyne* **48**: 411–37.

Staes, B. 1893. "Ο ΕΝ ΜΑΡΑΘѠΝΙ ΤΥΜΒΟΣ." *Mitteilungen des Deutschen Archäologischen Instituts, Athenische Abteilung* **18**: 46–63.

Stahl, H.-P. 1966. *Thukydides*. Munich.

Stahl, M. 1987. *Aristokraten und Tyrannen im archaischen Athen: Untersuchungen zur Überlieferung, zur Sozialstruktur und zur Entstehung des Staates*. Stuttgart.

Stevens, G. P. 1936. "The Periclean Entrance Court of the Acropolis of Athens." *Hesperia* **5**: 443–520.

Storch, R. H. 2001. "The Silence Is Deafening: Persian Arrows Did Not Inspire the Greek Charge at Marathon." *AAntHung* **41**: 381–94.

Strauss, B. S. 1984. "Thrasybulus and Conon: A Rivalry in Athens in the 390's B.C." *AJPh* **105**: 37–48.

1987. *Athens after the Peloponnesian War: Class, Faction, and Policy, 403–386 BC*. Ithaca, N.Y.

1996. "The Athenian Trireme, School of Democracy." In J. Ober and C. W. Hedrick (eds.), *Demokratia: A Conversation on Democracies, Ancient and Modern*. Princeton, N.J. 313–25.

2000. "Democracy, Kimon, and the Evolution of Athenian Naval Tactics in the Fifth Century BC." In T. H. Nielsen, P. Flensted-Jensen, and L. Rubinstein (eds.), *Polis and Politics: Studies in Ancient Greek History Presented to Mogens Herman Hansen on his Sixtieth Birthday, August 20, 2000*. Copenhagen. 315–26.

2004. *The Battle of Salamis: The Naval Encounter That Saved Greece – And Western Civilization*. New York.

2009. *The Spartacus War*. New York.

Stronk, J. P. 1995. *The Ten Thousand in Thrace: An Archaeological and Historical Commentary on Xenophon's Anabasis, Books VI.iii-vi-VII*. Amsterdam.

Stylianou, P. J. 1988. "How Many Naval Squadrons Did Athens Send to Evagoras?" *Historia* **37**: 463–71.

1998. *A Historical Commentary on Diodorus Siculus, Book 15*. Oxford.

Taplin, O. 1983. "Tragedy and Trugedy." *CQ* **33**: 331–33.

Taylor, M. C. 2002. "One Hundred Heroes of Phyle?" *Hesperia* **71**: 377–97.

Testard, M., and J.-L. Brunaux. 2004. "Don, banquet et funérailles chez les Thraces." *L'Homme* **170**: 165–80.

Theodossiev, N. 1998. "The Dead with Golden Faces: Dasaretian, Pelagonian, Mygdonian and Boeotian Funeral Masks." *OJA* **17**: 345–67.

2000a. "The Dead with Golden Faces II: Other Evidence and Connections." *OJA* **19**: 175–209.

2000b. *North-western Thrace from the Fifth to First Centuries BC*. Oxford.

2011. "Ancient Thrace during the First Millennium BC." In G. R. Tsetskhladze (ed.), *The Black Sea, Greece, Anatolia and Europe in the First Millennium BC*. Louvain. 1–60.

Thomas, R. 1992. *Literacy and Orality in Ancient Greece*. Cambridge.

2000. *Herodotus in Context: Ethnography, Science, and the Art of Persuasion.* Cambridge.

Thompson, W. E. 1985. "Chabrias at Corinth." *GRBS* **26**: 51–57.

Titchener, F. 2003. "Cornelius Nepos and the Biographical Tradition." *G&R* **50**: 85–99.

Tod, M. N. 1950. *A Selection of Greek Historical Inscriptions.* Oxford.

Todd, S. C. 1990. "The Use and Abuse of the Attic Orators." *G&R* **37**: 159–78.

Topper, K. R. 2007. "The Symposium and its Past in Athenian Vase Painting, ca. 530–450 B.C." PhD diss., Harvard University.

Traill, J. S. 1975. *The Political Organization of Attica: A Study of the Demes, Trittyes, and Phylai, and their Representation in the Athenian Council.* Princeton, N.J.

Tsetskhladze, G. R. 1998. "Who Built the Scythian and Thracian Royal and Elite Tombs?" *OJA* **17**: 55–92.

Tsiafakis, D. 2000. "The Allure and Repulsion of Thracians in the Art of Classical Athens." In B. Cohen (ed.), *Not the Classical Ideal: Athens and the Construction of the Other in Greek Art.* Leiden. 364–89.

Tuplin, C. 1982. "The Date of the Union of Corinth and Argos." *CQ* **32**: 75–83.

Tuplin, C., and V. Azoulay. 2004. *Xenophon and His World: Papers from a Conference Held in Liverpool in July 1999.* Stuttgart.

Tzvetkova, J. 2008. *History of the Thracian Chersonese (from the Trojan War to the Time of the Roman Conquest* (in Bulgarian with an English summary). Veliko Tarnovo.

Ustinova, Y. 1996. "Orgeones in Phratries: A Mechanism of Social Integration in Attica." *Kernos* **9**: 227–42.

van de Maele, S. 1980. "Démosthène et Cléon à Pylos." In Jean-Benoît Caron, Michel Fortin, and Gilles Maloney (eds.), *Mélanges d'études anciennes offerts à Maurice Lebel.* Quebec. 119–24.

van Wees, H. 1995. "Princes at Dinner: Social Event and Social Structure in Homer." In J.-P. Crielaard (ed.), *Homeric Questions.* Amsterdam. 147–82.

1998. "Greeks Bearing Arms: The State, the Leisure Class, and the Display of Weapons in Archaic Greece." In N. Fisher and H. van Wees (eds.), *Archaic Greece: New Approaches and New Evidence.* London. 333–78.

2004. *Greek Warfare: Myth and Realities.* London.

2006. "Mass and Elite in Solon's Athens: The Property Classes Revisited." In J. H. Blok and A. P. M. H. Lardinois (eds.), *Solon of Athens: New Historical and Philological Approaches.* Leiden. 351–89.

Vanderpool, E. 1966. "A Monument to the Battle of Marathon." *Hesperia* **35**: 93–106.

1968. "New Ostraka from the Athenian Agora." *Hesperia* **37**: 117–20, 398.

Venedikov, I. 1961. *The Panagyurishte Gold Treasure.* Sofia.

Vidal-Naquet, P. 1999 [1968]. "La tradition de l'hoplite athènien." In J.-P. Vernant (ed.), *Problèmes de la guerre en Grèce ancienne.* Rev. ed. Paris. 212–41.

Vokotopoulou, I. 1982. "Phrygische Helme." *Archäologischer Anzeiger* **93**: 497–520.

1985. *ΣΙΝΔΟΣ: ΚΑΤΑΛΟΓΟΣ ΤΗΣ ΕΚΘΕΣΙΣ.* Thessaloniki.

Von Salis, A. 1926. *Das Grabmal des Aristonautes.* Berlin.

Vos, M. F. 1963. *Scythian Archers in Archaic Attic Vase-Painting.* Groningen.

Wade-Gery, H. T. 1932. "Thucydides the Son of Melesias: A Study of Periklean Policy." *JHS* **52**: 205–27.

1951. "Miltiades." *JHS* **71**: 212–21.

Walbank, M. B. 1978. *Athenian Proxenies of the Fifth Century, B.C.* Toronto.

Wallace, M. B. 1970. "Early Greek 'Proxenoi.'" *Phoenix* **24**: 189–208.

Wardman, A. E. 1959. "Tactics and the Tradition of the Persian Wars." *Historia* **8**: 49–60.

Warner, R., and M. I. Finley. 1972 [1954]. *Thucydides: History of the Peloponnesian War*. London.

Webber, C. 2011. *The Gods of Battle: The Thracians at War, 1500 BC–AD 150*. Barnsley.

Whitby, M. 1984. "The Union of Corinth and Argos: A Reconsideration." *Historia* **33**: 295–308.

White, R. 1991. *The Middle Ground: Indians, Empires, and Republics in the Great Lakes Region, 1650–1815*. Cambridge.

Whitley, J. 1988. "Early States and Hero Cults: A Re-Appraisal." *JHS* **108**: 173–82.

Will, E. 1960. "Chabrias et les Finances de Tachos." *REA* **62**: 254–75.

Williams, D. 1991. "Onesimos and the Getty Iliupersis." *Greek Vases in the J. Paul Getty Museum* **5**: 41–64.

Wiseman, J. 1978. *The Land of the Ancient Corinthians*. Gothenburg.

Woodcock, E. C. 1928. "Demosthenes Son of Alcisthenes." *HSCPh* **39**: 93–108

Woodhead, A. G. 1960. "Thucydides' Portrait of Cleon." *Mnemosyne* **13**: 289–317.

1962. "Chabrias, Timotheus, and the Aegean Allies, 375–373 B.C." *Phoenix* **16**: 258–266.

Worthington, I. 1991. "Greek Oratory, Revision of Speeches and the Problem of Historical Reliability." *C&M* **42**: 55–74.

Yunis, H., ed. 2001. *Demosthenes: On The Crown*. Cambridge.

Zelnick-Abramovitz, R. 2004. "Settlers and Dispossessed in the Athenian Empire." *Mnemosyne* **57**: 325–45.

Zhivkova, L. 1973. *Das Grabmal von Kasanlak*. Sofia.

Zournatzi, A. 2000. "Inscribed Silver Vessels of the Odrysian Kings: Gifts, Tribute, and the Diffusion of the Forms of 'Achaemenid' Metalware in Thrace." *AJA* **104**: 683–706.

INDEX

INDEX

Alexander III (the Great) of Macedon, 29, 30, 45, 122, 171, 179, 232, 234, 274, 286, 292, 295, 296

alopekis (Thracian cap), 151, 196, 203

ambition, 114, 115, 117, 129, 130, 133, 134, 164, 223

Thrace as an outlet for, 43, 50, 115. *See* refuge

Amphipolis, 11, 12, 41, 47, 88, 127, 128, 138, 167, 218, 219, 262, 287, 290, 291

its foundation, 77–78, 257–60

Amyntas of Macedon, 58, 126, 127, 128

Anabasis (work of Xenophon), 15, 110, 111, 115, 116, 145, 169, 170, 180, 301, 309, 312

Anaxibius, 116, 121, 122, 123, 164, 281

Antalcidas, 123, 125, 250

Apollonia, 27, 28, 311

Apsinthioi (Thracian tribe), 10, 59, 239, 241, 243

Aratabazus, 294

archaeology. *See* material finds

archē, 63

Archelaus of Macedon, 102

archers, archery, 44, 87, 114, 161, 193, 195, 207, 242, 245, 246, 248, 260

Archibald, Zofia, 6, 8, 9, 10, 13, 24, 25, 26, 36, 51, 52, 56, 69, 70, 71, 72, 75, 87, 124, 126, 127, 157, 179, 180, 201, 214, 219, 229, 254, 256, 257, 258, 261, 292, 293, 299, 300, 301, 302, 306, 307

Archidamus, 250

Archinus, 265, 267, 268, 271, 272

Ares, 145

Argilus, 78

Arginusae, battle of, 266, 305

Argos, the Argives, 56, 120, 130, 131, 132, 304, 313, 314

Ariobarzanes, 167

Aristagoras of Miletus, 11, 33, 37, 77

aristocratic ethos. *See* aristocrats, aristocracy

aristocrats, aristocracy, 44, 54, 57, 58, 60, 61, 66, 67, 106, 109, 110, 119, 138, 152, 174, 176, 178, 179, 183, 191, 196, 197, 225–26, 231

Aristonautes naiskos, the, 201–3, 204

Aristophanes, 1, 2, 12, 17, 41, 82, 145, 146, 147, 159, 160, 164, 176, 200, 213, 228, 250, 261, 262, 302, 309

his coinage of *Thraikophoitai*, 2

Aristotle, 20, 148, 282

art, 191–208

its value as evidence, 25

Artaxerxes I, 34, 276, 294

Artemis, 146, 151, 219. *See* Bendis

Asclepius, 154

aselgeia, 142, 143

Aspendus, 97, 121, 162

Athena, 54

Athenaeus, 20, 54, 212, 213

Athenaiōn Politeia (Aristotelian), 20, 21, 53, 54, 55, 56, 101, 174, 175, 177, 196

its value as a source, 21

Athenian Empire, 93, 94, 98, 109

athletic competition, 146, 176, 217, 221, 227

Athos Peninsula, 8, 222

Attic Stelai, the, 107–8, 155

authority. *See* exousia

autonomy, 5, 30, 32, 35, 37, 39, 97, 116, 152, 157, 215, 257, 274, 295

Axiochus, 106, 108, 109

Axius River, 6, 8, 12

Bacchae (play of Euripides), 159

Balkans, the Balkan Peninsula, 30, 157, 183, 185, 186, 191

bandits, banditry, 61, 149. *See* raids, raiding

banquets. *See* feasts, feasting

barbarians, barbarism, 17, 61, 82, 87, 119, 128, 135, 143, 146, 147, 148, 149, 154, 156, 157, 161, 169, 171–72, 173, 193, 196, 216, 232, 253

basileus, basileis, 4, 6, 63, 141, 216, 231

Battus, 217

Bendideia, 150, 151, 152, 153, 154. *See* Bendis

Bendis, 43, 56, 75, 204–6, 264. *See* religion

her cult at Athens, 149–54

316

exousia, 47, 48, 52, 143, 182, 216, 232
extravagance. *See poluteleia*

feasts, feasting, 179, 180, 208–17, 221, 231
Ferrill, Arther, 237, 287, 303
foreign policy, Athenian, 41, 62, 69, 73,
    78, 98, 110, 124, 125
Forsdyke, Sara, 50, 54, 57, 58, 245, 246,
    303
fortification, 29
    of Alcibiades' estates in Thrace, 96
    of the elder Miltiades, 44, 64, 239–43
    of Hagnon at Amphipolis, 78, 258–60
    of Mycalessus, 80
    of the Spartans at Decelea, 79
frontier, 36, 40, 256
    Thrace as, 40
funeral rites, 221, 224, 229
funerary masks, 43, 56, 183–91. *See* gold

Gallipoli Peninsula, 7, 41, 44. *See*
    Chersonese (Thracian)
Ganos, 111
garrisons, 78, 95, 269
generals, generalship, 84–85, 93, 97, 99,
    119, 120, 123, 166, 238, 276, 290
    and democracy, 47, 48, 73
genos, 8. *See* tribe
Geometric period, the, 186, 187, 188, 190
Getai (Thracian tribe), 87
gift exhange, 116, 169, 180, 208–17, 231
gold, 41, 43, 183–91. *See* gold mines, gold
    mining
gold mines, gold mining, 5, 12, 13, 14, 53,
    56, 57, 66, 70, 72, 73, 88, 89, 156,
    195, 256, 257, 297
gold vessels, 6, 24, 211–12
grain trade, 49, 59, 60, 93, 98, 136
graphē paranomōn, 265. *See* law, law
    courts
graphē xenias, 165. *See* law, law courts
Grave Circle A (Mycenae), 184
Great King (Persian), 32, 34, 37, 39, 94,
    109, 164, 213, 232, 282, 293, 296,
    297, 307
Grunium, 34, 37
guest-friendship. *See xenia*

Haemus Mountains, 8, 10, 30, 274
Hagnon, 42, 81, 85, 87, 100
    his foundation of Amphipolis, 12, 41,
        77–78, 257–60
    his possible cult at Amphipolis, 218,
        219
    his service for Sitalces, 78–79, 103,
        257, 260
    his ties to Alcibiades, 103
    his ties to Thrasybulus, 100, 105
    as *proboulos*, 79
Hanson, Victor Davis, 175, 236, 240, 275,
    304
Harpocration, 121, 163, 215
Harris, Edward, 18, 123, 126, 128, 129,
    134, 135, 167, 168, 304
Hebryzelmis (Thracian king), 124, 125,
    126
Hecuba (play of Euripides), 17, 143, 144
Hegesipyle, 66, 67, 88
Hegesistratus, 55. *See* Pisistratids
Hellenism, 33, 200
Hellenization, 189
Hellespont, the, 2, 7, 10, 14, 35, 37, 55,
    62, 65, 67, 72, 92, 93, 94, 95, 97,
    98, 116, 121, 122, 123, 138, 164,
    220, 221, 223, 227, 239, 273, 276,
    278, 297
helmets, 201–8
Heracles, 31, 222
Heraclides of Maronea, 36, 37, 114, 169,
    215
hermokopidai, 107–8, 155, 164
Hermolycus, 83, 84
herms. *See hermokopidai*
Herodotus
    his account of Marathon, 244
    his value as a source, 13–14
    his views on Thrace, 32, 43, 145,
        147–48, 217, 221, 224, 256
    and pro-Philaid bias, 62
heroes, heroic ethos, 25, 30, 40, 43, 141,
    179, 183, 188–90, 207, 209, 211,
    214, 233, 237. *See basileus, basleis*
Hesiod, 144
Hipparchus, 54, 55. *See* Pisistratids
Hippias, 55, 57. *See* Pisistratids

nobles, nobility. *See* aristocrats, aristocracy
nomos, nomoi, 14, 211, 217, 222
Notium, battle of, 35, 96, 97, 138, 163
numismatics, 24
Nymphodorus of Abdera, 75, 76, 127

Ober, Josiah, 49, 168, 175, 177, 178, 241, 269, 304, 308, 309, 312
Octavian (Augustus), 29
Odomantoi (Thracian tribe), 12, 261, 262
Odrysai. *See* Odrysian kingdom, Odrysians
Odrysian kingdom, Odrysians, 8, 9, 10, 15, 24, 26, 29, 32, 36, 42, 111, 118, 123, 124, 126, 136, 138, 144, 153, 157, 165, 172, 183, 200, 211, 214, 221, 229, 280, 286, 291, 292, 297
    their alliance with Athens, 74–75
    their economic ties with Greeks, 27
Odysseus, 149, 189, 229, 303, 307
Old Oligarch, the, 16, 112, 177, 288
oligarchs, oligarchy, 82, 85, 86, 94, 103, 113, 130, 161, 162, 272
oligarchy of 411, 79, 85, 91, 93, 101, 102, 104, 136
Olorus (father of Thucydides), 14, 66, 88
Olorus (father-in-law of the younger Miltiades), 14, 66, 70, 73
Olympia, Olympic Games, 171, 223, 226, 227, 228, 231
Onesimus, 104, 105, 243. *See* vase-painting
Ophryneum, 108
oracles, 11, 28, 59, 63, 154, 158, 217, 222, 256. *See* Delphi
oratory
    its value as a source, 18–19
orgeōnes, 152
Orpheus, Orphic religion, 29, 51, 154, 158, 299, 304
Osborne, Robin, 156, 177, 178, 197, 199, 236, 267, 301, 309, 310
ostracism, 50, 81
ostrakon, ostraka, 81, 313
outlet. *See* ambition; refuge
Ovid, 144
Owen, Sara, 218
Oxyrhynchus historian, the, 103, 272

Pactye, 35, 239
Pallene, battle of, 53, 58
Panagyurishte Treasure, 24, 212, 313
Pangaeum, Mt., 10, 11, 12, 41, 51, 53, 56, 57, 77, 156, 256, 258, 261, 297. *See* gold mines, gold mining
pankration, 83, 223
Parnes, Mt., 241, 269, 305
Paros, 47, 70, 138
Parthenon, 83, 197, 198, 199, 231, 308, 309
Parthenon frieze, 197
Pelium, Mt., 87
Peloponnese, 45, 116, 296
Peloponnesian War, 5, 10, 12, 14, 19, 27, 33, 37, 42, 44, 60, 73, 74, 76, 79, 81, 88, 103, 104, 119, 144, 145, 153, 154, 179, 234, 236, 250, 263, 264, 266, 274, 301, 304, 306, 307, 311, 312, 314
peltasts, 25, 39, 44, 75, 81, 87, 98, 114, 118, 125, 145, 146, 167, 199, 231, 234, 235, 237, 250, 254, 260, 262, 264, 268, 273–77, 278, 280, 283
    as a complement to hoplites, 3, 279
    versus hoplites, 118, 121, 270, 277, 284–86
    as mercenaries, 3
peltē (3, 145, 234, 271, 283. *See* peltasts
Perdiccas I of Macedon, 75, 127
Perdiccas II of Macedon, 128
Pericles, 31, 70, 74, 91, 100, 176, 200
    and Hagnon, 78
    his settlement at Brea, 11
    his unusual political success, 73, 139
Perperikon (in Bulgaria), 29
Persae (play of Aeschylus), 257
Persia, the Persians, 38, 45, 65, 67, 68, 71, 73, 92, 93, 94, 101, 102, 109, 129, 133, 167, 179, 214, 220, 232, 293, 295
    as an alternative to Athens, 32–37
    as attractive to Athenians, 197
    as barbarians, 146
    and Conon and Iphicrates, 120, 122
    and Egypt, 39
    at Marathon, 238, 244, 245
    warfare of, 237
Persian Wars, 6, 56, 67, 314